Asian Perspectives on Teacher Education

Research into teacher education is dominated by Anglophone literature, with the inevitable result that teacher education in non-English speaking regions of the world largely remains unexamined. This book fills the gap in the existing literature and comprises twelve invited contributions from an international panel of educationists. To provide the reader with a clear structure, this book offers a detailed introduction and afterword which brings together the various themes examined in each chapter. The contributions offer perspectives on teacher education in the Asian region, perspectives which, until now, have been missing from contemporary debate on teacher education. Presenting research from Australia, Japan, the USA, the People's Republic of China, the Republic of Korea and Vietnam, this book examines the varied situations teacher educators experience in their own countries; in so doing the researchers identify resonances and dissonances in comparison with the dominant Anglophone research literature on the same subjects.

This book is an important contribution to the comparative study of teacher education in the first decade of the twenty-first century, giving a voice to an important sector of the international community of teacher educators.

This book was published as a special issue of *Journal of Education for Teaching: International research and pedagogy*.

Shin'ichi Suzuki is Professor Emeritus, Waseda University, Japan.

Edward R. Howe is Senior Lecturer in the Faculty of Education at Utsunomiya University in Tochigi, Japan.

Asian Perspectives on Teacher Education

Edited by Shin'ichi Suzuki and Edward R. Howe

LONDON AND NEW YORK

First published 2010 by Routledge
2 Park Square, Milton Park, Abingdon, Oxon, OX14 4RN

Simultaneously published in the USA and Canada
by Routledge
711 Third Avenue, New York, NY 10017

Routledge is an imprint of the Taylor & Francis Group, an informa business

First issued in paperback 2013

© 2010 Taylor & Francis

Typeset in Times New Roman by Value Chain, India

All rights reserved. No part of this book may be reprinted or reproduced or utilised in any form or by any electronic, mechanical, or other means, now known or hereafter invented, including photocopying and recording, or in any information storage or retrieval system, without permission in writing from the publishers.

British Library Cataloguing in Publication Data
A catalogue record for this book is available from the British Library

ISBN13: 978-0-415-56037-5 (hbk)
ISBN13: 978-0-415-85266-1 (pbk)

CONTENTS

Abstracts   vii

Introduction   1
Shin'ichi Suzuki

1. Teachers' role in the transition and transmission of culture   11
   Yuri Ishii and Mari Shiobara

2. Alternate routes in initial teacher education: a critical review of the research and policy implications for Hong Kong   26
   Kwok Chan Lai and David Grossman

3. Teacher education in a global context: towards a defensible theory of teacher education   41
   Richard Bates

4. Educators in American online universities: understanding the corporate influence on higher education   58
   Miki Yoshimura

5. Developing a 'feedback cycle' in teacher training: local networking in English education at Keiwa College   69
   Joy Williams, Akiko Shibanuma, Yoko Matsuzaki, Aiko Kanayama and Atsumi Ito

6. Gender inequality among Japanese high school teachers: women teachers' resistance to gender bias in occupational culture   81
   Tomomi Miyajima

7. Teacher induction across the Pacific: a comparative study of Canada and Japan   95
   Edward R. Howe

8. Reform of teacher education in China   109
   Xiaoguang Shi and Peter A. J. Englert

9. Early childhood teacher education in China   122
   Jiaxiong Zhu

10. English education and teacher education in South Korea   131
    Seongja Jo

11. Development of primary English education and teacher training in Korea 142
    Shiga Mikio

12. Educational reform and teacher education in Vietnam 156
    Takashi Hamano

    Afterword 170
    Shin'ichi Suzuki

    Index 177

Abstracts

Teachers' role in the transition and transmission of culture

Yuri Ishii and Mari Shiobara

Globalisation is evident in every aspect of human activity. As a result of crossborder information exchange, school music education policies in Asian countries have developed various trends. This paper investigates how these trends are adopted in music education policies and how they are influencing music teachers in Asian countries. The paper argues that the recent policy shifts in these countries reflect their desire to catch up with the global trend of educational values rather than responding to the realities of teachers in each respective country. It is also argued that the emphasis on cultural diversity has doubled music teachers' task in many Asian countries because teachers now have to cope with two different types of music: western music as a global common musical language as well as their own traditional music as the source of their national identity.

Alternate routes in initial teacher education: a critical review of the research and policy implications for Hong Kong

Kwok Chan Lai and David Grossman

In this article Hong Kong's policy on initial teacher training is used as a case study of the interplay between international trends and local policy. Traditionally initial teacher preparation in most countries has been based in higher education institutions. In recent years alternative routes for initial teacher education have proliferated in the United States and the United Kingdom. Meanwhile university-based pathways to teacher certification have been criticised as deterring talented candidates from entering the profession. The authors argue that these trends have had significant impact on Hong Kong's policies for initial teacher preparation. In Hong Kong untrained teachers have served as a convenient buffer to meet teacher demand for many decades. It was only in 1997 that the new Hong Kong Special Administrative Region government announced the policy objective of requiring all new teachers to be degree holders and professionally trained. However, this policy was short-lived. There is substantial evidence that government policy has been influenced by the development of alternative routes of teacher preparation elsewhere. This case study can provide useful insights for policy formation elsewhere.

Teacher education in a global context: towards a defensible theory of teacher education

Richard Bates

This paper examines some of the effects of globalisation on education and teacher education. In particular it considers the contradictory demands of economic and cultural forms of globalisation, and between globalisation and localisation. Attempts to construct an 'education space' in Europe and Asia are considered and various responses of teacher education systems are outlined. A defensible theory of teacher education is presented around the transformation of curriculum, pedagogy, assessment and the practicum: one that might allow a creative response to the contradictions of globalisation.

Educators in American online universities: understanding the corporate influence on higher education

Miki Yoshimura

As many higher educational institutions offer their courses online, college professors are faced with new challenges: pedagogical shift, a different type of relationship with students, and a need for redefining their role. Measurable goals and enforced accountability are challenging the conventional ways of which universities operate today. This paper explores the world of online education and the influence of corporate culture by paying special attention to the teachers' perspectives. The researcher observed virtual classrooms provided by American proprietary higher educational institutions that offer extensive courses online and conducted interviews with online instructors who teach at such institutions.

Developing a 'feedback cycle' in teacher training: local networking in English education at Keiwa College

Joy Williams, Akiko Shibanuma, Yoko Matsuzaki, Aiko Kanayama and Atsumi Ito

Keiwa College, a small liberal arts college in Niigata, Japan, has developed a number of on-campus and community-based teacher training programmes to benefit our students in the teacher education course in the Department of English and Communication and in-service English teachers in the area. These programmes provide students with opportunities to observe classes and acquire real classroom experiences both on campus and at local schools before they start the teaching practice. Local English teachers are also offered some practical workshops to enhance their English proficiency as well as their teaching skills. The authors call these interactions between the college and the community the 'feedback cycle'. This paper introduces some of the programmes they have developed for the feedback cycle over the years.

Gender inequality among Japanese high school teachers: women teachers' resistance to gender bias in occupational culture

Tomomi Miyajima

This study explores gender inequality in the occupational culture of Japanese high school teachers with special focus on women teachers' resistance to gender-biased practices. It examines the effectiveness of official and informal teacher training programmes in raising awareness of gender issues. Through an ethnographic case study conducted in five high schools in Gifu and Aichi, Japan, this study explores (1) the characteristics of the teaching community, and (2) the role of formal and informal teacher education in the occupational socialisation of new teachers. Moreover, by applying critical feminist perspectives, the study highlights (3) gender inequality within the occupational culture and myriad forms of women teachers' resistance to gender-biased practice. In drawing policy implications, the study examines (4) the effectiveness of teacher training programmes in raising teachers' awareness of gender issues.

Teacher induction across the Pacific: a comparative study of Canada and Japan

Edward R. Howe

This paper compares and evaluates teacher induction in Canada and Japan, following an overview of each educational system and an assessment of higher education in each region. Based on the author's personal teaching experience and research, suggestions for educational reforms are made to enhance the role of teachers. Teachers need opportunities to learn from one another and to benefit from the accumulated wisdom of generations of skilled practitioners. Moreover, teachers need time for collaboration, planning and reflection. Canada's strengths lie in well-developed pre-service teaching programmes. However, graduates are left to 'sink or swim' in their critical first year of teaching. In contrast, Japan's comprehensive yearlong internship offers an effective apprenticeship induction model with an emphasis on assistance rather than assessment.

Reform of teacher education in China

Xiaoguang Shi and Peter A.J. Englert

For more than 20 years the People's Republic of China has engaged in a significant transformation of its economy and social institutions, including its education system. This article provides a general picture of what changes have taken place in Chinese teacher education at a time of rapid transition from central control to devolved and distributed management and decision making, along with the country's shift from a planned economy to a socialist market one. Two major topics of this work focus on how institutions of higher and teacher education respond to the challenges of the changing environment, and on the major trends, priorities and direction of recent education reform. Embedded in the discussion are issues such as the merger and amalgamation of institutions, teachers' professional development under the auspices of market and knowledge economy, educational information, internationalisation and others, and their effects on Chinese teacher education both in the short and the long term.

Early childhood teacher education in China

Jiaxiong Zhu

This paper reviews early childhood teacher education in the People's Republic of China in the past years and raises the issues about teacher's education in the future. With thinking about early childhood education reform in China, unevenness in development in different areas and regions, and disparity in resources and programming among teacher education programmes at different levels, teacher education is confronted with great challenges. New policies and teacher education programmes have to be concerned more ecologically with how to have improvements in the real context. The countermeasures and strategies to deal with the problems of early childhood teacher education are identified.

English education and teacher education in South Korea

Seongja Jo

The spread of the English language is a global phenomenon, but it has a particular resonance in South Korea, where English is second only to Korean as a common language. The paper examines the current educational context in South Korea and the policy and practice issues that arise within this context regarding teacher education in English as a second language.

Development of primary English education and teacher training in Korea

Shiga Mikio

In 1997 English became a compulsory subject in Korean elementary schools. The education of English teachers for the elementry level was accelerated. The training curriculum was reformed according to the educational objective to enhance students' oral communication skills in English. Coupled to this change, the introduction of English Teacher Assistants is now also being reinforced to stimulate lively classroom discussions in English. This paper is based on the actual situation promoting English education and examines the characteristics of English education *vis-à-vis* the Japanese situation, which is said to lag behind Korea's. The paper examines various differences of social background and different approaches to equal opportunity and identifies some problems of early English education in countries like Korea and Japan where English is not used in daily life.

Educational reform and teacher education in Vietnam

Takashi Hamano

This paper examines the current state and a challenge faced by teachers and teacher education in Vietnam, and analyzes international aid projects providing support to teacher education there. It is necessary to grasp changes in teacher education in Vietnam in the context of the current comprehensive reform of education, which has been greatly influenced by world trends. In Vietnam today, improving the quality of basic education has been given a high priority, in line with the global movement for Education for All (EFA). The main task for improving the quality of education in Vietnam is the effective implementation of the new curriculum adopted in 2002. Teacher education is the key to completing this task. It is important for teachers to learn new methods of instruction, and teacher education needs to be strengthened to allow them to acquire these new methods. A great deal of international assistance is provided for the promotion of this type of teacher education. Projects in this area are provided by the World Bank, Belgium, and Japan. This paper analyzes these projects, and examines the challenges facing international assistance for teacher education.

Introduction

Shin'ichi Suzuki

Saitama-ken, Japan

Global learning

So-called globalisation has greatly influenced learning and school education. In Asia most nation-states have adopted policies for globalisation. The policies and the background policy orientations vary from country to country. However, it is common in Asian countries that they plan educational reforms and put them into practice. In China, Korea, Vietnam, Japan and other nations on the Pacific Rim, several measures for innovating school education and renewing teaching qualifications are needed. In addition, in almost all of the countries in the regions, teachers' professional responsibilities are put under stringent public scrutiny.

Within the global contexts of school education, learning is significantly important. The doctrine of lifelong learning became more or less dominant over the countries concerned. Its importance was interpreted in various international contexts toward the end of the last century. One example in theory of learning was the reappraisals of Vygoytsky (1896–1934) and Piaget (1896–1980). The counterpart to such a reappraisal was the Freirean movements for adult literacy which spread among the developing countries. An institutional response to the importance of learning can be seen in the report prepared for UNESCO (1996) by the International Commission on Education for the Twenty-First Century. The Report (*Learning: The treasure within*) postulates education as a necessary utopia. Designing the future society of human beings as learning communities, where the aims of, and the means to, ideals and moral values could be realised *facta non verba* through multicultural communication, the author of the introductory chapter, Jacques Delors, proposed new conceptions of learning; namely, learning to know, learning to do, learning to live together and learning to be (pp. 22–23).

Paraphrasing these four pillars into pedagogy, we may have various theories of teaching and learning. Some may prefer constructivist viewpoints of learning to conventional schemes of it, and others may choose the structural dynamics of learning. Those who think it essential to take into consideration the outcomes from cognitive and brain sciences might assert to building a renewed pedagogy of affordance (Sasaki 2000). Despite the possibilities for adopting or developing new pedagogical theorem and framework of teaching, any pedagogical approach to the four pillars may necessarily evoke some asymmetrical senses of cultural congruity between what can be learned and what ought to be learned, and between what can be expected and what can be realised. In this book, Ishii and Shiobara, and Bates focus on this aspect of pedagogy. It is simply because all human learning is at once cultural and universal in the sense that learning as it takes place in the brain is objectively universal, but what goes concomitantly with learning is necessarily personal. All learners are at once human beings in general and socio-cultural beings in particular. In other words, even the four pillars of learning have their own social, historical and cultural backgrounds. The cultural and academic background of the four pillars is entirely European which, ironically, can be shown in the UNESCO Report's chapter on Asian views on learning and human development (UNESCO 1996, pp. 239–46).

Teaching and educational idioms

So far as teaching is concerned, there arise the conflicting, if not contradictory, cultural conceptions of teaching. They vary from culture to culture. Given a culture, there can be observed always at least two views on teaching: permissive progressivism or oppressive essentialism, for example. In the Asian, particularly in the East Asian contexts, teaching has not been seen as a formative activity, but rather one of 'pressing', instilling, and indoctrinating. Even when new education movements reached these countries in the past, for example, the most enthusiastic attitudes of people arguing for alternative approaches waned in the long run when faced with the stubborn cultural and political regimes ruling over the scholastic teaching and learning. Looking back at the steps of learning Buddhism, Confucianism and endogenous knowledge, it was first rote-learning, then lecturing and annotative and explanatory approaches on the third stage. Referring to Jaspers' *Erziehungsformen* (1923), which are genuinely European, such an Asian teaching and learning pattern on the first stage could be equivalent to his definition of *Scholastische Erziehung*, and second stage learning may partially correspond to *Meistersbildung*. There would have been scarce opportunities for Asian teachers and Asian learners to undergo together truth-finding dialogues defined as *Sokratische Erziehung* (Jaspers 1923). Such a contrast between the European and the Asian teaching–learning paradigms might hint at both the possibility and impossibility of universal learning formalised in the report mentioned above.

How to overcome such a dilemma in teaching–learning paradigms is a provocative question of academic interest to researchers and professors serving in teacher education. Ishii and Shiobara, and Hamano emphasise the importance of renewing theory of teaching in their contribution to this book. I would suggest a theorem for teachers to develop their own teaching formula which may fit the teaching roles within respective socio-cultural circumstances in the Asian, or East Asian countries, as follows:

(a) teachers teach children all that is productive in thinking,
(b) teachers teach all that is essential for children to sustain their life,
(c) teachers teach children how to identify for themselves a vocational career and sexual maturity,
(d) teachers teach children how to live historically in their specific local communities, in their societies and in the wider world (Suzuki 1998).

Pedagogical interpretations of the theorem can be multifarious but the core issue regarding the intellectual development of children is how to motivate and enhance reasoning, which is itself a latent capability for a child to enrich experience and to develop intellectually. Teacher education faces the tasks of providing initial and acting teachers with appropriate programmes by which teachers should fully cope with brave tasks of 'new teaching and learning'.

Shifts in teacher education

In most of the East Asian countries like Japan, the People's Republic of China (PRC), Korea and Taiwan, the providers of initial teacher education are universities or colleges of higher education. However, there has been an institutional shift among these countries. Japan decided to introduce a higher advanced institute of professional teacher education and training in the sector of graduate schools. The open entry to the teaching profession, a guiding principle, has not yet been abandoned owing to its historical importance, but weight is now laid on the professional capabilities of teachers. Less emphasis is given to the liberal arts.

Alternatively, in Korea and China, including Taiwan, however, the state governments decided to unite the universities and the colleges of education and the former normal universities and colleges were reorganised into a comprehensive university complex, where not all students are registered as candidates for the teaching profession. In one form or another, Korea and China chose the open entry principle of teacher education just when Japan changed (if not abandoned) this principle. It is common, of course, for future teachers to be educated at higher education institutions at the university level (see Shi and Englert, Jo and Shiga, in this book). However, globally, it can be observed that some alternative modes or methods of teacher education become more and more prevalent among countries like the USA, UK, Australasia, and Europe. That is the pattern of the multiple systems in England, or the pattern of what might be seen as amateurism in recruiting teaching/mentoring staff from schools. No academic background or professional training is required. This pattern has been introduced owing to assertions that teacher education and training at universities is not fully evidence-based and in some cases is not accountable for the funds granted by the public authorities and private organisations (see Lai and Grossmann in this book). It is important to recognise the doctrines and the consequences of introducing the General Teaching Councils in the UK and the American Association of Colleges for Teacher Education (AACTE) in the US so that readers may make a fair assessment of these countries' policy choices.

Teaching profession and nations

Teaching as a profession has for long been controlled by nation-states. All nation-states provide schools to educate children to be future national citizens of the state. Schooling has been closely related to nation building. In addition, teaching can be biased in line with the indigenous cultures in which teachers grow. In one sense, 'globalism' itself is a sort of civilisation bias in the sense that it has been brought into international economies and politics by the hyper-information industry and by the more advanced nation-states. Against the global contexts of dominant cultures and languages, and against neo-nationalism, it is a crucial task for researchers to answer the question of how to secure teaching being at once universal and yet responsive to indigenous cultural drives.

During the period of the 1980s, an assumption defined as the grammar of modernity was accepted by many social scientists and it became prevalent through various discourses on modernity and modern nation-states. This position could be summarised as arguing that:

(a) modern nation-states are outcomes from the modern processes of history in the west,
(b) the modern nation-state became also the model of political modernisation outside of Europe, and
(c) all the nation-states required having national people, national territory, and national independence with self-determination.

All nation-states had to have, as political devices of modern governance, (1) national people(s), (2) national language(s), (3) national culture(s), (4) national religion(s), and (5) national education. National education required (1) national schools, (2) national school books, and (3) national teachers. Thus, nationalised education was in need of selecting contents of teaching and training teachers for national schools.

The content of teaching was authenticated in many cases by the secular and/or religious authorities. In order to make their inhabitants 'nationalised people' the states introduced universal popular education by ways of establishing national schooling systems. The contents of school education, based on traditional knowledge and skills and imported advanced knowledge and technology, were made compulsory and were taught by teachers who were licensed by the public authority. The licensing system of the teaching profession has been controlled by the secular (sometimes ecclesiastical) principles of the governance and the government of the country, particularly after the dawn of modernity in respective countries. The governance being based on democracy, teachers could have relatively autonomous independence through the whole history of modernisation, but in most cases teachers were given the status of public servants strictly controlled by the state or by the local governments that employed teachers. Such a pattern of teachers' dependence on public authentication has prevailed over the East Asian countries. The trends of teacher education reforms in Asia still show such a dilemma seen in the contradictory roles of teaching: the teacher as both professional learning facilitator and authorised transmitter of approved knowledge.

Nowadays, nation-states can behave like individuals in international trade and commerce, where education itself is a kind of good supplied on the national and international markets. As the General Agreement on Tariffs and Trade (GATT) declares, vocational qualifications are more like commodities of which anyone can be a buyer or a consumer. In this sphere, as Hardt and Negri (2000) indicate, most markets cross over the boundaries of nation-states and qualifications may come to be transnational. In this situation, the governments of nation-states have to enhance the quality of their education and learning in order to cope with competitive markets and to adjust intra-societal institutions to accommodate the drive towards globalisation in both commerce (industry) and culture (learning). At this point one can see teachers having to deal with new tasks and hence the importance of their renewed education and training.

National policies and teacher education

In the East Asian region, public education so far has had to cope with several socio-economic and socio-cultural issues which bring common tasks to school education.

Each country has its own tasks of innovating and improving initial teacher education and organising the further development of its teaching profession. In Vietnam, for example, it is urgent for the political leaders to reset the state and the government in line with market socialism, as is also the case with the People's Republic of China. Vietnam needs a highly educated manpower so that it may, as a nation-state, quickly adjust itself to the dynamic world politics and world economy. It was often the case that the state deferred sending well qualified human resources to the teaching sector. As a result the teaching sector was left to take a back seat to industry, commerce, and public management. However, on the occasion of a recent international seminar on teaching standards organised by UNESCO, the delegate from Vietnam asserted the importance of developing allowance schemes for teachers as a way of assisting local authorities in attracting highly educated men and women to schools (UNESCO 2004). Moreover, Vietnam accepted the UN policy of Education for All (EfA) and has started implementing the national policies in practice. Hamano (in this book) examines the governmental tasks of developing appropriate school curricula fitted to EfA in Vietnam and the actual job environments of teaching from the viewpoint of the pupil–teacher ratio in primary education in particular. Educational reforms in Vietnam have gradually improved the school conditions but it is still a considerable task for the government to innovate teacher education in order to have enough qualified teachers.

In South Korea, the primary principle of state management has long been one of initiating human resource development. The first fundamental law of human resource development was enacted in 2002. Before this law the government had already proposed the five year development plan for 2001–2005. In 2006 the second five year plan was introduced. The plan showed four leading strategies for the Korean society: (1) the country could cope with international competition with highly advanced human resources, (2) enhancement of lifelong learning for all people, (3) solutions of social, economic and educational gaps among people by ways of providing more opportunities and better welfare service, (4) improvement and development of infrastructures for human development. The second five year plan was supported by a succession of state budgets, which amounted to 51 billion won. In this plan education is crucial in the sense that the aims should be achieved by a new institutional innovation of lifelong learning and rehabilitating teachers as new professional facilitators.

In 2006 in the People's Republic of China, the government proposed the revised and extended five year plan of national economic development. The plan is comprehensive, including three educational priorities: (1) stable national development by way of education and science, (2) human education for securing personal maturity, and (3) further development of compulsory education, vocational education and training, and higher learning. The government declared its support for these strategies by much more investment in education, amounting to 4% of GDP (Chinese Government 2006). The features of educational planning were as follows:

(1) lifelong learning – (a) free one year course of vocational training for the upper secondary school leavers, leading to vocational qualifications; (b) physical training service for the young adults; (c) introducing the Beijing English Test system,
(2) primary and secondary education – (a) more resources for developing rural primary schools; (b) sustaining high quality education for personal development of children and the young,

(3) educational partnership between state government and local authorities – (a) joint fiscal support for school development in rural areas; (b) joint collaboration for the betterment of teachers' salary and pension,
(4) teacher education and training – (a) legislation of teachers and teaching qualifications; (b) legislative provisions for teachers' status.

The government enacted the Teachers' Law. The Law classifies all the qualified teachers into five groups: first, second, third, and higher. The criteria of classification are (1) academic career, (2) competency, and (3) experience. The professional status of teachers is divided into three: advanced class (higher class), middle class (first class), and primary class (second and third class). The criteria and classificatory standards are prescribed in two Teacher Assessment By-laws issued already in 1986.

With these policies announced, teacher education in the PRC faces new but pertaining and persistent problems. Shi and Englert describe and explain what kind of innovations of teacher education have been attempted (in this book) However, in practice, particularly in the rural areas, the shortage of primary school teachers is very marked. Wu (2007) discusses a new proposal on teaching practice. The proposal is termed Teaching Practice Center (TPC). TPC can be an institution where practising students from universities or colleges will be sent to rural primary schools which are in high need of teachers. Practicing students help school teachers in teaching and in managing classrooms and the school in which they are placed. The TPC can also offer opportunities both for school teachers and university teacher educators to discuss the knowledge base for teaching and how to advance learning on education. The scheme is intended to enhance a scientific approach to education. The TPC plays the pivotal role as a regional teacher education organisation. Such a proposal indicates how the PRC has recognised how urgent it is for the government to advance academic and professional teacher education in its genuine sense.

International policies and regional literacy

Not only in Vietnam but in all Asian countries, Education for All (EfA) is an important priority area in educational administration. It has been widely circulated and accepted among countries in East Asia. EfA may have a closer relation to the Four Pillars of Learning (FPL). However, when FPL refers itself to the Asian contexts of learning, FPL meets ideas and ideals of learning that have come from historical contexts of knowledge and cultures which confront and contradict Asia's. In China the public examination system called Ke-Ju served in educating and selecting the elites for government officers from common people for more than 15 centuries (sixth to twentieth century). The system was exported to the surrounding regions including the Korean peninsula, the Japanese archipelago and Vietnam. All of the countries in these regions established their own public examination systems long before the modernisation era. From the middle of the nineteenth to the middle of twentieth century, all the countries in the region were affected by Western cultures and their militant forces. In addition, China and Korea were invaded or controlled by Japan. From the view point of scripts, all the countries had used the Chinese square characters (*Han-Zi*, in Chinese), which are ideographical. In Japan some were changed into phonogram called *Kana* (*So-Kana, Hira-Kana* and *Kata-Kana*). In Korea the expression of phonogram was invented. In Vietnam, Chinese *Han-Zi* was abolished in 1954 and *Quoc ngu* (national language) re-introduced, which was originally devised by a French minister Alexandre de Rhodes (1591–1660) during the seventeenth century. *Quoc ngu* is, however, a mixture of Chinese *Han-Zi* and old *Annamese*. Consequently, after absorbing cultural impacts from the West, the Asians in their regions had a complex order of letters and literacy structure. Namely, people used a complex of letters: the indigenous system of ideograph – phonogramic symbolic signs, combined with European tongues. A list of some of the state-specific letter frameworks reveals the complexity of the situation:

> Korea=Chinese+Japanese+Koreans+European languages,
> China=Chinese+Japanese+European languages,
> Vietnam=Chinese+Vietnamese+European languages (French, particularly), and
> Japan=Chinese+Japanese+European languages.

With such complex literacy preconditions, the examination paradigm of *Ke-Ju* worked and still does in the East Asian counties. That is, a determinant factor of accelerated examinations on all levels of learning and schooling, which can be observed in Asian countries (Bray 2003). In introducing and disseminating the notions of FPL into the countries concerned, there can probably be some deformations of the international ideas of the agenda.

English, global literacy?

There are a number of common tasks for Asian countries who wish to develop the rich prospective programme of English teaching because English is nowadays the main mediator in almost all national human activities. Pan-en-English can be a troublesome issue form any but is an imperative for those concerned with worldwide communication regardless of asymmetric idioms and semantics of various kinds. Therefore, all countries in East Asia have adopted such policies as (1) introduction of English as a school subject for primary schools and (2) the enhancement of English ability of secondary and advanced students, together with providing adult learners with opportunities to enrich their experiences in communication with English-speaking foreigners. Korea led off earlier than others in the Asian contexts, and has introduced English to its primary school curriculum. As a result it became the priority for the government to provide initial and experienced teachers with several courses in learning English as ESL. Jo and Shiga (in this book) describe and explain what sort of policies are chosen and how they are implemented.

Japan also introduced a policy for English in primary schools and not a few native speakers of English were hired as Assistant Language Teachers (ALT) by the local authorities. The government held up standard Japanese people who speak English in 2003, and encouraged schools to develop plans for teaching English. According to the survey conducted by the Japanese Ministry of Education, Culture, Sports, Science and Technology (MEXT) in 2006, 95.8% of state primary schools had developed a new curriculum of English for the third–sixth grade pupils (MEXT 2007). The Local Education Authorities initiated programmes of English studies. However, the frequency for school children to hear any native speakers talk English was low: an opportunity a month on average (MEXT 2007). The government also supports local authorities in developing some types of 'magnet schools' for teaching English to primary school children (http://www.mext.go.jp/a_menu/shotou/kenkyu). Of late (2008) the Monbusho (Ministry of Education) has discussed the issue of the English curriculum for primary schools. Education and training of initial teachers of

English for primary schools have also been placed on the table for discussion at some of the country's Universities of Education.

E- and digital literacy, a new lingua franca?

Against such a political, historical and cultural background of learning, and internationalisation, a new dimension of learning has emerged in the intellectual sphere of information and communication technology (ICT): so-called e-learning. In the e-learning sphere literacy is not limited to English but is opened out to become a more collective literacy. Collective literacy is self-reflexive. Within the dimension of international communication, any collective literacy can easily lead to a mutual misconception of an utterance which is made from multi-standpoints. Even within one language sphere, some complex reactions can be made between the senders of information (teachers) and the receivers (students). Yoshimura (in this book) examines the contextual multi-dimension of e-learning schemes. The paper illustrates both the urgency for schools, colleges and universities to adjust to the expanding e-learning situations and the possible irrelevance of the schemes to genuine learning.

Despite such a dilemma, for example, in South East Asia, ministers of education have often met together to talk about integrating ICT into their educational systems covering schooling and lifelong learning. Malaysia discussed at length their plans to improve the ICT capabilities of their schools, to develop required infrastructures, and to guide teachers and pupils/students to the ICT culture (SEAMO 2007). The case is the same with East Asian countries. In each of the grand education programmes of the countries in the regions, teachers and facilitators were supposed to be well prepared for e-learning, not only in its positive prospective but warned of its negative aspects. Teacher education in this sense is complex because it is not possible for people to escape from inventions of new forms of expressions and representations based on new media, although cultural systems of coding and decoding human symbols are not universal, resulting in the politicians' claims for specific forms of national education.

E-learning depends on e- or digital literacy. E/d-literacy has multifold functions:

(1) manipulation of tools and signs,
(2) critical reading and interpretation,
(3) creative expression,
(4) acquiring multiple systems of coding (and decoding),
(5) understanding of media technology,
(6) insightful understanding of socio-economic and cultural environments which embrace all signs, forms and letters, and
(7) capability of searching information for learning (Yamanouchi 2003).

If we define 'literacy' as the abstract manipulation of information represented by and in symbols, signs, shapes, letters and scenes, literacy may have a meaningful structure consisting of (a) intentional (b) manipulation (c) of forms and space. If so, e/d-literacy has a wider functional structure, which includes of course the conventional literacy of the three Rs. E/d-literacy should contribute to developing new learning spheres, sometimes ubiquitous and sometimes articulated. Learning in and out of classrooms relies much on e/d-literacy. Teacher education and training should comply with it defined as a new lingua franca. All Asian nations are quick in understanding the importance and potential of e-learning. They had investigated and invested significant funds in the development of e-learning system.

National and individual identity in Asia

Public education, so far in East Asia, has to cope with several issues which cast shadows over most of school education. Among the issues the most serious is separation of younger generations from their traditional cultures. In modern societies, more people were separated from locales where once they would have had their own livelihood. In the so-called post-modern societies people are living in the hyper-information sphere as it were, where all areas, including education, tend to be commercialised and consumerism is so compelling and acquisitive that people may easily be remoulded in such a way that they are removed from all the customs and habits that are indigenous and genuinely ethnic to their society. It can be a political threat for any country which intends to retain its traditional and cultural identity. Therefore, all East Asian countries are eager for, and busy with, re-introducing highly nationalised principles of refurbishing societies by way of educational reconstruction. Such educational reconstruction, starting in the 1980s and resulting in hyper-national reorganisation of the systems in the 1990s, has brought other issues of learning in all countries concerned. Ishii and Shiobara's paper (in this book) illustrates what has happened regarding aesthetic education among many Asian countries by way of throwing light on music education as a case study. Their comparative studies indicate the various gaps and dilemmas in music education, which should be observable throughout the countries of Asia. Teacher education faces a crisis distilled from 'innovation' itself. Bates (in this book) analyses what kinds of situations schooling and teacher education now face after several successions of educational reconstructions have been implemented nationally and internationally.

In this book, Ishii and Shiobara discuss teachers' roles as cultural transmitters. Music lessons in Asian schools are especially prone to the double bind of tradition and 'modernity' that is represented by the European traditions. They write that teachers now have to cope with two different types of music, Western music as a global common musical language and their traditional music as the source of their national identity. In this sense, national public education in the Asian regions share a dominant common issue of exclusive identities between generations, genders, and nationalities. This book raises the kinds of issues that may well not be specific to the Asian context. Teachers, and thus teacher education, need revolutionary self-renewal crossing the boundaries of nations and regions.

References

Bray, M. 2003. *Adverse effect of private supplementary tutoring.* Paris: IIEP.
Chinese Government. 2006. *The 11th year development plan.* http://www.moe.gov.cn/edoas/website18/info21284.htm.
Hardt, M., and A. Negri. 2000. *Empire.* Cambridge, MA: Harvard University Press.
Jaspers, K. 1923. *Die Idee der Universitaet.* Berlin: Springer; revised ed. 1946, enlarged ed., with K. Rossman, 1961, *Daigaku no Rinen* (Japanese edition, trans. A. Mineshima, 1955), Tokyo: Mori Rishosha.

MEXT. 2007. *Survey on teaching English at state primary schools.* Tokyo: MEX. http://mext.go.jp/b_menu/houdou/19.

Sasaki, M. 2000. *Ahodannsu eno Shotai* [Invitation to affordance – evolving human cognitions]. Tokyo: Seido-Sha.

SEAMO. 2007. *ICT integration,* conference in November 2007. http://www.seamo.org/index.php.

Suzuki, S. 1998. Kyoshoku no saiko-chiku e [Toward redefinition of teaching job]. In *Kyoshi-Kyoiku no Kadai to Tenbo* [Issues and prospects of teacher education], ed. S. Suzuki, 163–201. Tokyo: Gakubun-Sha.

UNESCO. 1996. *Learning: The treasure within,* Report to UNESCO of the International Commission on Education for the Twenty-first Century. Paris: UNESCO Publishing.

UNESCO. 2004. Regional seminar on teacher education – on standards of qualifications. *Nguyen Than Son, Country Discussion Paper,* Background and Working Documents.

Wu, Xiao-rung. 2007. *Chihou ni okeru Kyouiku-Jisshu Sentaa* [Teaching practice centre in rural area], proposal made by the University of Shi Nan, in *Kenkyu Nennpo* [Annual Research Bulletin]. Tokyo: Nicchuu-Kyoiku Kenkyu-Koryuu Kaigi [Japan–China Forum for Education].

Yamauchi, Y. 2003. *Dezitaru Shakai no Riterasii* [Literacy in digital society]. Tokyo: Iwanami.

Teachers' role in the transition and transmission of culture

Yuri Ishii[a] and Mari Shiobara[b]

[a]Faculty of Education, Yamaguchi University, Yamaguchi, Japan; [b]Music Education, Tokyo Gakugei University, Tokyo, Japan

Globalisation is proceeding in every aspect of human activities and school education is also influenced. The most obvious influence may be the emphasis on Information and Communication Technology (ICT) education. The acquisition of ICT skills, however, is not so profound when considered in the light that so many countries are sharing exactly the same views on the introduction of ICT into their school curriculum. What is caused by globalisation is not just the diffusion of ICT skills, but also the spread of the values that regard ICT as an important element of school education.

A similar symptom exists in music education policies in Asian countries. There are some common trends, which indicate that certain values are now shared among music education policies of many Asian countries. These are an emphasis on the purpose of education as the development of children's total human quality rather than mere transmission of skills and knowledge by rote learning, the encouragement of a learner-centred approach, the introduction of authentic assessment, the integration of existing subjects, and the assertion of cultural specificity.

The purpose of this paper is to investigate how these values are adopted in music education policies and how they are influencing music teachers in Asian countries. Through the discussion, the paper argues that the recent policy shifts in these countries reflect their desire to catch up with the global trend of educational values rather than to respond to the realities faced by teachers in their respective countries. The paper also argues that the emphasis on cultural specificity has doubled music teachers' tasks in many Asian countries because teachers now have to cope with two different types of music, western music as a global common musical language and their traditional music as the source of their national identity.

Trends in Asian music educational policies

Many Asian countries have experienced curriculum revisions since the 1980s and there are common features in their policies. One such feature is their emphasis on education for the development of children's total human quality. The emphasis can be found in policies for music education, too.

The purpose of music education, though the wordings are slightly different, in both Thai and Hong Kong[1] curricula links music education with creativity, the ability to analyse and appreciate music, and self-expression (Tanaka et al. 2006). The Japanese curriculum refers to expression and appreciation for the sake of developing students' sensibility (Monbusho 1998). In the curricula of the Philippines and Taiwan, music education is expected to contribute to 'the total development' and the development of a 'well-rounded character', respectively (Tanaka et al. 2006). The philosophy of the Malaysian curriculum aims at the holistic development of intellectually, spiritually, emotionally and physically balanced individuals, and the objectives of music education include items such as the development of self-expression, creativity, the value of cooperation and a positive attitude toward trying as well as those more directly linked with learning music (Kementerian Pendidikan Malaysia 2002). The People's Republic of China (PRC) is currently trying to shift from exam-oriented education to quality education and music education is expected to enrich children's emotional experience and develop aesthetic sentiments of a good quality in them (Nishizono and Dong 2003). That overlaps with the total development of children's personality. The Republic of Korea (South Korea) is also moving towards education that 'cultivates fully each learner's personality and creativity' (Ministry of Education Republic of Korea 1999, 169) and music is expected to raise children's quality of life through total human development (Murao, Go, and Park 2003).

The emphasis on education for children's total development is linked with the promotion of learner-centred education. In the current music curriculum of Japan, children's learning through their own experience is emphasised more than before (Ishii, Shiobara, and Ishii 2005) and the current curriculum of the People's Republic of China includes respect for children's individuality and the importance of a co-workable teacher–student relationship (Nishizono and Dong 2003). The South Korean curriculum published in 1997 states that musical learning must be based on musical experience and students must be given opportunities to give presentations. In the area of understanding music, students are expected to develop creativity, the ability of problem-solving through participation and the ability of self-learning (Murao et al. 2003). In Thailand, although not specifically about music, the National Education Act in 1999 clearly states that 'teachers, instructors and administrators must change their roles from guiding and knowledge transferring to helping, promoting and encouraging learners in acquiring knowledge' (Pitiyanuwat and Anantrasirichai 2002, 7).

The third example is the introduction of the concept of 'authentic assessment'. A distinction drawn by Gipps between performance assessment and authentic assessment is as follows:

> Authentic assessment implies that the assessment is authentic to the learning activity we wish to promote and/or that the context of the assessment is authentic rather than artificial. Authentic assessment is always performance-based ... so it is in effect a special case of performance assessment. (Gipps 1996, 259)

Assessment in Asia used to be synonymous with summative assessment for the purpose of the comparison and selection of students. Nowadays, policies demand performance-based authentic assessment that is useful for the improvement of individual students' learning.

The Philippines employs self-assessment by students after every lesson (Tanaka et al. 2006). This is expected to facilitate two other forms of assessment by teachers: formative assessment and summative assessment. The curriculum of the PRC encourages formative and summative assessment (Nishizono and Dong 2003) and the use of various types of assessment such as students' self-assessment, students' mutual assessment and assessment by a third party (BEING.Org.cn 2005a, 2005b). In the assessment, not only knowledge and skills, but also attitudes and eagerness are supposed to be assessed clearly and objectively (Cheng 2005). In Hong Kong, assessment includes formative assessment such as immediate responses to students' performances and compositions as well as summative assessment that is accomplished mainly through final examinations in listening and performing (Tanaka et al. 2006). The Malaysian national curriculum explains that assessment will help students to raise their standard of achievement and teachers to prepare appropriate lessons (Kementerian Pendidikan Malaysia 2002). It suggests various ways to carry out the formative and summative assessments during course work and exam periods. Some examples are: interviews, demonstrations, quizzes, multiple-choice tests, discussions, portfolios, reflection and reports. The South Korean curriculum states that the assessment result should be used for the improvement of teaching and the assessment should take various forms (Murao et al. 2003).

Emphasis on clear and objective assessment is shared by Taiwanese and Japanese policies. Taiwan has introduced competence indicators for the 'arts and humanities' (Tanaka et al. 2006). Since Japan has switched from an assessment based on students' relative performance to that based on their absolute performance, teachers are now expected to have clear criteria that should be used for the assessment and devise clear ways to assess children based on the criteria. The assessment must cover the following points that are prescribed by the Ministry of Education and Science: interests, eagerness and attitudes; musical perception and devices for expression; skills for expression, and ability for musical appreciation (Monbusho 1996).

The integration of the art subjects as part of curriculum integration is also a feature often found in contemporary Asian curricula. For example, South Korea adopted the integrated curriculum in the first two years of primary education for six- to eight-year-olds in the 1995 curriculum revision (Murao et al. 2003). It integrated conventional subjects into five groups including Korean language and mathematics as two independent subjects. Music is mainly taught in the group that includes art and health education as other elements (2003). Thailand adopted the integrated curriculum policy in 1990 and divided conventional subjects into five areas in primary education, five subjects in lower secondary education and nine subjects in upper secondary education (Pitiyanuwat and Anantrasirichai 2002). Music was integrated with other conventional subjects into the area of 'character development' at primary level, the subject of 'personality development' at lower secondary level and the subject of 'art' at upper secondary level (Pitiyanuwat and Anantrasirichai 2000). After the revision in 2000, the curriculum was reorganised into eight subject groups of learning and music was included in 'art' with other areas of art (Pitiyanuwat and Anantrasirichai 2000). Taiwanese primary and lower secondary school curricula integrated music with visual art and drama as the 'arts and humanities' learning area in 2001 and now upper secondary school curricula is moving in the same direction (Tanaka et al. 2006). In the Philippines, the fourth to sixth years of primary education, which is for nine- to 12-year-old children, has an integrated subject consisting of arts, physical education, home economics and livelihood education. Secondary education has an integrated subject that includes physical education, health and music (Marinas and Ditapat 2000; Tanaka et al. 2006). In the current curriculum of the PRC, while music exists as an independent subject, an integrated subject 'arts' that includes music, art, drama, dance and film is also provided (BEING.org.cn 2005a, 2005b).

Japan has not introduced an integrated art subject but the possibility of the integration of music and art into something like 'self-expression' has always been discussed among policy makers since the 1990s (Shiobara and Ishii 1998). Indeed, the period of integrated studies was established in 1998 in order to promote the learning of interdisciplinary themes and the element of music education can be included, for example as a part of the learning of local cultural heritage, if a school so chooses.

Besides the features mentioned above, there is also a common trend of the assertion of cultural specificity in Asian countries. As a subject that deals with musical culture, music curricula directly reflect this assertion. In Asian countries, national identity in music education has been maintained in a different way, through the use of locally composed western-style pieces with lyrics in local languages. The recent trend indicates that this approach is no longer enough for the assertion of national identity. During the 27th International Society for Music Education (ISME) World Conference, a panel discussion was held on how teaching local traditional music is encouraged in music. The handout distributed at this discussion can be summarised as follows:

- Thailand: Thailand is the strongest in traditional instrumental teaching in each of the local cultural instruments ... schools have Thai traditional musical instruments for music classes.
- Malaysia: the curriculum includes music of all cultures in Malaysia ... In secondary school, traditional ensembles like Cak Lempong and Gamelan were made compulsory for students who choose music.
- The Philippines: Philippine music in its three mainstreams is present in the primary and secondary school curriculum.
- Taiwan: the localisation policy to include elements from 13 indigenous languages as well as Mandarin in 1993 and 1994 is reflected in the music teaching materials, mainly singing and music appreciation materials.
- Hong Kong: the government pushes the Chinese music very much by curriculum reform and in-service training since 1997.
- Japan: Japanese music has been more positively introduced into music classrooms since 2002 (Tanaka et al. 2006).

By 'more positively introduced' in the Japanese curriculum we mean that it includes actual instrumental playing, or at least touching instruments, in lower secondary schools. This represents a great difference from the previous curriculum that remained at an appreciation level (Ishii et al. 2005).

In the PRC, the music curriculum has stressed national identity since the 1990s. A national objective, written in 1992, is 'to ensure that students learn the superior national musical productions of our country' in order to nurture 'their sense of national dignity and pride' (PLC 1997, 78). Subsequently, in the primary school curriculum that was in effect in 1997, out of 143 pieces of music for appreciation, 32 pieces were traditional Chinese music and many of the songs were Chinese folk songs (Nomura and Nakayama 1997). The new curriculum announced in 2001 succeeded this policy. For example, fundamental educational principles for lower secondary school curriculum include 'treasuring national music' and the contents for appreciation include Chinese national music and folk music (Cheng 2005).

The South Korean curriculum emphasises its national musical heritage not by the number of the pieces of traditional music, but by inserting features of Korean music into pieces (Murao et al. 2003).

The implication of the policy trends

There is more than one message in these policy trends. The most obvious one is the shift of the whole meaning of school education from education for the sake of qualification to education that is meaningful for the development of each child's personal qualities. In many Asian countries, school education has been criticised for its exam-oriented, teacher-centred nature that resulted in children rote learning. The most well known examples may be Japan, South Korea and the PRC. Even in music education, which is relatively free from exam pressures, cramming knowledge and skills have been practised. The emphasis on education for children's total development is meant to remedy the defects of such exam-oriented education. In order for education that supports children's total development, children need to be enabled to learn depending on their own interests and capabilities. Hence the encouragement of learner-centred, process-oriented teaching methods and performance-based authentic assessment for the purpose of helping children's learning.

Besides the necessity to solve the actual problem of rote learning, the shift from exam-oriented education to education for children's total development has an implication of a shift from developing country status to industrialised country status, too. As Dore (1976) writes, education for qualification and rote learning have been regarded as features of a developing country. So, it is natural if policy makers of Asian countries regard such features of their educational system as something to eliminate and aim at education for children's total development as their target.

The integration of subjects also has a double message. On one hand, it is closely linked with the implementation of a learner-centred approach that should allow children to learn according to their interest without being restricted by subject boundaries. At the same time, it also means adopting the trend started in Europe and the United States. The integration of music education with other subjects in particular with those of art subjects has been discussed among Anglo-American music educationists since the late 1970s. They have supported the view of the arts as a unique form of knowledge proposed by philosophers such as Langer and Dewey. For example, Abbs defines music, literature, drama, visual art, dance and film as constituting a generic community of knowledge united by the process of making, performing, presenting and evaluating. He believes that through participating in these artistic processes children develop a special kind of perceptual understanding that leads to artistic knowledge (Abbs 1987). This kind of argument is often used for the justification of a place of music in a common curriculum along with the other art subjects. Lawton (1988) states that the aim of music and arts education is to develop students' understanding of the various 'meanings' that constitute the living culture. In the United States, music curriculum guidelines proposed by the Music Educators National Conference are partly presented in the National Standards for Arts Education (Consortium of National Arts Education Associations 1994) along with dance, theatre and visual arts education. Thus, these common features can be interpreted as Asian countries' effort to adopt what they consider the global standard of good school education.

Finally, the common trend of the assertion of traditional musical culture is based on the global trend of multiculturalism. When Japan introduced music education into schools in the late nineteenth century, it tried hard to westernise its musical culture in order to be admitted as a member of the modernised world. After the defeat in World War II, it again chose western classical music as the goal of music education. This history of Japanese music education reflects the values of that time when western culture was regarded as the ultimate form of human culture. This view started to change only after the importance of cultural diversity was recognised by the Ministry of Education in 1959 (Monbusho 1959). Since then, the emphasis on multiculturalism for the sake of a peaceful coexistence of culturally different peoples has become much stronger and in the contemporary world, it is now mainstream. In educational policies as well, cultural specificity has become an important element to be recognised as a country that respects the ideal of multiculturalism. Hence local traditional music that most reflects the cultural uniqueness of the country is an important focus in music education.

Influence on teachers' realities

The policies discussed above are supposed to be implemented and their implementation takes specific forms in each country. How they are implemented in each country determines the extent to which teachers are influenced by the new initiatives.

For example, in order to shift from an exam-oriented, teacher-centred approach to a process-oriented, learner-centred approach, Japan has reduced the content of the curriculum, established 'the period of integrated study' and promoted the new concept of learning ability by introducing assessment based on absolute performance of children. What affected music teachers' practice most was the introduction of 'the period of integrated study' and assessment based on absolute performance. 'The period of integrated study', though separate from the subject of music, resulted in reducing the instruction hours of music because time allocated to some other subjects had to be sacrificed in order to create time for this new element. For example, the lack of time was the problem most often mentioned by the four Japanese music teachers interviewed by the authors in 2006.

One of these teachers explained that since musical performance by children is needed at various occasions such as festivals and ceremonies, music teachers have to squeeze practice time for these events into their regular music lessons. With fewer instruction hours, it has become difficult for teachers to find time to devote to this. What is fortunate for Japanese teachers may be the understanding of their colleagues about the importance of the subject of music. They are not asked by other teachers to sacrifice time allocated to music lessons to other subjects. Two teachers admitted that a partial remedy to this problem is that colleagues sometimes offer some of their hours to compensate. This exchange of time is never reported to the local education authority.

The new concept of assessment is also a problem pointed out by Japanese teachers and teacher educators at almost every occasion. Japanese teachers that the authors interviewed were diligent teachers who were seriously making efforts to implement the assessment policy. They talked enthusiastically about how to carry out performance assessment based on the five viewpoints provided by the governmental policy without sacrificing too much instruction time for it. What troubles them most is the assessment of 'interests, eagerness and attitude towards music' and 'ability of music perception'. The policy does not provide any list of children's performances by which teachers can assess their interest, eagerness and attitude towards music. An interviewee considered possible ways of assessing 'ability of music perception' such as children's writings about their feelings and the observation of children's facial expressions, but realised that if children write about their feelings toward a piece of music, it would not be the assessment of musical perception, but more likely an assessment of their writing skills. If some children do not change their facial expressions even when they understand and are emotionally moved by the music, the ability of music perception cannot be assessed from their facial expressions correctly.

Another teacher pointed out the contradictions that performance-based assessment includes. For example, the total score based on the five viewpoints of a child's performance does not necessarily match the teacher's own impression of a child's progress so teachers may adjust the results according to their impression. Therefore, the results of the assessment vary between teachers and the marks children get from one teacher may differ dramatically from what they got from their previous teacher.

Thus, teachers who are trying to implement the policy seriously cannot help questioning the feasibility and validity of the assessment suggested by the policy. Ironically, teachers who do not take the policy seriously do not even notice the difficulty and assess children's perception of music, eagerness, interest and attitude using their own judgment. Other teachers who do not approve the policy from the beginning simply ignore it and just pretend as if they were following the policy. One interviewee revealed that this was often the case among Japanese music teachers.

Teachers in Hong Kong also have difficulty with implementing assessment policy. For them, the most difficult element of assessment is the formative assessment of composition that requires them to immediately make appropriate comments on students' compositions on the spot (Tanaka et al. 2006).

In the South Korean assessment policy, it is recommended that the ability to appreciate music be assessed by students' presentations and writings on what they felt and thought about the music they listened to. If teachers do not question the policy, they will not have any problem with the assessment, but if they start questioning its validity, they will face the same issues as previously mentioned regarding Japanese teachers.

In the PRC, teachers are supposed to assess eagerness and attitudes in a clear and objective way. However, unlike the case of Japan, none of the presentations, papers by Chinese researchers available to the authors nor teachers and teacher educators interviewed considered it to be a critical issue (altogether, two lower secondary school teachers, two primary school teachers, two teacher educators and a graduate school student were interviewed between August 2006 and January 2007). A possible explanation is that the new assessment policy has not yet been seriously tackled by Chinese teachers. If the climate until the early 1990s in which assessment objectives and strategies were not given due consideration (Leung 1994) remains, teachers are not likely to pay attention to the issue. Indeed, one Chinese teacher educator explained to the authors in January 2007 that research on assessment has just begun and teachers are still assessing students' skills based on their own impressions and students' musical knowledge and appreciation is evaluated through written examinations.

According to Xie, Li, and Zhao (2006), the hottest issues for teachers are the adjustment to the new curriculum and the problem of its weaker emphasis on basic skills and knowledge. Another Chinese teacher educator interviewed mentioned the gap between what teachers had been taught about the new curriculum policy at university and the realities of schools to which they were assigned as the biggest problem. The shift to the new curriculum policy introduced is thus causing confusion among teachers. Indeed, other research on Chinese teachers' anxiety, regardless of their subjects, indicates that the shift of the very concept of education, which creates a contradiction between exam-oriented education and the ideal of quality education, is the most important issue for them (Ihicmi 1999; Kurosawa and Zhang 2000).

The contradiction is deep-rooted in Chinese society where a severe urban/rural economic gap exists. Because of the gap, poor farmers hope to move to cities in order to secure a higher income, but are not allowed to do so freely. Poor parents hope their children are able to enter university in a city area and get a job there. It is natural that such parents put pressure on teachers so that their children get good marks in examinations and get a passport to university (Chen 2005). Music education, which is not an exam subject, tends to be taken lightly and its instruction hours are often sacrificed in favour of exam subjects. Such practice has been noticed and criticised by the authority ('Curriculum guides for primary and secondary schools in Shanghai' 1994), but still exists and as a Chinese graduate school student in music education told us in 2006, music teachers themselves take it for granted that their lessons are sacrificed for this purpose.

The urban/rural gap has also made a difference to the qualities of teachers in these areas. Since salaries are low and sometimes delayed in rural areas, teachers do not want to work in a rural school (Brahmstedt and Brahmstedt 1997; Chen 2005; Cheng 2005). While there are sufficient musically trained teachers in cities, many teachers without musical training are teaching music in rural schools. For example in Yancheng City, half of the music teacher posts were vacant in 1995 (Chen 2005). Without proper training, the employed teachers have to depend solely on textbooks.

The problem with the quality of teachers is not only related to rural teachers without musical training. Music teachers' inability to accompany children's singing and playing is pointed out by teacher trainers and a competition of music teaching ability is held for the purpose of improving quality of music teachers (Cheng 2005; Gan and Wang 2006). A lower secondary school music teacher also mentions too much formality in music classes as a problem of current music education in the PRC (Xie et al. 2006). Although the subjects are not limited to music teachers, the results of a questionnaire to Chinese teachers in an in-service training session also indicated that teaching method is an area in which teachers themselves are much interested (Kurosawa and Zhang 2000).

In Malaysia, the subject of music was established in the state school system in 1983. The addition of music as a non-exam subject indicates an attempt to enlarge the role of school education from preparing for examinations to developing children's various abilities. However, neither schools nor teachers are coping well with the shift. Although music is compulsory at the primary level, it becomes an elective subject from the lower secondary level. Only a small number of schools that can provide proper music courses offer them (Ghazali and McPherson 2006). The number of musically trained teachers is also limited and in order to compensate, music teachers' schedules are overloaded. Many Malaysian schools are operated in two shifts and teachers of other subjects teach only either morning or afternoon sessions, but music teachers often have to teach both. The government is trying to increase the number of music teachers by offering short courses to 3000 teachers of other subjects during school holidays (Ghazali and McPherson 2006), but not much can be expected of these hastily trained music teachers in terms of quality. As in the PRC, music lessons are often sacrificed in order to create extra instruction hours for exam subjects and musically trained teachers are often assigned to teach exam subjects other than music (Ghazali and McPherson 2006). All of these indications suggest that the subject of music has not yet secured its status as an indispensable element in the Malaysian school education system.

The influence of the integrated subject of arts being introduced also differs depending on how it is implemented. In the PRC an integrated subject was introduced, but conventional art and music have also remained as separate subjects, leaving schools the option of choosing how to approach these subjects. In South Korea, the integration was implemented only in the first two years of primary education and mainly consisted of music, art and health education with an allocation of six periods (240 minutes) per week (Murao et al. 2003). This allotment of time for instruction seems reasonable if each of the original subjects was allotted two periods before the integration.

If the integration includes upper grades and secondary education where a specialist teacher usually teaches music, the influence becomes larger. Reducing instruction hours is also a critical issue for teachers. This is what happened in Thailand after the integration was implemented in 1990. According to Maryprasith's detailed study of secondary school music teachers in Bangkok in 1998, some teachers perceived the curriculum integration as the devaluation of music by 50% because at their schools the time for the integrated subject 'arts and life' remained one period a week, despite doubling the contents. They expressed their worry about students' superficial learning of each area and the teachers' inability to teach the area they had not been trained for (Maryprasith 1999). Eight years after the integration was implemented, teachers were still very negative about being forced to teach unfamiliar areas.[2]

Taiwanese teachers share the same experience as Thai teachers. Taking the flexibility given to schools into consideration, time for the integrated subject is somewhere between two and 4.5 periods (one period = 40–45 minutes) per week (Oku 2003). If the minimum is adopted at a school, teachers have to teach music, visual art and drama within less than three periods a week. Besides the shortage of time, Taiwanese primary and lower secondary school music teachers are struggling with visual art and drama that are now included in the integrated 'art and humanities'. Although the government both at primary and secondary education level provides 30-hour in-service training sessions, it is still hard for musically trained teachers to teach other areas (Tanaka et al. 2006).

Teaching local traditional music

Just as with other common features, the influence of emphasising cultural specificity on teachers also varies depending on how it is implemented and what kind of local musical cultures each country has.

In Japan, Taiwan and Hong Kong where local musical culture has already been westernised, music educators did not pay much attention to their own traditional music in the past. The same applies to teacher education and teachers in these places are not really qualified to teach local traditional music. In Japan, where the actual experience of traditional music has been introduced at the lower secondary level, enthusiastic music teachers of both primary and secondary education started learning traditional musical instruments either privately or by attending in-service training sessions. For more difficult instruments, they need to make arrangements with volunteers who can come to the school and demonstrate the instruments.

Schools are not ready for teaching traditional music, either. Since schools do not have enough traditional musical instruments for all children to play, teachers are making efforts in various ways. A teacher interviewed has students buy their own Japanese bamboo flutes instead of western recorders despite the risk of the next teacher being unable to teach them. Another teacher has children make bamboo musical instruments by themselves. In some school districts, there is also a system to circulate traditional musical instruments among schools in the district. Given these obstacles, according to a Japanese teacher we interviewed in 2006, many teachers simply play a CD of traditional music in order to complete that part of the curriculum.

In Taiwan not only Chinese, but an additional 13 other diverse cultures are recognised and although there are singing and appreciation materials, the problem is teachers' lack of experience in teaching such music (Tanaka et al. 2006). What is fortunate for teachers is that they are not required to teach students how to play traditional instruments. Even traditional Chinese music, which is the mainstream of traditional music in Taiwan, is not required to be performed by students (Tanaka et al. 2006). So teachers are still free from the burden of learning these instruments or having to secure traditional musical instruments for their students.

In Hong Kong, the Education Department introduced the appreciation of Chinese music into the curriculum and ran courses on Chinese musical instruments for music teachers in the 1980s, but these initiatives were not successful (Law and Ho 2004). The emphasis on Chinese traditional music has been strengthened since the handover in 1997, but still teaching such music remains at the level of appreciation (Law and Ho 2004).

The PRC is becoming more and more like these countries in terms of westernising musical culture. Because of the break in music education due to the Great Cultural Revolution, music education in the PRC is trying to catch up with the rest of the world by promoting children's acquisition of western musical theory as well as the ability to appreciate western classical music, while at the same time recognising their own diverse national musical heritage.

The consequence is the overcrowded content of music textbooks and teacher training programmes. A Japanese researcher asserts that it does not seem realistic that all the contents about musical theory are actually taught by teachers and understood by children because the contents are advanced enough for a book for a specialist of music (Tobe 2000). The interviewed teachers also mentioned the difficulty of playing so many pieces for appreciation and the heavy task of preparing music lessons. In teacher training programmes at university, music education students are required to learn the piano and a traditional musical instrument. However, even for the piano, which is the most popular instrument among teacher trainees, a Chinese teacher educator asserts that the training is far from satisfactory (Cheng 2005). The problems she points out are: many students learn the piano for the first time at university; the teaching method is for professional players and not suitable for beginners and teacher trainees; though piano is compulsory for the first two years, time for practice is insufficient; there are not enough pianos and practice rooms; and there are only a limited number of courses on teaching piano accompaniment (Cheng 2005). Taking these points into consideration, it is not realistic that students without any previous experience develop the ability to play both instruments sufficiently well within several years.

Another problem is providing musical instruments for children at school (Brahmstedt and Brahmstedt 1997). Liu (2006) introduces teachers' efforts to create alternative musical instruments and suggests that by replacing traditional musical instruments with alternative instruments, the problem of the shortage of musical instruments in rural areas will be alleviated.

The realities of teachers described above have resulted in the poor implementation of the policy that requires teachers to secure 20% of instruction time for traditional music. At the practical level, since teachers are better at western music, they tend to teach western music more than traditional music (Xie et al. 2006).

In Malaysia traditional music is included in the curriculum, but actual playing of traditional musical instruments is not compulsory at the primary school level. At lower secondary school level, if a student chooses a music course, playing a traditional musical instrument is compulsory. Therefore it is the secondary school teachers who need to be able to play traditional musical instruments. In theory, there should be no problem because at secondary education level, only schools that can provide music courses have them. However, problems remain, such as musically trained teachers' weakness in music they have not been trained for (Ghazali and McPherson 2006) as well as the shortage of active musicians who can play traditional music (Tanaka et al. 2006).

An inadequate availability of musical instruments is also a problem. During the authors' visit to a state secondary school in Kuala Lumpur, three music teachers pointed out the lack of funding in order to buy enough musical instruments and maintain the air-conditioned music rooms for western and Malaysian music. The problem of not having enough proper equipment is more serious in rural areas and it affects teachers' enthusiasm because even if they have proper training for music teaching, insufficient equipment does not allow them to do what they would otherwise be able to do (Ghazali and McPherson 2006).

In terms of the influence of the emphasis on traditional music, Thailand is an exceptional case because it already had a policy emphasising Thai music and so has not really been affected by this aspect of the recent trends in music education. School education has a strong tradition of teaching Thai music and teachers are more qualified to teach Thai music than western classical music (Maryprasith 1999). Teachers are even allowed the freedom of ignoring western classical music they are not good at. Teacher educators have pointed out the shortage of teachers trained in western music as a problem (Tanaka et al. 2006) and there is pressure from parents who want their children to have the opportunity of learning to play a western musical instrument (Maryprasith 1999). However, since national policy does not impose instruction in western music as part of the curriculum, teachers have no incentive to learn western music themselves.

Teachers are not concerned about their weakness in western music, but rather worry about losing Thai-ness in music (Maryprasith 1999) and their problem is a shortage of traditional musical instruments, which has become an obstacle to teaching Thai classical music (Tanaka et al. 2006). Particularly in culturally diverse rural areas, it is difficult for schools to obtain specific musical instruments and find music teachers who can teach that specific music (Tanaka et al. 2006).

As discussed so far, the emphasis on local traditional music has increased teachers' tasks in many Asian countries where the music curriculum has been centred on western musical theory and western-style pieces and teachers themselves are not familiar with their traditional music. Even in Thailand where teachers are relatively well trained in Thai music, it is impossible for teachers to teach all of its diverse traditional musical cultures as the recent trend of multiculturalism demands.

Conclusion and further realities

What has become clear from the comparison of the curriculum policies and teachers' realities is the gap that exists between them. Many Asian countries have introduced music education policies that have common features. However, common features in policies do not necessarily lead to common practices in classrooms because the strategies of policy implementation, training teachers and the perception of music education in society generally vary among countries.

Child-centred approaches and authentic assessment are encouraged for the purpose of shifting the goal of school education from preparation for examinations to children's total development, but in countries where success in examinations greatly influences a child's opportunities, heavy pressure from society on teachers to teach for examinations remains. If teachers themselves are exam-oriented, they have difficulty understanding the meaning of the new curriculum policy and if they understand the meaning of the policy, they have to confront the pressures from parents. Where new assessment policies are imposed on teachers, they have to put the policy into practice somehow no matter how unrealistic the policies may look. Their problem becomes larger if they are not given enough time for this additional task. Where integration of art subjects was implemented, time and staff were the critical issues. If sufficient instruction hours are secured and teachers who are trained in different areas can teach as a team, there is not as much of a problem.

Dealing with the difficulties posed by introducing traditional music depends on how teachers are trained and whether time and equipment are provided. In many countries, since teachers are trained in western music and schools are equipped with western musical instruments, poor teacher training in traditional music and inadequate supply of traditional musical instruments emerged as the biggest obstacles. However, in countries where the instruction of such music is up to schools or teachers, the problems remain relatively marginal.

Thus, the gaps between the policies and teachers' realities are neither homogeneous nor single-layered. There are: the gap between the written policies and policy makers' commitment to actually secure appropriate resources for their implementation; the gap between educational policies and other policies of the country; the gap between the values reflected in the policies and the values in society in general; the gap between what teachers are expected to do and what they are trained for; the gap between the values written in abstract words in policies and their feasibility; and finally, the gap between the ideal type of traditional music and real contemporary musical cultures in Asian countries.

Is it the teachers' role to try to implement the policies as they are? The gaps between the policies and realities and insufficient governmental initiative to bridge them imply that the educational policies were never really intended or even expected to be completely implemented. Rather, the policies seem to exist in order to display the educational ideal of a country and confirm that the country is following the global trend. Their alienation from local diverse realities is a matter of course. Teachers' roles then are to judge the feasibility and the adequacy of the global trends of policies in the light of their own realities and decide how they best develop the musical abilities of the children they are faced with, with all the implications this has for teacher educators.

This paper finishes with a reminder that the problems mentioned above are only part of the problems faced by music education in schools. This is due to the fact that a large number of generalist teachers, who also teach music, have been excluded from the analysis.

Notes

1. Hong Kong is part of the PRC, but since its cultural experience is quite different from the main land in terms of westernisation, this paper treats Hong Kong separately.
2. There seems to be some variation of instruction hours depending on individual schools, but since Maryprasith's study covers virtually all lower secondary schools in Bangkok, teachers' comments are considered to have some generality. The Thai curriculum was revised in the 2000s, but integrated arts still exists as 'art group studies'. For the information on the existing subjects, see Sedgwick (2005).

References

Abbs, P., ed. 1987. *The living powers: The arts in education*. London: Falmer.
BEING. Org.cn. 2005a. *The National Curriculum Standard: The Curriculum Standard for Music*. http://www.being.org.cn/ncs/music/music.htm.
BEING. Org.cn. 2005b. *The National Curriculum Standard: The Curriculum Standard for Arts*. http://www.being.org.cn/ncs/fine-arts/fine-arts.htm.
Brahmstedt, H., and P. Brahmstedt. 1997. Music education in China. *Music Education Journal* 83, no. 6: 28–30, 52.
Chen, J. 2005. Sohoku kisokyoiku no hatten katei ni okeru mujun to sono taisaku [The contradiction in the process of developing basic education in Northern Jiangsu Province and its remedy]. In *Education in contemporary China under the reform and opening-up policy: Case of Jiangsu Province*, ed. H. Abe. Tokyo: Toshindo.
Cheng, Y. 2005. *Chugoku Shihan Daigaku ni Okeru Ongakuka Kyoin Yosei ni Tsuite no Kosatsu: Shokyu-sha karano Piano Kyoiku ni Shoten o Atete* [A study on music teacher training at Chinese Normal University: The case of beginners' Piano Training]. Unpublished master dissertation. Tokyo: Tokyo Gakugei University.
Consortium of National Arts Education Associations. 1994. *National Standards for Arts Education: What every young American should know and be able to do in the arts*. Lanham: Rowman & Littlefield Education.

Curriculum guides for primary and secondary schools in Shanghai. 1994. *Chinese Education and Society* 27, no. 1: 43–78.

Dore, R. 1976. *The diploma disease: Education, qualification and development*. London: George Allen & Unwin.

Gan, L., and Z.X. Wan. 2006. The role of music teacher in schools in 21st century: Musician, educator or researcher?: A reflection on the Fourth National Music Class Competition in mainland China. Paper presented at the 27th International Society for Music Education World Conference, Kuala Lumpur, Malaysia, 16–21 July.

Ghazali, G.M., and G.E. McPherson. 2006. Children's motivation to learn music: The Malaysian context. Paper presented at the 27th International Society for Music Education World Conference, Kuala Lumpur, Malaysia, 16–21 July.

Gipps, C. 1996. Assessment for learning. In *Assessment in transition*, ed. A. Little and A. Wolf. London: Pergamon.

Ichimi, M. 1999. Chugoku sohsitsu kyoiku no yukue: sono kaikaku kaiho seisaku ni okeru ichizuke o megutte [Where Chinese quality education is heading: Its position in reform and openness policy]. In *Education in contemporary China under the reform and opening-up policy: Case of Jiangsu Province*, ed. H. Abe. Tokyo: Toshindo.

Ishii, Y., M. Shiobara, and H. Ishii. 2005. Globalisation and national identity: A reflection on the Japanese music curriculum. *Globalisation, Societies and Education* 3, no. 1: 67–82.

Kementerian Pendidikan Malaysia (The Ministry of Education Malaysia). 2002. *Huraian Sukatan Pelajaran Sekolah Rendah: Pendidikan Muzik* [The description of the primary school education policy: Music]. http://www.ppk.kpm.my.

Kurosawa, K., and M. Zhang. 2000 *Gendai Chugoku to Kyoshi Kyoiku* [Contemporary China and teacher education]. Tokyo: Akashi Shoten.

Law, W.W., and W.C. Ho. 2004. Values education in Hong Kong school music education: A sociological critique. *British Journal of Educational Studies* 52, no. 1: 65–82.

Lawton, D. 1988. *Education, culture and the National Curriculum*. London: Hodder and Stoughton.

Leung, J.Y.M. 1994. Editor's introduction. *Chinese Education and Society* 27, no. 1: 3–7.

Liu, L. 2006. Music education network by non-governmental efforts in China: Brief introduction to the characteristics of the Hong Xiao Music Education Networks. Paper presented at the 27th International Society for Music Education World Conference, Kuala Lumpur, Malaysia, 16–21 July.

Marinas, B.O., and M.P. Ditapat. 2000. Curriculum development. In *Globalization and living together: The challenges for educational content in Asia*. Final report of the Sub-Regional Course, organized by the International Bureau of Education and the Indian Ministry of Human Resources Development. Paris and New Delhi: UNESCO and Central Board of Secondary Education. http://www.ibe.unesco.org/publications/regworkshops.

Maryprasith, P. 1999. *The effects of globalizaton on the status of music in Thai society*. Unpublished PhD thesis. London: Institute of Education, University of London.

Ministry of Education Republic of Korea. 1999. Review of national policies on education: Follow-up to OECD's education review of Korea. In *Education in Korea 1999–2000*, ed. Ministry of Education Republic of Korea.

Monbusho (The Ministry of Education). 1959. *Chugakko Ongaku Shidoso* [The guidebook for teaching secondary schools: music]. Tokyo: Toyokan Shuppan-sha.

Monbusho (The Ministry of Education). 1996. Shogakko jido shido yoroku: kaku kyoka no gakushu no kiroku [The record of instruction for primary school pupils: The record of learning of each subject]. In *Shogakko Shakai Shido Shiryo: Atarashii Gakuryokukan ni Tatsu Shakaikano Gakushu Shido no Sozo* [Primary school instruction resource: The creation of social studies instruction based on the new view on learning abilities]. Tokyo: Toyokan Shuppan-sha.

Monbusho (The Ministry of Education). 1998. *Shogakko Gakushu Shido Yoryo* [Primary school course of study]. Tokyo: Okurasho Insatsukyoku.

Murao, T., I. Go, and S. Park. 2003. Kankoku [South Korea]. In *Ongaku no Karikyuramu no Kaizen ni Kansuru Kenkyu: Shogaikoku no Doko* [A study on the improvement of music curriculum: Trends in other countries], ed. Kokuritsu Kyoiku Seisaku Kenkyu-jo. http://www.nier.go.jp/kiso/kyouka/kyouka15.pdf.

Nishizono, Y., and F. Dong. 2003. Chugoku [China]. In *Ongaku no Karikyuramu no Kaizen ni Kansuru Kenkyu: Shogaikoku no Doko* [A study on the improvement of music curriculum: Trends in other countries], ed. Kokuritsu Kyoiku Seisaku Kenkyu-jo. http://www.nier.go.jp/kiso/kyouka/kyouka15.pdf.

Nomura, K., and Y. Nakayama. 1997. Present music education in China: With special reference to an analysis of Music Kyogaku-Taiko and textbooks in elementary schools. *Nihon Kyoka Kyoiku Gakkai-shi* [Journal of Japan Subject Education Society] 20, no. 2: 39–48.

Oku, S. 2003. Taiwan. In *Ongaku no Karikyuramu no Kaizen ni Kansuru Kenkyu: Shogaikoku no Doko* [A study on the improvement of music curriculum: Trends in other countries], ed. Kokuritsu Kyoiku Seisaku Kenkyu-jo. http://www.nier.go.jp/kiso/kyouka/kyouka15.pdf.

Pitiyanuwat, S., and A. Anantrasirichai. 2002. Curriculum and learning reform in Thailand. Paper presented at Invitational Curriculum Policy Seminar, School based curriculum renewal for the knowledge society developing capacity for new times, Hong Kong, 14–16 November. http://ci-lab.ied.edu.hk/clprogram/icp/Curriculum-andLearning-Reform-in-Thailand.pdf.

PLC. 1997. An (experimental) curriculum plan for all-day primary schools and lower middle schools in the nine-year mandatory educational system. *Chinese Education and Society* 27, no. 2: 68–96.

Sedgwick, R. 2005. Education in Thailand. *World Education News and Reviews*, March/April. http://www.wes.org/ewenr/PF/05mar.

Shiobara, M., and Y. Ishii. 1998. Can Japanese children survive in the 21st century?: Toward new values for education in Japanese education reform in the 1990s. *Kiyo VISIO* 25: 143–49.

Tanaka, K. et al. 2006. School music education in Asian countries: Basic information and current issues. A talk delivered at the 27th International Society for Music Education World Conference, Kuala Lumpur, Malaysia, 16–21 July.

Tobe, T. 2000. A comprehensive study in music education between Japan and China: A survey through the textbooks. *Bulletin of Tokiwa Junior College* 29: 37–49.

Xie, J., W. Li, and X. Zhao. 2006. Facing up: Problems of music education in mainland China. Paper presented at the 27th International Society for Music Education World Conference, Kuala Lumpur, Malaysia,16–21 July.

Alternate routes in initial teacher education: a critical review of the research and policy implications for Hong Kong

Kwok Chan Lai[a] and David Grossman[b]

[a]Strategic and Academic Planning, Hong Kong Institute of Education, Hong Kong, China;
[b]Faculty of Languages, Arts and Sciences, Hong Kong Institute of Education, Hong Kong, China

Introduction

Worldwide there is little debate over the need for a high quality teaching force. It would thus seem that teachers should be among the most knowledgeable and skilled in a society, and that they should have more education (in most cases a first degree at minimum) than is the mode within their society. This is reflected in the often substantial requirements for entry into the profession. Traditionally initial teacher preparation in most countries is based in universities or higher education institutions (HEIs), requiring the students to undergo full-time academic course work and supervised student teaching before they obtain teacher certification or Qualified Teacher Status (QTS). In a summary of teacher education practices in APEC countries (Cobb 1999), three general approaches were identified:

   A. Sub-degree certificate or diploma programmes in normal colleges, normal schools, and colleges of education established for the purpose of training teachers. These programmes are usually for elementary teachers and emphasise pedagogical preparation more than subject area preparation in programmes that are generally two to four years in length.
   B. Bachelor's degree programmes, usually three to four years in length, housed at general, multipurpose universities, with greater emphasis on subject matter preparation, and relatively less on pedagogy.

C. Master's degree and/or fifth-year programmes of one or two years' duration designed for graduates with a bachelor's degree who receive a master's degree or postgraduate diploma.

We would label the above as the traditional pathways to teacher certification. In recent years, however, non-traditional pathways or alternative routes for initial teacher education (ITE) have been growing in number internationally. These alternative pathways refer to a wide range of non-traditional programmes, from emergency certification for immediate employment as a teacher to programmes that prepare individuals who already have at least a bachelor's degree and considerable life experience and want to become teachers. They include school-centred initial teacher training and employment-based teacher training for non-qualified serving teachers; and specialised teacher recruitment programmes such as Teach for America in the USA and Teach First in England. They are specifically designed to recruit and prepare university graduates of non-education fields or mid-career changers for teaching and to allow them to acquire their teaching qualifications more rapidly than in traditional modes.

In the case of Hong Kong, untrained teachers have served as a convenient buffer to meet teacher demand for many decades. It was only in 1997 that the Chief Executive of the new Hong Kong Special Administrative Region (HKSAR) announced a policy objective of requiring all new teachers to be degree holders and professionally trained in the 'foreseeable future'. However, this policy was short-lived. There is substantial evidence to support the claim that the wavering in government policy has been influenced by the developments of alternative routes of teacher preparation elsewhere. In this context in this article we examine the interaction between local policies on and international trends in teacher preparation. The policy shift in Hong Kong is used as a case study of the long and difficult process of teacher professionalisation and may provide useful insights for other parts of the world.

Background: the growth of alternate routes in ITE

As cited above, in recent years non-traditional pathways or alternative routes for initial teacher education have proliferated in the US and the UK (Furlong 2005; Berliner 2006), and are advocated in a number of European countries (Eurydice 2004) and Australia (Parliament of Victoria 2005). The impetus for this development has been largely attributed to the efforts of governments to alleviate critical teacher shortages in high need subjects and geographical districts. At the same time traditional university- or college-based pathways to teacher certification have been criticised as lacking quality and deterring talented prospective teachers from entering the profession (Walsh 2001; US Department of Education 2002).

Today alternative routes to certification have become a well established part of the education landscape in the USA and the UK. In the US teachers are traditionally prepared by college-based four-year degree in education programmes, though the requirements for certification or licensing after graduation vary greatly from state to state. Teacher shortages, particularly in the hard-to-staff subject areas and geographical districts, had traditionally been met by bringing in untrained teachers on emergency permits to take up the unfilled positions. In the past decade, a large variety of alternative routes to certification have proliferated in nearly all states in the US. It is estimated that approximately 50,000 people were issued with teaching certificates through alternative routes in 2004–2005, comprising approximately one-third of the new teachers in the US in that year. In 2006, 48 states and the District of Columbia reported that they were offering a total of 124 alternative routes being implemented in 619 programme sites across the country (Feistritzer 2006).

In the UK, the conventional routes of initial teacher training (ITT) consist of three- or four-year full-time undergraduate courses, i.e. the Bachelor of Education (BEd) or the BA/BSc in Education, and the one-year full-time Postgraduate Certificate in Education (PGCE) provided by the HEIs. All these routes lead to the QTS. Since the late 1980s, in line with managerialist reforms in the public sector, the government has exercised control over initial teacher education on an unprecedented scale. In 1993, it created the Teacher Training Agency (TTA), now called the Training and Development Agency for Schools (TDA), which had responsibility for setting the standards for the QTS and allocating funding to teacher education providers.

With an aim to set up a competitive market and attract people with work experience into teaching, the TTA was required to promote the development of school-centred and employment-based teacher education systems, such as the School-Centred Initial Teacher Training (SCITT) scheme and the Graduate Teacher Programme respectively (Furlong 2005). The TTA was authorised to approve any university, school or other organisation to be an accredited initial training provider in England. In 2005–2006, among the over 33,400 people recruited to ITT courses in England, 94.8% were enrolled in HEIs and 5.2% (1740 trainees) were recruited in SCITTs (DfES 2006). The biggest growth, nevertheless, has been in the numbers trained on employment-based routes, which have increased from 1790 in 2000–2001 (6% of the number of teacher trainees that year) to an estimated 7100 in 2005–2006 (17.5% of trainees) (DfES 2006).

The growth of alternative routes to teacher education in these countries has posed a fundamental challenge to university-based teacher education as schools, school-based consortia, for-profit organisations and community colleges now act as teacher education providers in their own right. In the US, Levine (2006, 36) describes that the franchise of America's colleges and universities on educating the nation's teachers 'is eroding as states deregulate requirements for becoming a teacher and non-university providers of teacher education mushroom'. The emphasis in teacher education has shifted from pre-service course work to on-the-job training, support and mentoring of serving teachers. Furthermore, governments and influential sections of the community have been increasingly critical of the effectiveness of university-based teacher education as well as the quality of their teacher candidates (Walsh 2001; US Department of Education 2002).

In order to understand the above developments, in the following section we examine government policies on initial teacher education in these countries in a broader context.

The policy context

As mentioned above, a major impetus for the deregulation of university-based training requirements and the development of alternative pathways has been the desire by governments to increase the supply of teachers to alleviate the chronic teacher shortage caused by teacher retirements and high attrition among new teachers. For instance, in the US, these measures are aimed to broaden the pool of prospective teachers in certain high need subject areas such as mathematics and science, special education, bilingual education, and in the most challenging schools in inner cities or rural communities (US Department of Education 2004; Berliner 2006). Similarly, in the UK, the non-traditional pathways are aimed to meet teacher shortages in a number of subject areas, such as mathematics, science and technology, and in certain geographical areas, such as London and the South East of England.

The proponents of alternative pathways consider that traditional teacher preparation systems are not providing enough quality teachers. Traditional programmes are perceived as too slow; inflexible in scheduling; and inaccessible to 'talented' graduates who have not studied education and mid-career professionals who wish to change their careers to become teachers (Hess, Rotherham, and Walsh 2005). In addition, favouring a market-based approach, these advocates consider alternative routes to be 'highly efficient' as schools could recruit and train only those teachers with the expertise that meet their specific needs and job openings (Buckingham 2005; Feistritzer 2006).

In both the US and the UK, the growth of alternative routes to teacher education has coincided with government efforts to carry out large-scale education reforms and standards movements to raise student achievement, in which teachers are considered as the key to success (Olson 2006). In this regard, traditional pathways are criticised about their inability to attract and prepare an adequate number of teachers of the desired quality (Walsh 2001; US Department of Education 2002). The proponents of alternative routes believe that the most important significant predictors of teacher quality are teachers' strength of subject matter knowledge and their own level of literary, and the education course work offered in universities is often unrelated to teacher effectiveness (Buckingham 2005). Furthermore, in the US, the passage of the federal 'No Child Left Behind' (NCLB) Act in 2001, which requires all teachers to be 'highly qualified' in their teaching field by the academic year 2005–2006, has further emphasised the importance of subject knowledge. Since the Act does not require teachers to have completed education course work based in universities, it has given further impetus to state governments to offer alternative routes to recruit qualified professionals from other fields.

In addition, some proponents of alternative routes believe that the quality of school-based or site-based models is better than traditional university-based models as the former can better cater for the practical needs of schools through making classrooms more central to teacher preparation. In other words, they found that many new graduates of the traditional model 'seem to lack practical teaching skills, as opposed to the theoretical foundations required to be an effective teacher' (Buckingham 2005, 3).

The above criticisms of traditional university-based teacher education and calls for a shift to alternative and school-based teacher education have led to highly politicised and polarising debates, particularly in the US. Supporters of the traditional model fought back against the criticisms by asserting that alternative routes are shortcuts to teacher education that tend to produce inadequately prepared teachers, who are then expected to take on the most demanding teaching posts (Berliner 2006). Instead, they argued that teachers need stronger preparation before they teach in disadvantaged schools with low-income children and minorities (NCTAF 1996). Furthermore, they believe that initial teacher education requires the transmission of a well-defined body of professional knowledge through prescribed and formal programmes, versus teacher 'training' which is narrow and utilitarian.

We will see that these debates are echoed in Hong Kong, but first we will introduce Hong Kong's teacher education system and then trace the development of policies on initial teacher education before and after the establishment of the HKSAR in 1997.

Teacher education in Hong Kong

Teacher qualifications

In Hong Kong, historically there has been no requirement that a candidate has to be professionally trained before they can enter teaching. Any person who wishes to teach in a school has to apply to the Education Bureau (EDB) (formerly the Education and Manpower Bureau (EMB)) for registration as either a 'Registered Teacher' (RT) or a 'Permitted Teacher' (PT). To qualify for registration as a RT, a person will have obtained a QTS through completion of an approved teacher education programme which may be a sub-degree level Certificate in Education, a bachelor's degree in education or a Postgraduate Certificate/Diploma in Education (PGCE/PGDE). For registration as a PT, a person only needs to hold the minimum academic qualification, i.e. a sub-degree qualification or an Associate degree, but does not need to possess any recognised teacher training qualification. In this regard, the PT status in Hong Kong is similar to the 'emergency certification' in the US. The difference is that there is no stipulation in Hong Kong that PTs must complete teacher training in a specified period to receive RT status. In fact, the requirements had been so lax that, until the year 2004, a PT was eligible for registration as a RT through mere accumulation of teaching experience and without undergoing training.

From the 1950s to the 1970s, untrained teachers or PTs had been regarded as a convenient buffer to meet the tremendous expansion in mass education. In 1974, the percentages of untrained serving primary and secondary school teachers, many of whom had only completed secondary schooling, were as high as 27.5% and 67.4%, respectively. The In-service Courses of Training for Teachers (ICTT) had played a key role in meeting the minimum training needs of thousands of unqualified non-graduate teachers during this period (Lai 2002). This state of reliance on untrained teachers and in-service training had basically remained little changed for several decades (Sweeting 1995). Nevertheless, with stabilisation in school enrolment and an increase in training capacity, the percentages of untrained teachers in both primary and secondary schools had decreased to 14% and 27%, respectively, in the year 1990.

Nowadays, most PTs will complete their professional training through part-time study in teacher education institutions in order to receive the RT status. Otherwise, a salary bar will be imposed on them within the first five years of service. Without a professional qualification, they are also not eligible for promotion to senior teaching posts.

Teacher preparation system

Similar to many places formerly under the British rule, before the late 1990s, teacher preparation in Hong Kong had traditionally been separated into the 'non-graduate' and 'graduate' tracks which had operated under the concurrent and consecutive models, respectively:

- *Concurrent model*: Government-run Colleges of Education offered two- and three-year full-time sub-degree level programmes, i.e. the Teachers' Certificate or Certificate in Education, to prepare 'non-graduate' teachers for primary schools and the junior levels of secondary schools. The candidates took education courses concurrently with subject studies.
- *Consecutive model*: The faculties of education of two comprehensive universities offered a one-year full-time PGCE/PGDE programme to prepare teachers for the senior secondary level. This model is also known as the '3+1' route as it focuses on professional training for graduates who have completed a three-year bachelor's degree with an academic major.

The Colleges of Education had faced a serious challenge in the late 1980s when the government rapidly expanded the provision of university education, which had greatly reduced the attraction of their sub-degree teacher education programmes. The concerns over the future of the Colleges and the quality of entrants to primary teaching had led to the *Education Commission (EC) report no. 5* in 1992 which recommended the amalgamation of the Colleges to form an autonomous institution, the Hong Kong Institute of Education (HKIEd) two years later. Furthermore, the Report also recommended the creation of graduate posts in primary schools to attract quality graduates into primary teaching. The upgrading schedule was initially slow as the plan was to have only 35% of primary teachers appointed to graduate posts by 2007.

With the creation of positions in primary schools for degree holders, primary teaching was no longer regarded as a career for non-graduates. Furthermore, the HKIEd had progressively replaced its sub-degree level awards in both primary and secondary education with bachelor's degrees and postgraduate diplomas. Its last cohort of Certificate in Education students graduated in 2004, signalling an end to the dual track of teacher preparation.

At present, initial teacher education is offered mainly in four HEIs funded by the University Grants Committee (hereafter UGC), i.e. the HKIEd and three comprehensive universities. Both concurrent and consecutive pathways are offered for the preparation of primary and secondary teachers. The former sub-degree Certificate level programmes have been replaced by four-year bachelor's programmes in education, i.e. a Bachelor of Education (BEd) or a BA or BSc in education. In this regard, the teacher preparation system in Hong Kong is largely similar to that in the United Kingdom.

The changing policy context in Hong Kong

In 1997, Hong Kong underwent a political transition from a British colony to a Special Administrative Region (SAR) of the People's Republic of China. The new Chief Executive, Mr Tung Chee Hwa, and the SAR Government were zealous in drawing up comprehensive blueprints to guide Hong Kong's social and economic development so as to meet the challenges of globalisation and a knowledge-based economy. Education was seen as pivotal to this development: the Chief Executive entrusted the EC to conduct a comprehensive review of the education system with a view to draw up a blueprint for reform for the twenty-first century (Hong Kong Government 1997). Based on EC's recommendations, education reforms in a number of areas, such as the school system, curriculum and assessment, have been launched in the past few years (Education Commission 2000).

The raising of the qualifications and competence of teachers were considered as crucial to realise the goals of the education reform. In the past decade, the government has been highly involved in setting the professional standards for new and serving teachers in the past few years. In 1997, it declared the policy objective of requiring all new teachers to be graduates and professionally trained in the 'foreseeable future' (see next section). Yet the main thrust has been on improving the standards of English language teachers. This has largely been in response to the concerns of the powerful business community which has been increasingly critical of the allegedly falling English standards of university and school graduates.

In the year 2000, the government decided to set up the *Language Proficiency Requirements* (LPR) for over 15,000 new and serving teachers of English and Putonghua (Mandarin) in both primary and secondary schools. Any new teacher who began teaching these two subjects from September 2004 would have to demonstrate, before taking up the responsibility, that he/she had already met the requirement. In addition, all serving teachers in these two subjects will have to meet the requirement before the end of the 2005/2006 school year. Those who failed to attain the requirement would not be allowed to teach the respective language subjects. The policy has resulted in prolonged confrontations with the largest teacher union in Hong Kong. At that time, the government apparently believed that ensuring teachers' language proficiency had a higher priority than requiring them to be professionally trained.

Before the LPR target was attained, the government adopted a report of the influential Standing Committee on Language Education and Research (SCOLAR) (2003) which recommended that all English and Chinese language teachers should also be well grounded in subject knowledge and pedagogy of their respective subject. The government stipulated that, starting from the 2004–2005 school year, all school principals are required to recruit language teachers who had both a degree in the relevant language subject and professional qualifications with a major in that language subject. If the new recruit does not have a relevant degree, he/she should complete a first degree/postgraduate level programme focusing on the subject knowledge of the particular language within five years. In the section below, we will note that the requirement for new language teachers is not consistent with the government's decision to put off the policy of requiring new teachers to be professionally trained.

'All trained, all graduate' requirement for new teachers

As mentioned above, the goal to improve teacher qualifications was given a significant boost when the Chief Executive announced the policy objective of requiring all new primary and secondary school teachers to be degree holders and professionally trained in the 'foreseeable future' (Hong Kong Government 1997). At the time it was a bold initiative as the percentages of newly joined teachers who were professionally trained in that year were only 62.8% and 29.4% at the primary and secondary levels, respectively. In addition, only 39.1% of the newly joined primary teachers possessed a bachelor's degree or above (Lai, Ko, and Li 2001).

To implement the new policy objective, the Chief Executive requested the UGC to conduct a thorough review of pre-service teacher education in Hong Kong, including the drawing up of a timetable for implementation and studying the implications of the new policy for the development of the higher education system and the role of the HKIEd (Hong Kong Government 1997). In 1998, he further announced in his policy address that the HKIEd would be developed into a degree-awarding institution and the sub-degree primary and secondary teacher education programmes offered by the Institute would be progressively upgraded to degree and higher level programmes (Hong Kong Government 1998).

At the same time, the Chief Executive had also asked the EC to consider plans to establish a General Teaching Council to address the issue of how to upgrade the professionalism and status of the teaching profession in Hong Kong, and to develop a professional training ladder for serving teachers (Hong Kong Government 1997). However, this policy has not been implemented and the government is still solely in charge of development of policies concerning teacher qualifications and registration.

Retreat from the 'all trained, all graduate' policy

Despite the Chief Executive's policy goal of an 'all graduate, all trained' profession in the 'foreseeable future', the government has hitherto refrained from setting a date to achieve this goal. The 1998 report submitted by UGC to the government was never released to the public (University Grants Committee 1998). By the following year the EMB had begun to describe the policy as a 'long term' target (Education and Manpower Bureau 1999). In addressing the Legislative Council, the former Secretary for Education and Manpower, Mr Joseph Wong said, 'while we have not set a specific date for the completion of the target, we are taking active measures to work towards the target' (LCQ 10 1999, 1345). In reality there is substantial evidence that the government actually retreated from the policy objective of requiring new teachers to be professionally trained. In October 2002, the Permanent Secretary for Education and Manpower, Mrs Fanny Law, admitted for the first time that the policy would not be met in the short term due to a lack of resources. Instead, the emphasis of teacher training would be on requiring untrained teachers to undergo training within their first two years of service (Chong and Poon 2002).

In response, a number of educators expressed their disappointment with the government's retreat from the policy at a time when 1100 untrained teachers were joining the teaching force, comprising 40.5% of the newly joined teachers in 2001. During a press conference organised by the HKIEd, the lead author of this paper pointed out that the government would miss a golden opportunity to implement the policy because the supply of trained teachers would increase sharply in the following years while the demand for teachers would drop due to the continual decline in birth rates. He also cautioned that Hong Kong would lag behind its neighbouring countries by not requiring its new teachers to be professionally trained. It would also be a big step backward in moving towards teacher professionalisation. As long as the professional status of teachers could not be established, it would be difficult to attract high quality candidates into the teaching profession. He proposed that the policy should be implemented in the primary and secondary sectors by 2005 and 2007 respectively. Temporary teacher licences could be issued to untrained teachers for a small number of subjects in which trained teachers were in short supply (HKIEd 2002). A similar view was also expressed by a school principal who contended that untrained teachers would face difficulties in carrying out the education reform and teachers in most subjects should be required to complete pre-service training (Chong and Poon 2002). In spite of the suggestions, the government insisted that implementing the policy in the short term was not realistic because of a shortage of resources (Hui 2002).

Influence by developments of alternative routes elsewhere

During the debate, a Deputy Secretary for Education and Manpower provided a revealing account of the government's thinking on why it did not want to require all new teachers to be professionally trained (Cheng 2002). Interestingly, a lot of his arguments were strikingly similar to those supporting the deregulation of teacher education systems and the development of alternative pathways to teacher certification elsewhere, particularly in the US.

Maintaining flexibility in teacher supply

On the supply side, the Deputy Secretary pointed out that implementing the policy was not realistic as there was an acute shortage of teachers in certain subjects, especially English language. In addition, flexibility was needed as past experience indicated that the supply of teachers would be affected by economic conditions – e.g. the number of entrants would be reduced by a thriving economy. Hence, it would be necessary to maintain a supply buffer to ensure that suitable personnel could still be recruited to fill urgent or unanticipated teaching vacancies.

Deterring talented people from becoming teachers

The EMB further questioned the desirability of imposing the training requirement as this would jeopardise teacher quality by deterring high-calibre students or professionals from becoming teachers (Hui 2002). Referring to the views of some school principals, the Deputy Secretary also claimed that:

> On the user side, the government is aware that when selecting teachers, school principals tend to place greater emphasis on a candidate's personal qualities and subject knowledge than on academic or professional qualifications alone. A rigidly-imposed, all-trained policy will unduly limit the ability of schools to select the right staff. (Cheng 2002)

Most disturbing of all, the Deputy Secretary then launched a blistering remark on the quality of graduates from teacher education institutions:

> The employment of untrained teachers, at a time when there is surplus of trained teachers in certain subjects, raises serious questions about the quality and relevance of existing teacher education programmes. This situation deserves closer analysis and reflection by the teacher education institutions. We certainly believe that teacher education institutions should ensure their graduates are equally, if not better, educated than their untrained counterparts. (Cheng 2002)

It is notable that a number of secondary school principals had concurred with the government's views. For instance, a principal was of the view that implementing the training requirement would deter mid-career changers and talented individuals from entering teaching (Chong and Poon 2002). Another said that 'recruitment flexibility is vital' as it would allow schools to recruit 'candidates they found suitable even though they might not have received any teacher training' (Ng 2002). Apparently, many preferred to employ university graduates with in-depth understanding of their school subject, irrespective of whether they had received professional training.

Preference for in-service training

Instead of requiring new teachers to be professionally trained when they enter teaching, the 'all trained' policy was reinterpreted to mean that new teachers should obtain training qualifications after a few years of teaching. The Deputy Secretary attributed this policy shift to the ongoing deliberation by the Advisory Committee on Teacher Education and Qualifications (ACTEQ) on the introduction of a period of internship for beginning teachers as a necessary condition for obtaining Registered Teacher status:

> [Initial] teacher education should entail substantial and comprehensive workplace experience. ... With the introduction of an internship period, the point of entry into the teaching profession can be redefined. ... With an induction and mentoring support programme for beginning teachers ... it is conceivable that academically-competent, degree-holding but untrained teachers could still be taken on board. (Cheng 2002)

In this regard, the EMB was no longer keen to draw up plans to ensure an adequate supply of pre-service trained graduates, but wanted to ensure that sufficient in-service training places would be provided for untrained teachers. Subsequently, it instructed teacher education institutions to shift the balance of initial teacher education provisions from the pre-service to the in-service route. At the same time, the institutions were advised to offer short courses on teaching methods and classroom management for untrained teachers before they enter teaching. The government claimed that it would require the 'teaching interns' to enrol in in-service teacher education programmes within two years of joining the profession (Chong and Poon 2002). However, up till now there are no policies requiring new teachers to undergo internship or to complete in-service training.

There is considerable evidence to demonstrate that the Hong Kong government's policies in initial teacher education have been considerably influenced by the developments of alternative routes of teacher preparation elsewhere and in particular from the US and UK. During a radio programme (in which the lead author of this paper participated), the Deputy Secretary for Education and Manpower waved a copy of the US Secretary of Education report as evidence supporting government policies in Hong Kong. In a meeting of the HKIEd Council, the Secretary for Education and Manpower (SEM), Professor Arthur Li, openly questioned whether teacher education institutions were vying for a 'monopoly' by advocating that teachers need to be pre-service trained. In a legislative session the SEM was more direct:

> To capture the best talents, the teaching profession must not be a closed system. Under the current legislation, university graduates without teacher training can enter the teaching force as permitted teachers. They should then pursue in-service teacher education to acquire their professional training. (LCQ 2 2003)

The arguments elsewhere for alternative pathways to teacher education have clearly influenced ACTEQ, the major government consultative committee on teacher education. While the then Chairman of ACTEQ emphasised that its thinking was still at a preliminary stage, the basic principles are clear in a paper which was recently made available to teacher education providers. It outlined a framework for ITE as follows:

- there should be 'multiple routes and multiple modes' of providing preparation for beginning teachers,

- it would be increasingly necessary to include second career teachers as target learners in ITE programmes,
- teacher education institutions should engage in stronger partnership with schools and develop collaborations with non-school partners,
- there will be a heavier emphasis on learning in practice in contrast to learning through lectures and examinations (ACTEQ 2006).

With the keen interest expressed by ACTEQ on mid-career changers, multiple routes, internship for untrained teachers and questioning the relevance of university-based teacher education, a number of teacher educators believe that the government will increase its intervention in ITE, advocate greater school participation in teacher preparation or even introduce school-based teacher education in the future. It will adopt and adapt alternative pathways to ITE similar to models from the US and UK.

Discussion

Hong Kong has a long history of depending on the supply of untrained teachers to meet the demand of schools. Lai's study (2002) demonstrated that though the remedial ICTT courses for unqualified teachers without degrees had all along been perceived by the community to be of dubious quality, they had lasted for five decades from the 1950s to the early 2000s as untrained teachers continued to join the teaching force in the absence of a government policy requiring new teachers to be trained. Lai concluded that the prolongation of these courses for half a century had illustrated the long and difficult process by which Hong Kong has been moving towards an 'all trained' teaching profession. According to Lai, 'The experiences showed that once remedial measures have been set firmly in place, there had been a tendency for the government to continue to rely on them to meet new quantitative demands. Quantitative considerations had perennially taken priority over qualitative ones' (Lai 2002, 9).

Similarly, secondary schools in Hong Kong have also depended on the supply of untrained university graduates, who later obtained their teaching qualifications through the part-time PGDE. Many secondary school principals were trained through the part-time route, which may partly explain their habitual objection over any attempts to impose a training requirement for new teachers.

The wavering policies on initial teacher education since the establishment of the HKSAR in 1997 deserve more careful study. The quick retreat of the HKSAR Government from the first Chief Executive's policy objective of an 'all graduate, all trained' requirement for new teachers has partly represented a perpetuation of the longstanding mentality of putting supply considerations over qualitative ones and by a lack of commitment to expand pre-service teacher education places to meet the target. However, the policy shift has apparently been entangled with an enthusiasm in the development of alternative routes to initial teacher education and the criticism of university-based teacher education elsewhere. In other words, the arguments adopted by proponents of alternative routes elsewhere have conveniently been borrowed by the policy makers in Hong Kong:

- Training requirements deter talented or highly qualified people from entering teaching.

- The academic standard of teacher education graduates is doubtful.
- Teacher education institutions should not pose hurdles to schools recruiting teachers that best suit their needs.
- A key predictor of teacher quality is the strength of his/her subject matter knowledge; whether a teacher has professional training is of secondary importance.
- Academically competent individuals need not undertake course work or just take short courses prior to entering teaching; they can acquire professional qualifications in the workplace with mentoring support.

The enthusiasm of Hong Kong policy makers in removing hurdles for talented individuals to enter teaching and breaking the 'monopoly' of HEIs is paradoxical as they have ignored the local context in which hundreds of individuals without any teacher training are recruited by schools every year. These teachers could readily acquire their professional qualifications through the completion of a part-time PGDE programme which is by nature a type of alternative route to teacher certification. In this regard, pre-service teacher education based in HEIs has never acted as a deterrent to non-education graduates and mid-career changers in Hong Kong. Furthermore, compared with alternative routes elsewhere, the requirements in Hong Kong are so lax that there is not even the need for untrained teachers to complete short-duration or crash courses before teaching in classrooms.

In the absence of a firm policy commitment, a large number of untrained teachers have continued to join the teaching force every year. In 2005, nearly 25% of the newly joined primary and secondary school teachers were still untrained. This situation has periodically caught the attention of the media and the legislative councillors. The EMB habitually responded to their criticisms by affirming that it was 'fully committed' to the 'all graduate, all trained' policy (Ng 2002), and that it had issued letters to all schools urging them to give priority to recruiting professionally trained teachers (LCQ 16 2003).

The formulation of government policies in education has not been coherent, a phenomenon which has been described by Morris and Scott (2003) as 'disarticulated'. For example, the government's adoption of the SCOLAR recommendation to require new language teachers to be professionally trained came as a surprise to the educational community as it was completely inconsistent with the government's previous insistence on not imposing the pre-service training requirement due to the critical shortage of English language teachers. This had probably reflected more the influence of the powerful members of SCOLAR than a government reversal in policy on initial teacher education. For instance, this training requirement was not mentioned at all in an article written by a senior EMB official on the upgrading of the qualifications of language teachers (Wardlaw 2005). Instead, he emphasised that 'all new language teachers joining the profession will be subject and teacher trained within 3 to 5 years'.

In the broader policy context, the past decade has been characterised by the government's increasing involvement in setting up the professional standards for new and serving teachers, formulating policies and guidelines about their professional development, external scrutiny of their work and strengthening of accountability systems (Lai 2005). Never before have the teaching profession and teacher education received so much monitoring and scrutiny from the government and its consultative committees. Furthermore, in the absence of a professional teaching body such as a General Teaching Council in Hong Kong, the teaching profession is unable to set standards for and self-regulate its new and serving members, leaving the government dictating the agenda.

Furthermore, despite the fact that various measures have been adopted in raising the qualifications of teachers, the government and its consultative committees have hitherto evaded the broader question of the attractiveness of the teaching career, which is in turn affected by teachers' social status and their conditions of work. This ignorance is similar to that in the United States (Berliner 2006). The absence of training requirements for people to obtain employment as teachers in Hong Kong has been considered as a condition that maintains teaching as a low status occupation and having a low level of professionalisation (Morris 2004). Paradoxically, the government intervention has often been done on the pretext of teacher professionalisation or advancing the professionalism of teachers. The development has been akin to what Furlong (2005) described in the UK as a shift from 'individualized professionalism' to new forms of 'managed' and 'networked' professionalism (Furlong 2005, 120).

University-based teacher education in many parts of the world, including Hong Kong, has faced increasing scrutiny of their quality and their relevance to the needs of schools (for example, see Furlong 2001; Levine 2006). Teacher educators in Hong Kong may benefit from the following critique by Yinger and Nolen (2003, 386) on the state of teacher education in the US:

> Teacher educators live in a new world. This is a world of accountability, competition, alternatives, and serious questioning of the need for university-based teacher education. Even five years ago, it was unthinkable that university teacher education programs would be facing serious challenges to their legitimacy and importance. Many teacher education faculty members still deny that such a threat exists, but they are wrong.

References

Advisory Committee on Teacher Education and Qualifications (ACTEQ). 2006. *Initial teacher education: A revisit*, crude draft 15. Hong Kong: Advisory Committee on Teacher Education and Qualifications.

Berliner, D. 2006. The dangers of some new pathways to teacher certification. In *Competence oriented teacher training: Old research demands and new pathways*, ed. F. Oser, F. Achtenhagen, and U. Renold. Rotterdam: Sense Publishers.

Buckingham, J. 2005. *Good teachers where they are needed*, Issue Analysis No. 64. St. Leonards, NSW: Centre for Independent Studies.

Cheng, Y.C. 2002. Teacher status revamp method seen as realistic. *South China Morning Post*, 9 November.

Chong, C.W., and S.H. Poon. 2002. Untrained teachers may be required to undertake training within two years. *Mingpao*, 28 October (in Chinese).

Cobb, V.L. 1999. *An international comparison of teacher education*. Washington, DC: ERIC Clearinghouse on Teaching and Teacher Education.

Department for Education and Skills (DfES). 2006. *Statistics of education: School workforce in England*. http://www.dfes.gov.uk/rsgateway/DB/VOL/v000633/index.shtml (accessed 11 August 2006).

Education and Manpower Bureau. 1999. *Quality education – policy objective for Education and Manpower Bureau*. Hong Kong: Printing Department.

Education Commission. 1992. *Education Commission report no. 5: The teaching profession.* Hong Kong: Government Printer.

Education Commission. 2000. *Learning for life, learning through life – reform proposals for the education system in Hong Kong.* Hong Kong: Printing Department.

Eurydice. 2004. *Keeping teaching attractive for the 21st century.* The teaching profession in Europe: Profile, trends and concerns report IV. Brussels: Eurydice.

Feistritzer, C.E. 2006. *Alternative teacher certification: A state by state analysis 2006.* Washington, DC: National Center for Alternative Certification.

Furlong, J. 2001. Reforming teacher education, re-forming teachers: Accountability, professionalism and competence. In *Education, reform, and the state: Twenty-five years of politics, policy, and practice,* ed. R. Phillips and J. Furlong. London: Routledge/Falmer.

Furlong, J. 2005. New labour and teacher education: The end of an era. *Oxford Review of Education* 31, no. 1: 119–34.

Hess, F.H., A. Rotherham, and K. Walsh. 2005. *Finding the teachers we need.* San Francisco: Policy Perspectives.

Hong Kong Government. 1997. *The 1997 policy address.* Hong Kong: Printing Department.

Hong Kong Government. 1998. *The 1998 policy address.* Hong Kong: Printing Department.

Hong Kong Institute of Education (HKIEd). 2002. *HKIEd's response to EMB's proposed changes to the Chief Executive's policy on new teacher qualification requirements.* Unpublished document.

Hui, P. 2002. Time ripe for teachers to be fully trained, says institute. *South China Morning Post*, 31 October.

Lai, K.C. 2002. Lessons learnt on the long road towards an all-trained profession – fifty years of in-service training for non-graduate teachers in Hong Kong. Paper presented at the Symposium on Learning from the Past, Informing the Future: Education Then, Now and Tomorrow, Hong Kong.

Lai, K.C. 2005. Bureaucratic control and the professionalism of Hong Kong primary teachers. *New Horizons in Education* 51: 1–8 (in Chinese).

Lai, K.C., K.W. Ko, and C. Li. 2001. *Profile of the teaching profession in Hong Kong in the 1990s.* Hong Kong: Office of Planning and Academic Implementation, Hong Kong Institute of Education.

Legislative Council Question (LQC) 2. 2003. *Qualification of newly inducted teachers*, 12 March. Hong Kong: Legislative Council. http://www.edb.gov.hk/index.aspx?nodeID=136&langno=1&UID=101181.

Legislative Council Question (LQC) 10. 1999. *Teaching posts to be filled by professionally trained and degree holders*, 17 November. Hong Kong: Legislative Council.

Legislative Council Question (LQC) 16. 2003. *Supply and demand of teachers*, 8 October. Hong Kong: Legislative Council.

Levine, A. 2006. Will universities maintain control of teacher education? *Change* 38, no. 4: 36–43.

Morris, P. 2004. Teaching in Hong Kong: Professionalization, accountability and the state. *Research Papers in Education* 19, no. 1: 105–21.

Morris, P., and I. Scott. 2003. Educational reform and policy implementation in Hong Kong. *Journal of Education Policy* 18, no. 1: 71–84.

National Commission on Teaching and America's Future (NCTAF). 1996. *What matters most – teaching for America's future.* New York: NCTAF.

Ng, T. 2002. HK lags the region in teacher training policy. *Standard Student*, 14 November.

Olson, L. 2006. Find more like this. *Teacher Magazine* 17, no. 5: 16.

Parliament of Victoria. 2005. *Final report: Step up, step in, step out – report on the inquiry into the suitability of pre-service teacher training in Victoria* (No. 115 Session 2003–2005). Victoria: Education and Training Committee.

Standing Committee on Language Education and Research (SCOLAR). 2003. *Action plan to raise language standards in Hong Kong: Final review report*. Hong Kong: Standing Committee on Language Education and Research.

Sweeting, A. 1995. An introduction to the history of teacher education in Hong Kong: In-service, pre-service, and lip-service. Paper presented at the Teacher Education in the Asian Region: International Teacher Education Conference, Hong Kong.

University Grants Committee. 1998. *Review of teacher education*. Unpublished report. Hong Kong: University Grants Committee.

US Department of Education. 2002. *Meeting the highly qualified teachers challenge: The Secretary's annual report on teacher quality*. Washington, DC: US Department of Education.

US Department of Education. Office of Innovation and Improvement. 2004. *Alternative routes to teacher certification*. Washington, DC: US Department of Education.

Walsh, K. 2001. *Teacher certification reconsidered: Stumbling for quality*. Baltimore, MD: Abell Foundation.

Wardlaw, C. 2005. Supporting language learning in Hong Kong – are we doing enough? http://www.emb.gov.hk/index.aspx?langno=1&nodeID=4085 (accessed 23 October 2006).

Yinger, R.J., and A.L. Nolen. 2003. Surviving the legitimacy challenge. *Phi Delta Kappan* 84, no. 5: 386–90.

Teacher education in a global context: towards a defensible theory of teacher education

Richard Bates

Faculty of Education, Deakin University, Victoria, Australia

Introduction

Teacher education is under scrutiny in virtually every country. In part this is a result of increasing public concern over the availability and quality of public education. Such education is seen by both individuals and states as a crucial factor in obtaining positional advantage in an increasingly integrated and competitive global economy. Simultaneously, increasing flows of ideas and people across national boundaries are subjecting traditional cultures to scrutiny and comparison. The result is that education systems are frequently subject to demands to combine technical and economic innovation on the one hand with social and cultural conservation on the other. The provision and preparation of teachers is, consequently, regarded as an issue of 'quality': quality defined as both 'technical competence' and 'socially acceptable values'. Sandwiched between the two great steering mechanisms of markets and money on one side and culture and tradition on the other, teacher education, like education more generally, needs a defensible theory that celebrates its contribution to the relative autonomy of individuals and education systems from both markets and traditions.

However, as teacher education itself becomes more globalised, most systems are preoccupied with pragmatic issues of enrolment and graduation; length of preparation; comparability of standards; mutual recognition; portability of qualifications and intercultural education. Political resolutions of these issues differ from state to state and are in some cases significantly influenced towards privatisation by intergovernmental organisations.

This combination of social and procedural issues underlies the current debate in teacher education and requires the development of a defensible theory of teacher education that supports the relative autonomy of teacher education from the pressures of markets on one side and traditions on the other.

Markets, cultures and education in the global village

Globalisation is ubiquitous and indeed frames much contemporary discourse in education and, particularly, in teacher education. Cheng, Chow, and Mok (2004), for instance, in their introduction to a volume on teacher education reform in the Asia Pacific, argue that

> The impacts of globalization, international competition, and local social-political demands have induced rapid changes in nearly every society in the Asia-Pacific region since the 1980s ... How teachers can be prepared and empowered to take up new roles and effectively perform teaching to meet the [resulting] challenges and expectations raised from education reforms and paradigm shifts in school education is a crucial concern in policy and implementation of teacher education in the Asia-Pacific. (Cheng et al. 2004, 3)

Similarly, Tatto, in a special edition of the *International Journal of Educational Research* devoted to teacher education, suggests that

> The influence of educational reform on teachers and their work is a result of global forces, mediated by local culture and directed, for the most part, at the institutions where teachers learn and work ... [where] formal and informal mechanisms of accountability are continuously created to secure compliance with globally determined standards of quality in teacher learning and practice. (Tatto 2007, 231–32)

Bates and Townsend, in their afterword to the *Handbook of teacher education*, observe that in the view of many commentators

> Economic globalization is ... reinforcing a centralised and standardised policy agenda across many political systems: one which argues that only if politicians seize control of public education can it be transformed from its current disorganised condition into an appropriate mechanism of modernisation in an increasingly competitive economy. (Bates and Townsend 2007, 727)

Thus a strong argument is built around the idea that education, and therefore teacher education, is currently being transformed to better serve the cause of competition in an emerging world economy; markets and money are the dominating structures to which education and teacher education must be subordinated in the ruthless competition for economic survival.

The problem here, for society and educators in particular, is that a global market economy is both de-socialised and inherently unstable. Despite the attempts of international capital to re-order labour and politics to serve such an economy (Harvey 2007) the order produced does not constitute a social system capable of providing a context for personal or social development over an extended period.

> The world of markets does not constitute a social system, but rather a field of strategic action in which actors strive to use an uncontrolled and even unknown environment ... Change replaces order as the framework for analysis and social action, because the field of strategic action is a constantly changing set of possibilities, opportunities and risks. (Touraine 2000, 27)

A global economy driven by markets, money and continuous innovation provides, therefore, an inherently unstable context for education and teacher education: an anarchy of risk.

Others, however, point to another facet of globalisation:

> ... [T]he effect of globalization has not only been in the economic domain, but also on the social and cultural content of nation-states, within and outside the developing world. Whole societies are being formatted on a globalized grid that has transformed

everything from music, art and culture to curriculum, pedagogy and assessment ... In terms of education, globalization has redefined how we teach, what we teach, where we teach, whom we teach – and even whether we teach. (Jansen 2007, 25)

There is, therefore, a cultural side to globalisation that also needs to be acknowledged. And, despite Jansen's concerns over the cultural homogenisation of the 'globalized grid', one of its manifestations is the increasing cultural diversity of many cities and nation-states (Townsend and Bates 2007, 7).

Globalisation therefore, both promotes the subordination of local cultures to 'global' culture and, simultaneously, contrives the increasing exposure of traditional cultures to one another.

One response to this cultural globalisation is an increased emphasis on the importance of local, particularly indigenous cultures. Some developing societies have policies directed towards the replacement of expatriate teachers with locals (Al-Hinai 2007). Other societies are seeking partnership and equity between indigenous and now dominant post-colonial, largely European, cultures (Greenwood and Brown 2007). For instance

Many Pacific people today believe that for the sake of cultural survival and continuity, schools (and in turn, teachers) should have a role in the transmission of the best of Pacific cultures, especially their languages, to future generations of Pacific people. (Thaman 2007, 57)

In the cultural sphere, then, there are trends towards (a) an emerging 'global' culture, (b) the increased juxtaposition of cultures and (c) the reassertion of local cultures – what Foucault (1980, 81) so wonderfully called 'the insurrection of subjugated knowledges'. Such cultural transformation has paradoxical effects leading, on the one hand to significant cultural conflict which, in its extreme form is argued to be a 'clash of civilizations' (Huntington 2002) or a 'clash of fundamentalisms' (Ali 2002) and on the other hand to processes of hybridisation and cosmopolitanism (Appadurai 1996; Pieterse 2001, 2006).

Indeed, if the *economic* context of teaching and teacher education reform is that of the anarchy of markets and their associated 'creative destruction' of tradition and social order (Touraine 2000; Harvey 2007), then the *cultural* context is that of an anarchy of cultures and their associated struggles for recognition (Fraser and Honneth 2003; Bates 2005).

The resulting competition between individuals and societies has brought a new emphasis on league tables and accountability through which success and failure may be judged and competitive and positional advantage organised and legitimated (Brown 2003). Teacher education is as subject to this process as other aspects of education.

Comparisons, competition and positioning: new accountabilities for teacher education

Education throughout the world is currently being reorganised, both within nation-states and between them. Teacher education is part of this reorganisation. As Tatto (2007, 232) suggests

This worldwide reform activity can be seen as an indicator of societies' economic, political, societal and cultural priorities. The regulation of teachers' education, development and work via current reform initiatives, increasingly appear accompanied by exogenous monitoring and accountability schemes at every level of the system ... Thus formal and informal accountability mechanisms are continuously created to secure compliance with globally determined standards of quality in teacher learning and practice.

While there is certainly a general move in this direction, the reorganisation of education to enable comparisons and competition and, hopefully, improved performance, is a process of particular concern to the First and Second Worlds. Education in the Third World can hardly hope to even enter such a competition for, as Broadfoot (1999, 228) points out

> ... in the 49 least developed countries of the world, 50% of the children are not in school: 50% do not finish the first 4 years of schooling: 60–80% of these have no place to sit and write and 90% learn in a strange language.

Such global disparities appear to be increasing rather than decreasing.

Within the First and Second Worlds, however, there are both tendencies towards convergence and the continuation of significant differences within and between states and systems. Convergence is largely driven by intergovernmental organisations (IGOs) such as the Organisation for Economic Cooperation and Development (OECD), the European Union (EU), Asia Pacific Economic Cooperation (APEC) and at another level, by the World Bank and the World Trade Organisation (WTO). Such convergence is encouraged through both policy documents such as the OECD's *The teaching workforce: Concerns and policy challenges* (OECD 2002) and through the construction of international league tables such as developed through the *Programme for International Student Assessment* (PISA 2006).

The OECD is probably the most influential IGO and during its initial period was concerned with issues of economic development, but also of social equity and cultural convergence (Henry et al. 2000; Lawn 2001, 2003). However, it is clear that during the 1990s the OECD saw a displacement of its social agendas by market considerations as a result of the dominance of neoliberal agendas driven in particular by the United States (Rizvi and Lingard 2006; Harvey 2007).

The result is a shift towards the centralisation of policy setting coupled with the devolution of responsibility for implementation and associated strong accountability mechanisms, a narrowing of curriculum focus and an increased emphasis on testing. Despite a commitment to devolution the shift is strongly away from principles of engagement and social democracy that might serve *cultural* ends towards principles of corporate management directed to *economic* ends.

One of the crucial mechanisms of such corporate management is that of audit and comparison. This is achieved in education through testing procedures and comparisons. Here, countries' performances are ranked against each other and the rankings used as a mechanism for driving policy and accountability through the various education systems. As Torrance (2006) suggests, however, these tests and their associated ranking procedures are highly selective in their focus (usually on reading, mathematics and science) and are generally restricted to what it is easy to measure and compare.

The result is a regime of testing, governance and accountability that aims to make learners, schools, systems and states as economically competitive as possible (Tonna 2007). This requires a corps of teachers that is focussed on producing 'trainability' in their students: the capacity to be readily and continuously trained and retrained in response to the instabilities of technology, markets, production and the (dis)organisation of work. 'Flexibility', 'creativity' and 'lifelong learning' become the mantra of such systems and teacher education becomes focused on the technical means of producing such commitments alongside a new biddability focused on the utilisation of information and communications technologies through which knowledge flows like money, dissociated from the knower (Bernstein 2000).

In this view of the world, education, like knowledge, becomes commodified, something that is to be bought and sold as a commodity or a consumable; a temporary possession of individuals who barter their transitory ownership in a market-place (Hartley 2002, 2003). Such a view also implies a valuation of teacher education in terms of its cost-effectiveness in facilitating such trainability and marketability in an essentially privatised economic system where individuals and institutions confront the market directly according to the cost-effectiveness of their individual utility in the production process.

The result for institutions of teacher education, as for higher education more generally, is an increased demand for flexibility, continuous retraining and mobility. This demand can only be achieved if such institutions can be made simultaneously subject to 'continuous improvement', more 'transparent' and comparable in terms of curriculum, pedagogy and certification.

A global market?

The World Trade Organisation would not seem to have an immediate relevance to such an agenda for teacher education. However, the recent rounds of negotiation over the General Agreement on Trade in Services (GATS) are focused precisely on creating global markets in such services as education. Unlike most other IGOs the WTO has no social agenda and is focused exclusively on the promotion of global trade in goods and services through 'successive rounds of negotiations to achieve a progressively higher level of liberalization' (WTO, in Robertson, Bonal, and Dale 2006, 233). Given that global public spending on education now exceeds one trillion dollars US per year it is not surprising that the WTO (or more precisely some states within it, such as the USA, UK and Australia) should see this as a prime area for marketisation and profitability. While the immediate impact of GATS negotiations (and other regional 'free trade' agreements) is on higher education institutions, the free trade principles apply equally to all education sectors except those completely financed and administered by the state and free of any commercial purpose. By these criteria virtually all education in all countries will eventually come under the GATS rules (Robertson et al. 2006, 235).

The effect of such rules is not only to establish a global education market for private providers but also to expose public institutions to the need to remodel themselves on the structures and financial models of private institutions in order to compete. As private institutions typically commit themselves to servicing the areas of lowest cost and highest demand, public institutions can be expected to become residual providers of high cost/low demand areas or to close down such offerings as they can no longer be cross subsidised from high revenue areas.

As such pressures mount, both individual countries and groups of countries are pressured to reorganise themselves to meet such potential competition. Awareness of the implications of this global competition is exemplified by the European Union's (EU's) commitment to the Bologna Declaration where the 'idea of a globalized world threatening European competitiveness is part of the discourse' (Barkholt 2005, 26; see also Westerheijden 2003, 280).

The Bologna Declaration's main proposal was to encourage conformity in the structure of degree programmes throughout Europe based upon a two-cycle structure of three or four year undergraduate degrees followed by two year professional degrees. Crucial to the success of such a structure are guarantees of 'quality' and 'equivalence' that would ensure 'value' as well as relevance to the labour market and portability between institutions and countries (van Vught, van der Vende, and Westerheijden 2002; Westerheijden 2003).

While some progress has been made towards these objectives (Haug and Tauch 2001; Feerick 2004) significant obstacles exist (Clement, McAlpine, and Waeytens 2004). This is particularly the case for teacher education. Despite optimistic scenarios provided, for instance, by the Association for Teacher Education in Europe (ATEE 2003):

> Recognition of academic qualifications beyond a lowest common denominator remains a matter of discretion, despite moves towards a commonly recognizable basis of Bachelor and Master university qualifications. There is little harmonization of initial training for any of the professions, and none at all for teaching. The picture is one of confusion. (Sayer 2006, 70–71)

Such a conclusion is borne out by other studies that report multiple and incommensurable programmes of teacher preparation across Europe (TNTEE 2000) and indeed more broadly (OECD 2005). Partly this seems to be due to different traditions in the preparation of primary and secondary teachers. Primary teacher preparation, despite being transferred into the higher education sector, maintains strong elements of the 'normal school' tradition which itself developed out of an apprenticeship model of teacher education emphasising 'the culture of teaching, studying and learning and on the importance attached to methodology courses and teaching practice' (TNTEE 2000, 15). On the other hand, secondary teacher preparation emphasised an academic tradition within which 'scientific knowledge in academic disciplines' was paramount (TNTEE 2000, 15). The debate between emphasis on professional knowledge versus emphasis on subject knowledge is widespread in teacher education, not only in Europe but also in Asia (Cheng and Chow 2004) and North America (Darling-Hammond and Bransgrove 2005). But, beyond this, barriers to standardisation can be seen as profoundly cultural.

Culture and tradition in teacher education

As I have insisted on a previous occasion,

> ... [I]t is culture that gives meaning to life. Culture is the framework that connects beliefs, values and knowledge with action. Culture is the context within and the material from which we form our societies and selves. (Bates 1992, 194)

This being so, the historical dimensions of cultures are frequently articulated through education as a celebration of cultural, especially *national*, identity. Indeed, schools and school systems often have their roots in attempts to produce and/or reproduce particular cultures. Many national systems of schooling have been constructed so as to create and maintain commitment to a particular state. And, despite arguments to the contrary, the nation-state is alive and well (Green 2006).

Such systems have been resisted by cultures that are either minorities within particular states and who resent the absence or misrepresentation of their culture within the national curriculum, or by cultures that cross state boundaries and are thereby divided by the artificial demarcation of official histories, values and commitments (Griffin 2000; Touraine 2000).

The result is that

> Education for the twenty-first century presents educators with a paradox; on the one hand the necessity to respond to a knowledge-based global economy is critical ... but, on the other hand, schools with a captive audience are exploited as sites for cultural reproduction and for the transmission of a 'shared cultural heritage. (Clay and George 2000, 206)

Increasingly, however, both nation-states and regional groupings are having to recognise the plurality of cultures within their borders. Typically they respond by developing 'multicultural' policies directed towards the recognition of difference while simultaneously promoting commitments to national or regional loyalties.

In this respect attempts by the European Union (EU) and the Association of Southeast Asian Nations (ASEAN) are particularly interesting. While 'Europe' and 'Asia' are general geographic denotations that encompass multiplicities of cultures and nation-states (many of whom have been in historical conflict), attempts are currently being made to promote overarching regional identities. Education is one of the main agencies charged with the creation of such identities and in both instances the reform of curriculum and of teacher education is a central concern.

Lawn (2001, 2003) describes the creation of a 'European educational space' within which the idea of Europe can be created and defined. Such an educational space is vital because

> Rising free from older ideas of territory and people, [Europe] is a political and cultural project, an idea and a conduit, a projection and a form, in which meaning is created, delivered and maintained ... Europe is not a place, [a] warehouse full of cultural artefacts, institutions and asymmetrical relations. Europe is a project, a space of meaning, a state in process, and education is the core technology in which governance, ordering and meaning can be constructed. Without education, there can be no Europe. (Lawn 2003, 325–26)

As Lawn goes on to suggest, 'Europe' is being constructed in much the same way as its preceding States. This process sees education as a prime means for developing a sense of shared history (through the construction of a European curriculum), pedagogy (through the construction of a European teaching force) and assessment (through the construction of compatible certification procedures). Nowhere was this agenda more obvious than in the European Commission's White Paper *Accomplishing Europe through education and training* (1997), which argued that 'If Europe is to remain at the driving edge, economic and political progress must be complemented by offering a European vision to her young people' (European Commission 1997, 1).

The difficulty facing such a project is the resistance of traditional cultures to such negation of existing individual and cultural identities, for while the European project continues at a bureaucratic level, at a cultural level Europeans are becoming more, not less, aware of differences in culture. The fluidity of population movements within the new Europe creates anew questions of what it means to be French, Polish, English etc. These questions necessarily translate into how such identities are to be managed within education systems and what particular demands the resolution of such issues might make on teacher education. For instance, as Sayer (2006) suggests

> Far from showing signs of convergence, specific policies and structures have, in some cases become more confined and exclusive. So in the United Kingdom, the national

> curriculum introduced to legislation for the first time in 1988 and operating with frequent modifications since 1992, was nationalist in intention, restricted the scope for local innovation and led to a required curriculum for teacher training which was centred on the enforced curriculum for pupils, with training institutions being inspected, graded and financed solely according to these criteria. The Department for Education and Employment ... set out required teacher competencies without reference to other EU member countries' views. (Sayer 2006, 67)

Moreover, the differences in official policy also establish differences in recognised languages as well as different notions of work, contract and service. The result is significant difference in what is meant by public service, corporate responsibility and how the profession or career of teaching is viewed (Sayer 2006).

Very similar processes are underway in ASEAN nations where attempts to forge a regional cross national/supra-national identity are also underway (Koh 2007). While this project derives again from a concern with economic competitiveness in a global economy, the charge given to the ASEAN organisation is to explore the role of education in promoting a shared regional identity. The priorities here would be to emphasise civic education as a major contribution to the acceptance of a multicultural society; multilingual education as a mechanism for enhancing cross cultural communication; and the creation of an overarching educational policy for the region that would shape the general direction of national education systems (Jones 2004).

The economic motivation and the procedural mechanisms advocated are quite similar to those adopted by the EU, in that a close specification of curriculum, a didactic pedagogy (albeit supported by new technologies) and centralised mechanisms of assessment and accountability combined with devolved management are seen as ways to enhance the production of useful skills in the student population.

Again, however, the issue of separate historical identities is highly problematic in this newly emerging Asian 'educational space' (Koh 2007). While some scholars, particularly in cultural studies, argue that there is a significant increase in inter-Asian cultural traffic and an emerging sense of 'the region' through the reworking of traditional cultures into a hybridised notion of 'Asia' the same problems remain. For instance, Lincicome cites the example of Malaysia where the education system is focused on the problem of creating a sens of 'a common national identity and national unity among numerically and economically unequal populations of Malays, Indians and Chinese [as well as] tribes like the Orang Asili' (Lincicome 2005, 198). The example of Singapore is also cited where textbooks in geography, social studies and history give only a 'short four page overview, of ASEAN as a region' (Lincicome 2005, 203). Such parochialism is particularly evident in curriculum, textbooks and pedagogy throughout the Asian region where conflicting accounts of national histories and relationships are presented (Nozaki, Openshaw, and Luke 2005).

There seem to be, both in Europe and Asia, conflicting struggles going on. At one pole of the struggle there are emerging national and supra-national elites driven by ideas of international competition in the global market and whose influence over national educational systems attempts to drive towards convergence. As Massey (2005) and Koh (2007) suggest, such convergence is being created through a new organisational architecture which brings together a network of networks in a new international 'space'.

> In this light, the ASEAN education space is an emerging form of networking where elite networks, represented by government and educational administrators and bureaucrats,

meet and discuss matters related to education projects. An elite ASEAN network has been in place for some time ... (Koh 2007, 185)

At the other pole of the struggle is the increasingly vociferous plurality of cultures within and across nation-states; a plurality that is demanding the articulation of their histories within the curriculum of educational institutions. This series of demands constructs another space

> ... [W]here heterogeneity and difference are not only permissible but the norm. In this space there are no prescriptive/normative rules that constrain what can or cannot be spoken or performed. Because heterogeneity and difference characterize [this space] we can no longer insist that the story of the world is the story of the 'West' alone, as there are multiple histories and trajectories through which the story of the world can be constructed and reconstructed. (Koh 2007, 185)

Two conflicting demands are therefore placed upon education systems and upon teacher education in particular. First, there is the demand from markets and money articulated through elite IGOs and networks for a common curriculum, common assessment, 'transparency', central policy-making and strong accountability in devolved systems of management. The purpose is to serve economic competition in the global market. Second, there is the demand from local communities for the articulation of their stories, histories and interests in an increasingly multicultural world where diversity and difference are increasingly obvious. This struggle is often labelled the struggle between globalisation and localisation (Robertson 1995). Teachers, and teacher educators are often seen as failing to respond to either of these pressures and teacher education is consequently under review almost everywhere.

Glocalisation and the reform of teacher education

In such a contradictory context it is not surprising that while there is a general move towards increased intervention in teacher education, the process and effects of such a movement show considerable diversity. Some of the diversity is due to historical differences; especially those between countries that have traditionally seen teachers as bureaucrats responsible for implementing a centrally determined curriculum, what Tatto (2007) calls a procedural approach (Chile, France and Japan, for instance) and those who have relied upon teachers' professional judgement within relatively autonomous schools (Denmark, Germany, England, for instance). Other differences are due to differences in political orientation and the management style adopted by various countries. Here some countries have been moving towards significantly increased control of what teachers teach and how they teach it (Chile, England, China, Mexico) while others have been moving to loosen bureaucratic controls over schooling (Japan, Guinea) (Tatto 2007). A third dimension of difference is in the implementation of policies where some countries, notably Germany and Guinea, have had considerable success, while others such as Japan and Mexico have faced insurmountable opposition from teachers and their unions (Tatto 2007). A fourth issue to affect such implementation is clearly the relative demand for teachers in some systems where there is a significantly ageing teaching force compared to others where there is an oversupply (OECD 2005). Issues of quality and quantity, the positioning of teaching within the overall context of the labour force, mobility and alternative routes into teaching all contribute to the complexity of the structural issues in various countries (OECD 2005).

Attempts by governmental organisations and IGOs to address this complexity through the establishment of working parties on standards, curriculum and management have led in many instances to the development of Teaching Councils charged with the task of standardising and controlling teacher education (OECD 2005, Ingvarson et al. 2006, Zammit et al. 2007). Many such institutions are concerned with the convergence and competition presumed by the argument over globalisation and economic competitiveness. But on the other hand, such pressures towards globalisation of the economic variety are challenged by those who see the processes involved as damaging to local cultures and particularly to concerns over social justice, equity, gender disadvantage, political and civil rights, and participatory democracy (Behabib 2006; Olssen 2006; Torres 2006). Here, the issues are partly about localisation but also about the need to address diversity and find ways of living together (Luke 2005, 22).

Struggle towards the 'new basics' for teacher education must clearly take account of both pressures. Developing a curricular, pedagogical and assessment capacity in teachers that will allow them to enhance the economic prospects of their students is a necessity. Similarly, developing a curricular, pedagogical and assessment practice that enhances their students' understanding and ability to participate in a heterogeneous cultural life is equally important. Moreover, as Touraine (2000) suggests, teachers and teacher educators also need a certain autonomy from both global and local, economic and cultural pressures. This predicament requires a defensible theory of teacher education.

A defensible theory of teacher education?

The work of schools can quite conventionally be considered as focused on three practices: curriculum, pedagogy and evaluation (what Bernstein referred to as their 'message systems'; 1975, 85). Each of these message systems is contestable and changes in the fields of production and of symbolic control within the wider society inevitably bring pressures to bear for change in the school (Bernstein 1990). States have quite elaborate procedures for ensuring that such changes take place and current changes to officially sanctioned curricular, pedagogical and assessment practices across education systems are evidence of this. Official sanctions regarding teacher education follow the same pattern.

Contemporary changes in official educational policy are justified by appeals to the effects of the transformation of production through the application of electronic and communications technologies on the one hand (a sort of competitive panic regarding productive competence) and by concerns for social order brought about by recognition of increasing disparities and antagonisms between social groups on the other (a sort of moral and behavioural panic regarding social cohesion). The response to these twin panics is to attempt the restructuring of educational message systems to focus on the production skills required by the 'new economy' (especially basic communications skills in literacy, numeracy and information technology) and the social and behavioural skills required by the 'inclusive society' (especially the construction of personalities which might maintain motivation, commitment and acquiescence under conditions of periodic or permanent poverty and exclusion).

As a result pressure is exerted on the curricular message system to restrict it to a skills oriented focus where what counts as knowledge is defined all but exclusively in terms of 'productive' knowledge. Pressure is exerted on the pedagogical message system for a visible pedagogy which implements the accumulation of productive knowledge but simultaneously for an invisible pedagogy which serves the purposes of moral and social order – embedding behaviours invisibly in the compliant performances of students. Pressure is exerted on the assessment message system through more frequent and public comparisons of performances of students, teachers, schools and institutions of higher learning according to universalised (but highly selective) criteria.

Curriculum and the problem of focus

One of the difficulties such systems of official direction and sanction face, is that the very technologies that supposedly require such controls act simultaneously to subvert them. For instance, while official knowledge is restricted and focussed on 'productive' knowledge, access to knowledge and information of all kinds through the World Wide Web allows continual transgression of officially imposed boundaries by teachers and students alike. For example, the official curriculum will increasingly be concerned with skill formation required by continuous innovation in technology and production in the global economy – especially in areas of communications, financial services, miniaturisation and biotechnologies – both medical and botanical. Access to and utilisation of the Web is fundamental to such activity. But those technologies which give access to the skills and information required by the global economy also give access to information on the negative 'side' effects of the globalisation of production: instability, gross inequalities, environmental degradation, political and economic repression. Moreover, while consideration of the social and ethical is excluded from official knowledge (whatever happened to sociology, history and philosophy in the teacher education curriculum?) access to the Web also gives access to unofficial knowledge regarding debates over the requirements of a global society: equitable development, human rights, access to communications technologies, freedom of association and expression, social, political and environmental action groups. The preparation of teachers must surely take these matters into account.

The problem of curriculum within such a context is clearly that of *focus*. Attempts to prepare teachers for a retreat into a skills-based version of the grammar school curriculum and its associated notions of pedagogical authority and rigid assessment are probably the worst possible 'solution' to contemporary difficulties, for they misconceive the nature of knowledge in the contemporary world and they profoundly mis-recognise the changes in authority relations brought about by the liberal-democratic traditions of Western societies. On the other hand, a curriculum that was more widely based and which brought students into contact with knowledge needed to construct both a global economy *and* a global society would be potentially more democratic and more defensible.

Pedagogy and the problem of motivation

The problem of pedagogy is not unrelated. If pedagogy is defined as 'what counts as valid transmission of knowledge' (Bernstein 1975) teachers must be prepared to face the key pedagogical problem of *motivation*. Here, the imitation of current practice or the attempt to return to a more authoritarian pedagogy is unlikely to succeed. As John Elliott puts it:

> If the traditional view of knowledge, reinforced by government policy and legislation, continues to be deeply embedded in school cultures within liberal democratic societies, then schools will fail as educational institutions, not because they are failing to maintain 'standards' but because they are failing to supply the culturally appropriate form of motivation for pupils to learn. The basis for such motivation resides in bestowing recognition and status on pupils as autonomous learners. The valuing of individual autonomy is deeply embedded in Western culture but becoming detached from the belief that the prior acquisition of stocks of objective knowledge is a condition of its realization. This is why traditional education no longer supplies motivation for individuals who seek recognition as autonomous persons. (Elliott 2000, 182)

The notion of students as autonomous learners implies a very non-authoritarian form of learning: one which the new technologies may, for the first time, make possible. If information of all kinds becomes widely available and accessible then the problem of pedagogy – what counts as valid transmission of knowledge – may take on a quite different form. The teacher may well be less concerned with didacticism and more concerned with helping students with relatively autonomous learning centred around personal creativity, values and commitments. But, as Taylor (1989) has argued, creativity, values and commitments are both individual *and* social constructions. They are indeed 'sources of the self' and fundamental to the making of identity, but they cannot be constructed without benefit of a social context. And how that social context is understood is vital for the construction of the self. Here the pedagogy of the teacher working with the autonomous learner, is most likely to address the issue of motivation through the careful (sometimes supportive, sometimes challenging) matching of knowledge with the students search for meaning. While the valid transmission of knowledge may often be prescribed by official discourse in quite narrow ways that limit motivation on the part of both student and teacher (often leading to withdrawal from engagement) it need not be so. A pedagogy which links knowledge with the process of construction of meaning and purpose in both individual and society would indeed be defensible.

Assessment and the problem of validity

Assessment is the third message system, one which Bernstein defines as 'the valid realisation of knowledge'. Official discourse clearly defines assessment as assessment of student performance against the constricted (officially defined) curriculum and its validity is judged in terms of compliance with that curriculum and the ranking of individuals in terms of their compliance. But this is a very narrow notion of assessment and one which rather misses the central problem of evaluation and the problems it faces in the contemporary world. For example: the rate of knowledge production and the rapid transformation of ways in which it is distributed faces users with a significant problem – how to judge the validity, dependability and utility of the almost infinite array of information which they can access. The central assessment issue for educational institutions had now become that of how teachers and learners are to devise ways of testing validity claims – of testing the validity of information and knowledge claims that are new to both. This is by no means a simple issue, but contemporary circumstances force the issue to the centre of the curriculum and pedagogy of educational institutions. The open curriculum and an autonomous pedagogy require tests for truth and utility that are centred around individual and social purpose. Assessment of pupil performance is necessarily replaced, or at least supplemented by the development and learning of techniques for determining the validity of knowledge claims from whatever source they arise.

In part, such validity arises from the tests derived from long-standing considerations in various intellectual disciplines (perhaps especially philosophy, aesthetics and ethics as well as history and science). This is why a liberal education that takes account of these traditions is important in teacher preparation. But the issue of *use* is also significant. If, for instance, the major difficulties facing a school or a community and the individuals within it are cultural and social, the utility of knowledge derived from production process may not contribute greatly to the motivation and learning of students. The use value of particular knowledge is an important aspect of the assessment of knowledge accessed through educational institutions.

Here the issue of localisation becomes important, for students inhabit local as well as global spaces. Global forces associated with economic and social change do shape local contexts but it is the local context that provides particular experiences that shape the activities of students and their families. In fact what Robertson (1995) calls 'glocalisation' is a more realistic label. Within such a concept that identifies and explores the interpenetration of the local by the global the utility and relevance of knowledge of various kinds might well be explored, addressing both the validity and relevance of such knowledge to the glocal economy and the glocal society. And this will be done within contexts that are, to a greater or lesser extent, changing as movements across religious, political, ethnic, cultural and geographical boundaries increase.

Considerations of this kind need to be incorporated into a defensible theory of teacher education (indeed, perhaps into a more general theory of education). They do, of course, need expanding and developing as well as relating to the ways in which subject knowledge is incorporated into the programme. They also need to be related to two further aspects of teacher education programmes. First, the practicum needs reconsidering and, second, the place of research in teacher activity becomes important.

The practicum and teacher research

The practicum as it is currently conceived tends simply to reinforce the previous socialisation of students into the conservative, authoritarian culture of traditional schools. This does not help to prepare students for the kind of agenda described above. One possible solution to this is to draw less on a 'teaching practice' approach and more on a 'critical case study' approach. Here, following MacDonald (2000) and Brennan and Nofke (2000), students would be encouraged to develop materials which document curricular, pedagogical and assessment practices in ways which illustrate the diversity of practice and open it up for analysis in its relationships to social, cultural and economic contexts and subject it to evaluation against the criteria outlined above.

This would lead directly to the engagement of students in research activity and further, allow them to develop links between research and practice that might later be sustained by the networks which have been shown, in a series of recent Australian studies (DETYA 2000), to enable considerable influence of research on practice. Such impact was, nonetheless, shown to be selective, being greatest where teachers actively sought research relevant to their immediate concerns (a finding which incidentally supports the arguments outlined above). What was described in this study was the way in which teachers actively engaged with the educational research community in seeking solutions to particular problems rather than simply becoming passive recipients of 'evidence-based' policy formation. Indeed the DETYA report *The impact of educational research* demonstrated clearly that where teachers were linked into networks with researchers the impact of research on practice was strong and pervasive.

Conclusion

The conclusion of this brief outline is that a defensible theory of teacher education depends upon a defensible theory of teaching which addresses the issues of curriculum focus, pedagogical motivation and the tests for truth in evaluation of knowledge claims. Defensible approaches to these problems have to take account of contemporary social as well as economic contexts rather than seek refuge in the mock heroism of tradition, and they need to take account of increasing awareness of social difference as well as processes of glocalisation. In addition, teacher education students need to engage in critically reflective research through a practicum which links case studies with the broader research and teaching communities as the basis for continuing professional development.

Such an approach to teacher education would not only be more comprehensible to students: it would also allow them some territory on which to build a defensible theory of educational practice within a professional community of teachers.

References

Al-Hinai, A.M. 2007. The interplay between culture, teacher professionalism and teachers professional development at times of change. In *Handbook of teacher education: Globalization, standards and professionalism in times of change*, ed. T. Townsend and R. Bates, 41–52. Dordrecht: Springer.
Ali, T. 2002. *The clash of fundamentalisms: Crusades, jihads and modernity*. London: Verso.
Appadurai, A. 1996. *Modernity at large: Cultural dimensions of globalization*. Minneapolis: University of Minnesota Press.
ATEE. 2003. Scenarios for the future of teacher education in Europe. *European Journal of Teacher Education* 26, no. 1: 21–36.
Barkholt, K. 2005. The Bologna process and integration theory: Convergence and autonomy. *Higher Education in Europe* 30, no. 1: 23–29.
Bates, R. 1992. Leadership and school culture. In *Cultura escolar y desarrolo organizativo*. Seville: Universidad de Sevilla.
Bates, R. 2005. An anarchy of cultures: The politics of teacher education in new times. *Asia Pacific Journal of Teacher Education* 33, no. 3: 231–41.
Bates, R., and T. Townsend. 2007. The future of teacher education: Challenges and opportunities. In *Handbook of teacher education: Globalization, standards and professionalism in times of change*, ed. T. Townsend and R. Bates, 727–36. Dordrecht: Springer.
Benhabib, S. 2006. Multiculturalism and gendered citizenship. In *Education, globalization and social change*, ed. H. Lauder, P. Brown, J. Dillabrough, and A. Halsey, 152–60. Oxford: Oxford University Press.

Bernstein, B. 1975. *Towards a theory of educational transmissions*. London: Routledge and Kegan Paul.
Bernstein, B. 1990. *The structuring of pedagogic discourse*. London: Routledge.
Bernstein, B. 2000. *Pedagogy, symbolic control and identity: Theory, research, critique*. Oxford: Rowman & Littlefield.
Brennan, M., and S. Nofke. 2000. Social change and the individual: Changing patterns of community and the challenge for schooling. In *Images of educational change*, ed. H. Altrichter and J. Elliott. Buckingham: Open University Press.
Broadfoot, P. 1999. Stones from other hills may serve to polish the jade of this one. *Compare* 29, no. 3: 217–31.
Brown, P. 2003. The opportunity trap: Education and employment in a global economy. *European Educational Research Journal* 2, no. 1: 142–80.
Cheng, Y., and K. Chow. 2004. Institutions of teacher education in Asia. In *Reform of teacher education in the Asia-Pacific in the new millennium*, ed. Y.C. Cheng, K.W. Chow, and M.M.C. Mok. Dordrecht: Kluwer.
Cheng, Y.C., K.W. Chow, and M.M.C. Mok, eds. 2004. *Reform of teacher education in the Asia-Pacific in the new millenium*. Dordrecht: Kluwer.
Clay, J., and R. George. 2000. Intercultural education: A code of practice for the twenty-first century. *European Journal of Teacher Education* 23, no. 2: 203–11.
Clement, M., L. McAlpine, and K. Waeytens. 2004. Fascinating Bologna: Impact on the nature and approach of academic development. *International Journal for Academic Development* 9, no. 2: 127–31.
Darling-Hammond, L., and J. Bransford, eds. 2005. *Preparing teachers for a changing world*. San Francisco: Jossey-Bass.
DETYA. 2000. *The impact of educational research*. Canberra: Commonwealth of Australia.
Dooly, M., and M. Villanueva. 2006. Internationalisation as a key dimension to teacher education. *European Journal of Teacher Education* 29, no. 2: 223–40.
Elliott, J. 2000. Towards a synoptic vision of educational change in advanced industrial countries. In *Images of educational change*, ed. H. Altrichter and J. Elliott. Buckingham: Open University Press.
European Commission. 1997. *Accomplishing Europe through education and training*. Luxembourg: Study Group on Education & Training.
Feerick, S. 2004. *Bologna process update*. Strasbourg: European Commission.
Foucault, M. 1980. *Power/knowledge*. Brighton: Harvester Press.
Fraser, N., and A. Honneth. 2003. *Redistribution or recognition?*. London: Verso.
Green, A. 2006. Education, globalization and the nation-state. In *Education, globalization and social change*, ed. H. Lauder, P. Brown, J. Dillabrough, and A. Halsey. Oxford: Oxford University Press.
Greenwood, J., and L. Brown. 2007. The treaty, the institution and the chalk-face: An institution-wide project in teacher education. In *Handbook of teacher education: Globalization, standards and professionalism in times of change*, ed. T. Townsend and R. Bates, 67–78. Dordrecht: Springer.
Griffin, K. 2000. Culture and economic growth – the state and globalization. In *Global futures: Shaping globalization*, ed. J. Pieterse. London: Zed Books.
Hartley, D. 2002. Global influences on teacher education in Scotland. *Journal of Education for Teaching* 28, no. 3: 251–55.
Hartley, D. 2003. New economy, new pedagogy. *Oxford Review of Education* 29, no. 1: 81–94.
Hartley, D. 2007. *A short history of neo-liberalism*. Oxford: Oxford University Press.
Haug, G., and C. Tauch. 2001. *Trends in learning structures in higher education*. Strasbourg: European Commission.
Henry, M., B. Lingard, F. Rizvi, and S. Taylor. 2000. *The OECD, globalization and education policy*. Oxford: Pergamon.

Huntington, S. 2002. *The clash of civilizations*. London: Simon & Schuster.
Ingvarson, L., A. Elliot, E. Kleinhenz, and P. McKenzie. 2006. *Teacher education accreditation: A review of national and international trends and practices*. Canberra: Teaching Australia.
Jansen, J. 2007. Learning and leading in a globalized world. In *Handbook of teacher education: Globalization, standards and professionalism in times of change*, ed. T. Townsend and R. Bates, 25–40. Dordrecht: Springer.
Jones, M. 2004. Forging an ASEAN identity: The challenge to construct a shared identity. *Contemporary Southeast Asia* 26, no. 1: 140–54.
Koh, A. 2007. Deparochializing education: Globalization, regionalization and the formation of an ASEAN education space. *Discourse: Studies in the Cultural Politics of Education* 28, no. 2: 179–95.
Lawn, M. 2001. Borderless education: Imagining a European education space in a time of brands and networks. *Discourse: Studies in the Cultural Politics of Education* 22, no. 2: 173–84.
Lawn, M. 2003. The 'usefulness' of learning: The struggle over governance, meaning and the European education space. *Discourse: Studies in the Cultural Politics of Education* 24, no. 3: 325–36.
Lincicombe, M. 2005. Globalization, education and the politics of identity in the Asia-Pacific. *Critical Asian Studies* 37, no. 2: 179–208.
Luke, A. 2005. Curriculum, ethics, metanarrative: Teaching and learning beyond the nation. In *Struggles over difference: Curriculum, texts and pedagogy in the Asia-Pacific*, ed. Y. Nozaki, R. Openshaw, and A. Luke. Albany: SUNY Press.
MacDonald, B. 2000. How education became nobody's business. In *Images of educational change*, ed. H. Altrichter and J. Elliott. Buckingham: Open University Press.
Massey, D. 2005. *For space*. London: Sage.
Nozaki, Y., R. Openshaw, and A. Luke. 2005. *Struggles over difference: Curriculum, texts and pedagogy in the Asia-Pacific*. Albany: SUNY Press.
OECD. 2002. *The teaching workforce: Concerns and policy challenges*. Paris: Organisation for Economic Cooperation and Development.
OECD. 2005. *Teachers matter: Attracting, developing and retaining effective teachers*. Paris: Organisation for Economic Cooperation and Development.
Olssen, M. 2006. Neoliberalism, globalization, democracy: Challenges for education. In *Education, globalization and social change*, ed. H. Lauder, P. Brown, J. Dillabrough, and A. Halsey. Oxford: Oxford University Press.
Pieterse, J. 2001. Hybridity, so what? *Theory Culture & Society* 18, no. 2–3: 219–45.
Pieterse, J. 2006. Emancipatory cosmopolitanism: Towards and agenda. *Development and Change* 37, no. 6: 1247–57.
PISA. 2006. *PISA – The OECD Programme for International Student Assessment*. Paris: OECD.
Rizvi, F., and R. Lingard. 2006. Globalization and the changing nature of the OECD's educational work. In *Education, globalization and social change*, ed. H. Lauder, P. Brown, J. Dillabrough, and A. Halsey. Oxford: Oxford University Press.
Robertson, R. 1995. *Glocalization: Time–space, homogeneity – heterogeneity*. London: Sage.
Robertson, S., X. Bonal, and R. Dale. 2006. GATS and the education service industry: The politics of scale and global reterritorialization. In *Education, globalization and social change*, ed. H. Lauder, P. Brown, J. Dillabrough, and A. Halsey. Oxford: Oxford University Press.
Sayer, J. 2006. European perspectives of teacher education and training. *Comparative Education* 42, no. 1: 63–95.
Tatto, M., ed. 2007. Special edition on educational reform and teacher education. *International Journal of Educational Research* 45, no. 4–5.

Taylor, C. 1989. *Sources of the self.* Cambridge: Harvard University Press.
Thaman, K. 2007. Partnerships for progressing cultural democracy in teacher education in Pacific Island countries. In *Handbook of teacher education: Globalization, standards and professionalism in times of change,* ed. T. Townsend and R. Bates, 53–66. Dordrecht: Springer.
TNTEE. 2000. *Green paper on teacher education in Europe.* Umea, Sweden: Thematic Network on Teacher Education in Europe.
Tonna, M. 2007. Teacher education in a globalized age. *Journal for Critical Education Policy Studies* 5, no. 1. www.jceps.com/print.php?articleID=88.
Torrance, H. 2006. Globalizing empiricism: What, if anything, can be learned from international comparisons of educational achievement? In *Education, globalization and social change,* ed. H. Lauder, P. Brown, J. Dillabrough, and A. Halsey. Oxford: Oxford University Press.
Torres, C. 2006. Democracy, education and multiculturalism: Dilemmas of citizenship in a global world. In *Education, globalization and social change,* ed. H. Lauder, P. Brown, J. Dillabrough, and A. Halsey. Oxford: Oxford University Press.
Townsend, T., and R. Bates. 2007. Teacher education in the new millennium. In *Handbook of teacher education: Globalization, standards and professionalism in times of change,* ed. T. Townsend and R. Bates, 3–24. Dordrecht: Springer.
van Vught, F., M. van der Vende, and D. Westerheijden. 2002. Globalization and internationalization: Policy agendas compared. In *Higher education in a globalizing world,* ed. O. Fulton and J. Enders. Dordrecht: Kluwer.
Westerheijden, D. 2003. Accreditation in Western Europe: Adequate reactions to Bologna Declaration and the General Agreement on Trade in Services? *Journal of Studies in Higher Education* 7, no. 3: 277–302.
Zammit, K., B. Sinclair, B. Cole, M. Singh, D. Costley, L. Brown, and K. Rushton. 2007. *Teaching and leading for quality Australian schools.* Canberra: Teaching Australia.

Educators in American online universities: understanding the corporate influence on higher education

Miki Yoshimura

Graduate School of Education, Old Dominion University, Norfolk, VA, USA

Introduction

Many higher educational institutions today offer students the option of taking courses online. College professors are faced with several new challenges, which are: a pedagogical shift, a different type of relationship with students, and a need to redefine their role (Couvillion 2002; Conceicao-Runlee 2001). Online teaching requires instructors to become facilitators of learning, for distance learning courses often assume a constructivist, learner-centred approach (Bastiaens and Kirschner 2007). Conventional didactic instruction does not thrive in an online environment. Furthermore, neo-liberal forces and corporate culture are sweeping higher educational institutions with more strenuous demands for student retention and accountability. Pedagogy seems to have been reduced to 'a matter of taste, individual choice, and job training' (Giroux and Mysriades 2001, 8).

What becomes of a college professor's job in this context? What are online educators experiencing in virtual teaching environments? The purpose of this article is to understand and describe the nature of online teaching through the perspective of online teaching professionals in higher educational institutions. A more specific purpose of this article is to examine the role of corporate forces in education as well as the neo-liberal politics and market fundamentalism.

This paper attempts a virtual educational ethnography that is identified by Lipman (2005, 319) as 'an educational ethnography that links micro with macro from an anti-imperialist, anti-neo-liberal position'. Virtual ethnography refers to the methodology for conducting ethnography in a virtual environment (Hine, 2000; Ward, 1999). This method was selected to obtain the naturalistic picture of the online learning environment and teaching in particular. This qualitative research was conducted over the three consecutive semesters at two online proprietary higher educational institutions in 2006. Non-participant observational data were gathered on a day to day basis, paying special attention to the communications between the instructor and the students mainly on discussion boards and chat windows. To supplement the data, interviews with three online teaching professionals were conducted either in person or by telephone. The interview participants were identified using a purposeful, homogeneous sampling method (Patton, 2002), with the sampling criteria being instructors who have taught online at post-secondary institutions.

Background to the study: education industry and online learning

Education industry

The history and evolution of online learning is documented elsewhere (Rosenberg 2001), and it is not the intention of this article to cover extensively how online learning evolved; instead, it will try to offer an analysis of commercial influence in education especially with regards to the development and evolution of online education.

In order to understand how the education industry emerged and developed, I would like to draw upon the White Paper from the Educational Industry Leadership Board (Sandler 2002) which provides a concise review of the education industry at the turn of the century. Until the 1990s, education had been the last sector in the American economy mostly untapped by private entities. There had been a growing demand by educators and parents for improved educational opportunities. These demands opened the door for private corporations to enter this largely untouched territory. Charter school legislation was first passed in 1991, providing a more favourable environment for schools and corporations to enter into contractual relationships. During the early stages of the emergence of education market in the 1990s, corporations began to offer solutions of school management systems and digitalised school supply procurement systems, as well as supplemental services such as ESL (English as a Second Language). In the late 1990s, the explosion of the information technologies and the internet delivered further market capitalisation opportunities for private corporations. Federal and privately funded initiatives to integrate technology into schools brought about a great opportunity for corporations to provide technology integrated solutions for schools. Educational platforms and portal services became popular commodities, and schools began to incorporate Instructional Management Systems and Student Information Systems to solve the issues related to standards, assessment and accountability. When teachers began to be held accountable for poor student performance, the professional development provider business was born and became very lucrative, generating $1.5 billion in revenue in 2001. The developing corporate educational industry continues to capitalise on the educational market, as they are able to leverage both the public demand for improvements in education and an environment which has become more accepting of for-profit involvement in schools.

Today, the education and training industry represents a $23 billion business, with leading corporations like Apollo Group (market capitalisation of $6.4 billion), owner of the University of Phoenix, and ITT Education (market capitalisation of $2.9 billion) which operates 87 technical institutes in 33 states with 48,000 students (Finance Review 2006). The education industry, as an emerging market, is expected to grow even further in the years to come.

Online learning

Grubb and Lazerson (2004) note that the expansion of the education and training industry was brought about with the rise of vocationalism in the United States; the purpose of education shifted from collective goals – the maintenance of democracy, the preparation of moral leaders – to private goals such as access to valued occupations. This is a fundamental shift in the purpose of education. As people began to seek education for specific personal purposes (i.e. improved employment opportunities), the common good (preservation of democratic values) became less and less important. There has also been a widely accepted notion that for-profit involvement is a positive phenomenon; it will bring about innovation and better management and accountability (Fein 2007). But is this really so? The bottom line goal for most corporations is to generate profit. Although educational corporations are often passionate about providing better education and improving educational quality, shareholders satisfaction oftentimes supersedes the satisfaction of their students or employees (faculty).

In 1892, the President of the University of Chicago created a correspondence school for individuals who could not afford to leave their homes and jobs to pursue higher education. Other schools followed suit. In 1998, Columbia University signed a contract with U.Next, an online education oriented company. Columbia professors would teach online and U.Next could identify them using the Columbia University brand name. Columbia would receive royalties based on class sizes with a minimum guarantee of 20 million dollars payable after five years. By the year 2000, education via the internet was already a 2 billion dollar business and growing 40% per year (Bok 2003). Today, almost all traditional higher education institutions are developing an Internet presence by going beyond simple Web sites and providing courses online. For-profit universities such as Apollo Group's University of Phoenix, Jones International University and Walden University are examples among many of the for-profit 'e-universities' (Rosenberg 2001).

Online learning is defined as 'any learning that is web-enabled', 'complete learning solution', and 'learning through amalgamation of technology' (Chadha and Kumail 2002, 32–33). There are many recorded benefits to online learning. Some of the strengths are described as having interactivity and flexibility and increased accessibility, as well as being able to deliver dynamic content (Goodyear 2001; Chadha and Kumail 2002). DeVries and Lim (2003, 3) describe the benefits as 'the asynchronous nature of the environment means that the student (or lecturer) can read a posting and consider their response for a day before posting it', and 'the written word encourages a deeper level of thinking'.

Online learning is said to have many advantages, but it is not a panacea. Online text-based communication is often accused of being impersonal and lacking expressive richness, and it requires technical access and competence in order to reap the benefits (Goodyear 2001).

Drawbacks are also numerous. Luke (2002) in *The virtual university?* argues:

> Digitalization cost more, not less. It really takes more people, not fewer. Optimal class size online often falls, not increases. Computer technology is rapidly obsolescing permanent cost, not a long paying investment. Students must work more, and far more actively, not less and much more passively. Hence, most distance learning is heavily

subsidized, like third world country airlines or old-time soviet military units, by other activities, and it often cannot face successfully a rigorous audit. (Luke, in Robins and Webster 2002, 270)

Knowledge and learning in an online environment

In the previous section, I referred to the word 'vocationalism'. In this section, I would like to expand on the notion of vocationalism in higher education and seek the meaning of knowledge and power in today's so-called 'knowledge society'.

Education is closely tied to economic opportunity (Grubb and Lazerson 2004), and receiving higher education has become perceived as an investment. Adult learners are keen on having flexibility and convenience (to overcome time and distance challenges), high quality and relevant education, and value for their money (Robins and Webster 2002). Hence online education draws favour, as one can participate in learning at one's convenience. Online education is now a popular option for people who seek to enhance their economic opportunities but are constrained by time and distance, like many adults with jobs and family.

In an online environment, there are virtually no extracurricular activities such as club activities, social events or athletics. Although it is a form of higher education, the kind of educational experience a student receives at an online institution is quite different from what they might experience at a traditional university. In a society where it is believed that knowledge is equivalent to power and educational achievements lead to economic prosperity, such activities that do not entail monetary value become less important. Online educational institutions therefore focus on the transfer of relevant knowledge and skills, and that is the commodity exchanged in online educational market.

In this regard, it is natural for universities to begin to put an increasing emphasis on the promotion of 'transferable skills' – the content with competencies – such as 'analytical abilities', 'problem solving', and 'communication skills', which is clearly about generalised forms of knowledge and expertise. This has been termed the 'de-referentialization' by Readings (1996, 17), where there no longer exist specific referents, or a specific set of things or ideas; his argument being that this process calls for a crucial shift in thinking that has dramatic consequences for the university. For Giroux and Myrsiades (2001, 36), it is the 'instrumentalization' of knowledge. They argue that this instrumentalisation of knowledge is what is undermining the meaning of higher education.

This de-referentialised or instrumentalised knowledge is certainly not the type of 'universal knowledge' that Comenius (1592–1670) envisioned (Chadha and Kumail 2002, 19). Education has become a kind of compartmentalised, standardised, packaging of pieces of information and contents that can be disseminated throughout the world, regardless of local context, culture or relevance. Robins and Webster (2002) refer to T.M. Porter, claiming that knowledge detached from the skills and close acquaintanceships that flourish in local sites becomes 'information' (Porter 1994). A world of information is, then, a world of knowledge detached from local contexts, 'a world of standardized objects and neutralized subjects' (Robins and Webster 2002, 321).

Regardless of the kind of 'knowledge' one is being exposed to, online learning presupposes a constructivist approach to learning (Bastiaens and Kirschner 2007).

Learning is not about merely acquiring the knowledge; rather, the learner is expected to actively engage himself/herself in constructing knowledge, and the educational practice is a task of 'facilitating' and 'orchestrating' the learning conditions for learners (Robins and Webster 2002, 107–8). In the e-learning context, learning is 'active, individual, cumulative, self-regarded, and goal-oriented' (Goodyear 2001, 72).

There is an existing, unspoken perception that how we learn is universal. Online courses assume autonomous learning, underpinned by constructivist learning theories and learner-centred approach. If learning style and culture are made universal, then online learning has enormous potential. As is described in Robins and Webster (2002, 217):

> For the commodity model, the issue is economy of scale. When customers are homogeneous, fewer fixed costs are required to produce goods that everyone wants. When consumers are heterogeneous, businesses and industries must find ways to segment the market to achieve economies of scale within each segment while still approximating each consumer's wants. With information goods like multimedia courseware, the pay-offs from a one-size-fits-all product are enormous.

The 'one-size-fits-all' perception in online learning has made the course design and course contents a pre-packaged, standardised commodity, ready to be traded and exported anywhere in the world. Standardised content ignores local culture, specificity and different learning styles. The commoditised learning becomes a political force for homogenising and marginalising variety and differences that exist in the world.

Otto Peters calls distance education 'the most industrialized form of learning' (Keegan 1994, 10). According to Peters, the structure of distance learning is determined by the principles of industrialisation, in particular by those of rationalisation, division of labour, specialisation, mass production, and cost-effectiveness, and is characterised by depersonalisation.

The course materials of the courses I observed were very well packaged. There were pre-made multimedia lectures and tutorials for the students. The course consisted mainly of (1) online discussion boards that the students were required to post every week, (2) online quizzes, which can be taken as many times as the student desired, (3) essay assignments and (4) optional chat sessions with the professor. The standardised course contents were provided to the instructor, along with a very detailed instruction manual and course syllabus.

The instructor has access to the statistical data of students, where (s)he could see how much time each student spent on each content area. Very few students spent time looking at the multimedia lectures; even the students who received As at the end of the class did not spend significant time with lectures. They knew exactly what to do to get a good grade with the course, and watching the lecture did not have any significant impact on their grade. The course is so clearly defined, calculated and compartmentalised that the instructor does not have to make any subjective decisions. The instructor is there to help the students consume the materials in the manner the *student* desires. The course is repeated term by term, and if the quality of the package is good, it can be repeated many times without any modification, and is thus very cost-effective.

Most students reported being on very tight schedules. In the introduction, students stated that they had full time jobs and were married with children. Several students were posting from the workplace. They stated that they were taking online courses toward a degree so as to upgrade their income potential. Students expressed their goals of taking online courses as 'changing employment' or 'trying to become eligible for a higher position at work'. The information they exchanged had little context, for they were scattered all over the United States and were accessing from different places and different time zones. Overall, the students seemed interested in getting the practical skills and knowledge that would lead to increased income.

Teacher–student relationship in online universities[1]

'Online is just another pedagogy', as one informant proclaimed during an interview. Teaching online is quite different from face-to-face teaching. The aim of this section is to depict online instructors' personal experiences, with the following themes emerging from interviews: (1) communication, (2) workload, (3) students and (4) their view of themselves.

Communication

Probably the biggest difference between online teaching and classroom teaching is the communication pattern. Most online classes are developed in such a way that the instructors never have to lecture in front of a classroom of students. The students are presented with a synthesis of materials (documents and multimedia files) and they discuss the materials in the form of a discussion board, where the instructor plays the facilitative role. The students and the instructor never meet in person, and it is difficult to nurture a student–instructor relationship.

Online teachers feel that they have to supplement the lack of personal touch in online communication by some other means in order to make the students feel that they are dealing with a human being, not a teaching machine. One strategy some teachers employ is to call the students at the beginning of the term.

> Some classes, if I have time, I will call them at home the first week of class to let them know that someone is really here and it's not some computer-generated response that they are getting, this is really me here and I am reading and grading their work. A lot of students have told me that they never had that happen before; they are just shocked that someone calls them. I think that they are paying a lot of money for these courses, and I think sometimes when you do that, that makes you more human to the students, that they are not viewing some monster at the other end [*sic*]. (Informant B)

> Plus the mere fact that they had a voice, the students don't feel that there is a real human, they don't feel the connection to the teacher as much online, so when they talk to you, it makes a difference. And one thing I did was that the first week of class I call all of them. I had so many students say that they really appreciated that because they really felt like they really had a professor. A personal touch made a huge difference. (Informant A)

Another way to compensate for the lack of personal touch is to be less formal in online communication. One instructor remarked that she uses a lot of 'emoticons'[2] in order to create the sense of personality.

> I significantly am less formal myself, and I also use lots of emoticons. (Informant A)

Another informant, who said that he is much less formal in online classes, had students post jokes as part of the self-introduction during the first week of the course. One student made a 'blond joke' and he replied 'Be careful, your teacher is blond'. And the student's response was 'lol' (an abbreviation for 'lots of laughter'). This represents the predominant tone of communication between the online instructor and the students. Had they been in the same room, the student would not have made that joke, knowing that his instructor is blond, and the teacher and the student may have had a different kind of relationship even if he had.

Workload

The impression of online teaching as being less demanding than classroom teaching is not necessarily so in reality. Since all coursework has to be word processed, many instructors feel that it is actually more work to teach online. Teachers are expected to give feedback to every single contact from the students, and the feedback oftentimes has to be made immediately. Teachers spend many hours grading papers and writing feedback.

> It is very time consuming. If you have 18 to 20 students, they have assignments sometimes 2 to 3 times a week, if you have 18–20 students, times 3 assignments per week, imagine, how much you are scoring. There have been times I have been up all night long, scoring assignments. (Informant B)

> It is definitely, definitely more work, and almost any instructor will tell you it's more work than in-seat. Anything that you would normally have said during lecture, you have to type and you have to write. (Informant A)

Some instructors are learning to be efficient. By creating several patterns of feedbacks and reusing them, they can give students personal feedback but not have to spend as much time constructing the feedback each time. An instructor also admitted that the time he saves by not having to sit in and lecture balances out the time he needs to spend on grading papers.

Students

Are online students different from traditional students? The answer to this question may be the result of the open door policy of many online proprietary higher educational institutions. As many higher educational institutions strive to make profits and survive, they have lowered their requirements for admission. Many instructors are startled at the poor writing skills of some students, and that they feel some students are not qualified or ready for college level work.

> You (the institution) have to continue to grow (student numbers) in each quarter. You have to have more and more and more and more. And this could stress them and they accept students who wouldn't ordinarily qualify for a college programme. (Informant A)

> Most students, their writing skills are not good, and they will be very upset if they don't get a 100% on everything. (Informant B)

There are three types of students, as one instructor categorised.

> You got the slackers, who think the class is going to be easier than in-seat, the ones who drop quickly. Then you got these working professionals, and sometimes they bite off more than they can chew, because they do think that online is easier, again. And you got these people who really understand what online is about, and see the flexibility factor, and they do really well. (Informant A)

Being an online instructor

When asked about the benefits of online teaching, every instructor replied that they enjoy the flexibility. They value the ability to work anytime, anywhere. One instructor even admitted that 'the only' benefit is flexibility. Another informant remarked:

> Independence, mobility, like I can be at the beach now, and I have my laptop with me I am in a wireless hotel, so I can travel, I can be sitting at the beach and have my wireless card in and look at the ocean, I can be with my family in West Virginia I can go to Las Vegas if I want to. Still teach and still have an income. When I get older if I don't have enough money to live on, this is something I could do as long as my mind is good, I have my mobility, my hand and things like that, I would be able to continue having an income. And I think this is the way to the future for high school. I heard that they are going to try to get online programmes for athletes in high school that they won't have to go to class. (Informant B)

Most instructors I have interviewed teach at a traditional university during the day. For them, having an additional source of income is like having an insurance policy, and they enjoy this supplemental income opportunity. One informant directly expressed his view:

> Currently I teach online just to supplement my income, because I have a full time job at a university. From my experience, talking with other instructors, I think that's what a lot of people are doing. Just supplementing income. (Informant C)

Online instructors are aware that they are in the 'education business'.

> You know, it's a business. I don't think the students see it, but that is the reality of it; it is a business. ... I see it as a business. I don't know if I really want you to use this in your thesis, but I see online teaching, and I see a lot of online professors see it as business, because a lot of people would teach at several colleges. But yet, universities, they have become a business. (Informant B)

Instructors often expressed frustration about the business-mindedness of the school they work for. So much emphasis is placed on student retention, and they are concerned about declining academic integrity.

> It is business first and then school. And if you can deal with that, that's great. And there is nothing wrong with that. They are really clear about that. As a faculty member, you also have to be clear about that. Too many people who come here aren't, and that we have a pretty significant turn over rate. I have been department head for 10 years. ... It's a business. If you lose students, you lose money. And that money has to be made elsewhere and therefore, one way to conserve some of that money is not to give raises to the faculty. (Informant A)

> I think about my academic integrity. I wonder how, let's say, somebody at a traditional institution, if they would view me, if they would see me as equal to a professor who is teaching in a public institution, or if they would see me as somebody who is somehow lesser. (Informant C)

Instructors oftentimes struggle with teaching online, but they are trying to do their best by adjusting their communicative and educative styles. The popular impression of online teaching is that it is an easier alternative to classroom instruction. As indicated above, this is not always the case. Online instruction requires that all materials be word processed and available electronically. There are also stringent requirements regarding the timely feedback given to student submissions. Indeed all student submissions require comments and feedback from the online instructor.

Some instructors feel that the lack of the need to prepare for classroom lectures more than balances the time demands relative to online instruction. But this opinion, while valid, is in the minority. The biggest disappointment for online teaching seems to be with the students' lack of writing and social skills and the 'businesslike' relationship they have with their schools, but they endure these challenges because they believe online is here to stay, and they appreciate the flexibility and extra income it offers.

Higher education at risk

Henry Giroux (2005) wrote that schools today closely resemble malls or jails, teachers are forced to adopt market values and their jobs are reduced to prepping students to take standardised tests. What I saw in the online classrooms reinforces this view, especially after interviewing instructors who are disillusioned and frustrated, but at the same time quite indifferent to the degree of corporate mentality that is prevalent in their working environment. Corporate ethos in higher education is altering the nature of academia and is having a profound effect on the very notion of education as public good.

It seems that the changes in higher education today come from three directions. First is from the schools that have become fearful of the disappearance of public funding and federal support. Second is the education industry that sees a great opportunity for profit in an unexploited emerging market. Third is the societal value that not only accepts but accommodates the goals and values of market fundamentalism and the people in the society who act as the promoter and the consumer of new educational values.

At the very base of this triangle, school, industry and the society, lies the corporate ideology of globalisation. Some call this phenomenon the corporatisation of higher education, and others use words such as commercialisation, commodifcation, marketisation, new managerialism, neo-liberalism and so on. Regardless of the term being used, what is evident is the growing concern that education as a public sphere is disappearing and is hampering the very existence of democratic society. Giroux and Myrsiades (2001, 31) contend that 'public spheres are replaced by commercial spheres as the substance of critical democracy is emptied out and replaced by a democracy of goods, consumer life styles, shopping malls, and the increasing expansion of cultural and political power of corporations through the world'.

Disappearing public funding in higher education has forced universities to seek corporate assistance. As a result, there is an increasing degree of internal and external control, surveillance and 'self-governmentality' (Robins and Webster 2002, 126). This means that universities have allowed the businesses to set the standard for intellectual activity, and this will quickly lead to 'liberal learning, individual autonomy, and cultural "building" being written off as inefficient, unproductive, and wasteful' (Luke, in Robins and Webster 2002, 267).

Increased corporate influence also means more emphasis on accountability and incorporation of cost accounting principles of efficiency in academic activities. Professors with research plans that are linked to profit generation are often granted more funds, and students become keen on getting their money's worth from higher education. Management courses that train students for high paying managerial jobs become popular, and humanities courses that do not lead to monetary benefits attract fewer students. As a result, humanities departments are downsized, and academic productivity goes down.

Robins and Webster (2002, 320) warn that:

> the 'traditional' ideals for liberal education have been replaced by a new discourse of rationality, efficiency, flexibility, competitiveness, and so on. ... Universities have to adopt a new managerial ethos because they are now involved in a new competitive game, both amongst themselves and with new kinds of 'for-profit' educational enterprises.

It is this corporate leadership that is transforming higher education today. The domination of corporate ethos means that management decisions are based on profitability. Knowledge becomes treated as 'property' or 'commodity' and pedagogy becomes a 'process' that has to be measured and be made as cost-effective as possible.

This trend must be understood as a present danger to higher education as a social good. Giroux and Myrsiades (2001) stress that education must not be confused with training, and that educators must resist allowing commercial values to shape the purpose of and mission of higher education. Their point is that higher education must be defended as both a public good and an autonomous sphere for the development of a critical and productive democratic citizenry. They warn that 'reducing higher education to the corporate culture works against the critical social imperative of citizens who can sustain and develop inclusive democratic public spheres' (Giroux and Myrsiades 2001, 2, 33).

Throughout this study, I have witnessed the degree of corporate influence in the online educational environment. As critics sound the alarm, the future of higher education looks bleak. The degree of governmental intervention and the balance of autonomy and accountability in higher education have to be openly discussed and negotiated. Robins and Webster (2002, 323) call for a 'cosmopolitan university, an institution committed to understanding the new global realities, and at the same time grounded in, and producing awareness of, its own local space'. As Newman, Couturier, and Scurry (2004) suggest, the success of American higher education depends on a shared understanding of what it is that higher education does for the society and the support, privilege, and respect that society provides in return.

Note

1. This section includes comments acquired from interviews with three online instructors. Informant A is a female instructor teaching public speaking and intercultural communication classes online. She is in her 30s, and has 11 years of teaching experience and started teaching online in 1997. Informant B is also a female instructor, in her 40s, who teaches sociology, psychology, and cultural diversity classes online. She has over seven years of teaching experience and started teaching online in 2005. Informant C is a male instructor in his 30s who teaches humanity courses online. He has been teaching for eight years, and has four years of online teaching experience.
2. Emoticons are symbols that convey emotions with typeface, for example, :-), :-(, and so on.

References

Bok, D. 2003. *Universities in the marketplace: The commercialization of higher education.* Princeton, NJ: Princeton University Press.

Chadha, G., and S.M.N. Kumail. 2002. *e-Learning: An expression of the knowledge economy*. New Delhi: Tata McGraw-Hill.

Conceicao-Runlee, S. 2001. Faculty lived experiences in the online environment. *Dissertation Abstracts International* 62, no. 4: 1296.

Couvillion, J.S. 2002. What is the experience of nursing faculty who teach online? *Dissertation Abstracts International* 64, no. 3: 1176.

De Vries, J., and T. Lim. 2003. Significance of online teaching vs. face-to-face: Similarities and difference. *Proceedings of World Conference on E-Learning in Corporate, Government, Healthcare, and Higher Education 2003*, 1044–47.

Fein, P. 2007. Vision for excellence. *Chronicle of Higher Education* 54, no. 6: 28.

Finance Review. 2006. Yahoo! *Finance Industry Review*. http://biz.yahoo.com/ic/766.html (accessed in November 2006).

Giroux, H. 2005. *Border crossing: Cultural workers and the politics of education*. New York: Routledge.

Giroux, H. 2006. *America on the edge: Henry Giroux on politics, culture, and education*. New York: Palgrave Macmillan.

Giroux, H., and K. Myrsiades, eds. 2001. *Beyond the corporate university*. Oxford: Roman & Littlefield.

Goodyear, P. 2001. Effective networked learning in higher education: Notes and guidelines. In *Networked Learning in Higher Education Project (JCALT) Deliverable 9* (vol. 3 of the Final Report to JCALT), 14–158. Center for Studies in Advanced Learning Technology, Lancaster University.

Grubb, W.N., and M. Lazerson. 2004. *The educational gospel: The economic power of schooling*. Cambridge, MA: Harvard University Press.

Hine, C. 2000. *Virtual ethnography*. London: Sage.

Keegan, D., ed. 1994. *Otto Peters on distance education: The industrialization of teaching and learning*. New York: Routledge.

Lipman, P. 2005. Reflections on the field: Educational ethnography and the politics of globalization, war, and resistance. *Anthropology and Education Quarterly* 36, no. 4: 315–28.

Martens, R., T. Bastiaens, and P. Kirschner. 2007. New learning design in distance education: The impact on student perception and motivation. *Distance Education* 28, no. 1: 81–93.

Newman, F., L. Couturier, and J. Scurry. 2004. *The future of higher education: Rhetoric, reality, and the risks of the market*. San Francisco: Jossey-Bass.

Patton, M.Q. 2002. *Qualitative research and evaluation methods*. 3rd ed. Thousand Oaks, CA: Sage.

Porter, T.M. 1994. Information, power and the view from nowhere. In *Information acumen: The understanding and use of knowledge in modern business*, ed. L. Bud-Frierman. London: Routledge.

Readings, B. 1996. *The university in ruins*. Cambridge, MA: Harvard University Press.

Robins, K., and F. Webster, eds. 2002. *The virtual university?: Knowledge, markets, and management*. Oxford: Oxford University Press.

Rosenberg, M.J. 2001. *E-Learning: Strategies for delivering knowledge in the digital age*. New York: McGraw-Hill.

Sandler, M.R. 2002. *The emerging education industry: The first decade*, White Paper for the Education Industry Leadership Board.

Ward, K.J. 1999. Cyber-ethnography and the emergence of the virtual new community. *Journal of Information Technology* 14: 95–105.

Developing a 'feedback cycle' in teacher training: local networking in English education at Keiwa College

Joy Williams, Akiko Shibanuma, Yoko Matsuzaki, Aiko Kanayama and Atsumi Ito

Department of English and Communication, Keiwa College, Niigata, Japan

Introduction

Keiwa College is a small Christian liberal arts college located between Shibata City and Seiro Town, in a rural area of northeastern Niigata Prefecture. It has altogether 800 students in three departments: the Department of English and Communication, the Department of International Studies, and the Department of Community and Social Welfare. The college was founded in 1991 to cultivate in students a broad and deep understanding of the human and natural worlds, communicative competence, and a spirit of volunteerism.

Until Keiwa was built there were no schools of higher education in the area. Both the local government of Shibata and the people in the community were eager to have a place for higher education. To meet their high expectations, Keiwa College has provided the community with evening courses, numerous lecture series, and student volunteer work in addition to programmes for the students on campus.

Our English language teacher education programme that started in 1993 has also been closely involved in the community services. This programme aims not only at producing conscientious and competent teachers of English who can play an active role in secondary school education in the community, but also aims at supporting our students' mental growth through contacts from local school teachers and students.

In order to meet this goal the teacher trainees at Keiwa have developed programmes unique to our school, in addition to programmes required by the

Japanese Ministry of Education, Culture, Science and Technology (hereinafter called Ministry of Education). We call these programmes as a whole a 'feedback cycle' between the college and the community. By this we mean the networking and the feedback born from the interactions between local schools and the college through its programmes in English education. Both groups in this interaction can develop understanding of some of the goals of English education by sharing teaching and learning experiences, discussing problem areas, and exchanging opinions.

Every year since the programme started, a number of its graduates have become teachers of English, surviving extremely competitive circumstances where the number of teachers to be employed has been drastically cut back due to a decrease in the total number of youth population in Japan.

This paper introduces some of the programmes we have developed for the 'feedback cycle'. In the first section, we will discuss practical initial education for student trainees. In the second section, we will discuss programmes for teachers in the community.

A communicative approach is central to Keiwa's English language programme. Full-time native speakers of English teach 60% of all English classes, which, for this size of a college, is rather exceptional in Japan. Thus students who proceed to higher levels show considerable progress in English proficiency, particularly in skills of listening and speaking. However, for the students to become competent and caring teachers, they need more opportunities to improve their teaching skills, to obtain 'hands-on' experiences, and to be more directly involved in the education of junior and senior high school students.

Our teacher trainees participate in an internship programme at local junior high schools on a weekly basis throughout their second year. This internship programme provides students with basic knowledge about the actual teaching environment. Then the on-campus Teaching Assistantship Programme is introduced when they become junior year students. As Teaching Assistants to native speaker mentor teachers in first year oral communication classes, teacher trainees become familiar with 'classroom English', class time management skills, and have an opportunity to interact with younger students. With these experiences the trainees are better prepared for the mandatory teaching practice required by the Ministry of Education at secondary schools.

We also encourage trainees to do voluntary work at primary schools where they use games and songs in English to introduce English to children. We support these volunteers by providing them with courses in English Education for Young Learners in our curriculum.

'Refresh Seminars' discussed in the second section of this paper provide in-service training for local teachers of English by giving them opportunities to develop their own language skills as well as to participate in workshops featuring communicative approaches to language education. This kind of communication among teachers in primary, secondary and university education – which is uncommon in Japan – has proved to be an important way for the college to learn about and respond to local needs.

We believe Keiwa's teacher education programmes have led to ongoing development of creating a more dynamic 'feedback cycle' between the college and the community.

Pre-service teacher training programmes at Keiwa College
Background
In the following section the pre-service training programmes that are offered to the students in the college's Teacher Training Course will be discussed. In one

programme the teacher trainees are Teaching Assistants (TA) in English classes at the college. In the other programme students are given opportunities to be TAs in local secondary schools. Before introducing these programmes, it may be useful to briefly provide some background information in regards to English education in Japan.

In Japan compulsory education is from grades 1 through 9 and students generally begin formal English classes in the seventh grade, or first year of lower secondary school. After lower secondary school almost all students go on to upper secondary schools. In order to enter the upper secondary schools of their choice, students must pass competitive entrance exams. After upper secondary school, entrance into top ranked colleges and universities is determined by test scores in each institution's particular entrance exam, or by the student's scores in the exams provided by the National Centre for University Entrance Examinations.

In all of these exams, English is one of the required subjects, thus many Japanese students study English in school, and in after-school 'cram schools', where the goal of instruction is passing exams. Questions in these exams tend to be of a discrete point and passive nature, therefore classroom practice has tended to rely on the 'grammar translation' method, memorisation and rote learning.

However, education in Japan is currently in a period of transition. The decline in the youth population of Japan is having an effect on entrance policies at secondary and tertiary schools, and in conjunction with this change there are shifting views about the goals and approaches of English language study. In recent years the Ministry of Education has emphasised the importance of communicative competence and the importance of English in cultivating international understanding. Many English teachers are re-examining former goals and approaches to English language learning. Teacher trainees today are at this 'crossroads' in changing attitudes toward English education.

The Teaching Assistant Programme in college English classes

Most educators would agree that pedagogical knowledge, strong subject area knowledge, effective communication skills, understanding of human growth and development, effective skills in teaching as well as classroom management, and a sense of ethics are the essential attributes of effective teachers. These attributes cannot be developed simply by taking courses in an academic setting. It is during the period of teaching practice, and then through ongoing, and reflective classroom experience, that young teachers can move from the theories learned in their education courses to obtaining the many skills necessary in the actual teaching environment. In Japan, however, the period of pre-service training has been fairly limited.

In recent years the Japanese Ministry of Education has required four weeks of teaching practice. However, before 2000 the duration of teaching practice in Japan was only two weeks and was completed during a student's senior year at college or university. The focal point of this two-week teaching practice period was the demonstration lesson conducted by the teacher trainee. This class is observed and evaluated by other teachers, including faculty advisers from the university or college. This two-week period of teaching practice was inadequate and many student teachers felt ill-prepared. We believed our teacher trainees needed more support in order for them to gain classroom experience and gain confidence in their own capabilities as teachers. The Teaching Assistant Programme at Keiwa College began as a way to help student teachers acquire some of the skills, mentioned above, before they began the required teaching practice.

It is with these objectives that our Teaching Assistant Programme began informally in 1997. It was hoped that by working cooperatively with trained 'native speaker' mentor teachers, student TAs would get more practical in-class experience, would become familiar with English expressions used in the classroom and they would be introduced to more communicative approaches to language teaching. Teacher trainees would also become more comfortable in the classroom situation, become sensitive to learner needs as well as gain more confidence in their own English skills. This programme has now been incorporated more formally into the college's teacher training course for third year students and now college credit can be earned for participation in the programme.

In the Keiwa College TA Programme, students in the English Teacher Training Course work as assistants in the Basic and Level One English Oral Communication courses in the core language curriculum. The Oral Communication classes meet three times a week for 60 minutes per class session. (Many of the university classes in Japan meet only once a week for 90 minutes.) By Japanese standards, language classes at Keiwa College are fairly small, averaging about 15 to 20 students per class. Students are streamed into proficiency level classes based on results of a placement test administered to incoming first year students at the beginning of the academic year. These oral communication classes are taught, in English, by teachers who have degrees in Teaching English to Speakers of Other Languages (TESOL). Emphasis is on language skills needed for communication and class activities are generally 'learner-centred' with students practising language structures in various pair and group activities. Assessments are holistic; students' grades are based not only on results of coordinated listening comprehension tests and speaking evaluations, but also on students' active participation in class.

Third year students in the Teacher Training Course are introduced to the college Teaching Assistant Programme during academic guidance at the start of the school year. Students are given the following suggestions of what their role can be as a TA in an English language class: model dialogues; demonstrate language activities or games; interpret vocabulary and explanations in Japanese as needed; participate in language activities with the students; assist students or respond to questions; be observant and help students who lag behind in class activities; be an English language learner 'role model' for the younger students. In general their role is to help students become comfortable with a more communicative approach to English instruction. After discussion of these points, students are assigned to the Oral Communication class that fits in with their course schedules. Thereafter the TAs work directly with their respective mentor teachers in making lesson plans and determining the various activities that the TAs will be involved in.

Over the years the TA Programme has gone through a number of modifications as we adjust to changes in the Ministry of Education's policies, the needs of the students in the Teacher Training Course as well as the needs of local schools. Ongoing feedback, in the form of questionnaires from the TAs as well as informal meetings with the mentor teachers, has indicated that this programme has provided valuable experiences for the student TAs and given much appreciated support for the mentor instructors.

Mentor teachers and TAs have mentioned the following benefits of the programme:

1. With a TA in the class, there was a better sense of communication between the students and the teacher. Having a TA in the class created a more comfortable, non-threatening learning environment and students were able to more easily ask questions and get clarification of language points from the TA.
2. Students were able to get more individual attention, thus learner differences could be more directly addressed.
3. Class time could be used more efficiently because the more complicated instructions for a language activity could be quickly provided in Japanese, thus students could spend more time engaged in the particular English language task.
4. The TAs were role models for the lower level students as English learners who have gained competence through classes in the English language programme at the college. Students in the lower level classes could get a real sense of how their English skills would develop as they progressed to higher levels in the English language programme.
5. The TAs gained confidence not only in regards to their own English skills, but also in their perceptions of themselves as English teachers.
6. Through this kind of 'learner-centred' type of language class the TAs became conscious of the importance of motivation in the learning process, as well as the importance of addressing a wide range of student learning styles and strategies.
7. The TAs could become familiar with team-teaching activities and skills.

Of course with the TA Programme there are also problem areas and concerns, such as the lack of time for mentor teachers and TAs to discuss lesson plans together, the sporadic attendance of some TAs which make it difficult for the mentor teacher to plan for a TA role in the class. These problems are being addressed through continued communication between the participating mentor teachers and TAs.

The Teaching Assistant Programme at Keiwa College is very much a 'work in progress'; the programme continues to evolve as circumstances in the college change and also with our greater understanding of the needs of the teacher trainees. We are particularly interested in finding out whether or not our teacher trainees perceive their TA experience as significant career support toward their future work as teachers in secondary schools.

In the academic year of 2006, questionnaires were given to the 16 third year TAs and 85 first year students who had TAs in their classes. Results of these questionnaires indicate that a large percentage of the TAs felt their experience in the Level I classes contributed to improving their own English skills, introduced them to a variety of teaching approaches, and helped them learn how to interact with students in a class setting. The experience seems to have given the teacher trainees a stronger sense of confidence not only in their own English, but also in their abilities as future teachers. The students who had TAs in their classes also appreciated the extra support that the TAs could offer. They mentioned that if they had questions related to class work, it was often easier to ask the TA rather than the regular teacher. Others seemed to view the TAs as role models; the younger students were impressed by the TAs' English abilities and aspired to be like them. This ongoing feedback is crucial as we seek to develop the programme to better meet the needs not only of our students, but also the needs of local schools.

Over the years the Ministry of Education has suggested various objectives for English education and in 2002 another new goal was proposed. The objective of English language classes was now to 'cultivate Japanese with English abilities'. Perhaps as a way to achieve these goals, since 2006 a listening comprehension component has been incorporated into the exam provided by the National Centre of University Entrance Examinations. The Ministry of Education is also suggesting that English language be formally introduced in primary schools. It is not yet clear whether introducing a listening component in the national entrance exams will change teaching practice at secondary schools and thus turn out students with greater abilities to communicate in English. There is also much debate about if, how, and when English language should be introduced into curricula at the primary level.

These are just a few of the issues that English language teachers today will need to consider. We hope that students who have been TAs, with more 'hands-on' classroom experience, will become more effective teachers. We also hope these teacher trainees will develop flexible teaching approaches and will be better able to adjust to various school situations. It is important for our teacher trainees to be capable of making the transition from the learning environment at the college to the environment at secondary schools. Hopefully these teacher trainees will also perceive their future teaching roles as that of 'facilitators' in a more student-centred approach to language instruction. In this atmosphere students may cultivate new learning strategies which will encourage the use of English as a means of communication rather than English just as an exam subject.

Most of all we hope that our teacher trainees will feel more empowered as effective communicators in English and as competent English language teachers. It is hoped that students who go through the college TA experience will be able to integrate more innovative and communicative teaching approaches within the educational setting at secondary schools. Their ability to do this will help them have a constructive role in the ongoing discussions related to English language education in Japan.

Local networking

The start of local networking

In this section, we will introduce the Teaching Assistant Programme at Seiro Middle School (equivalent to lower secondary school) which was the first of the local networking programmes that we developed in cooperation with schools in the community. Seiro Middle School is well known for adopting an educational policy featuring a 'subject-centred' educational plan which is unique in Japan. This new school is equipped with new information technology and encourages community support in its management and was part of a one hour project 'Education in the 21st century' broadcast by NHK in 2001.

Just when we in the college were concerned about the fact that students needed more actual teaching experiences, we learned that Seiro Middle School was considering recruiting student teachers to assist pupils' English learning. We developed a plan with the teachers to send our students to assist teachers in classes of

English language. Thus we started this programme in April 2000, and the college received a Grant-in-Aid from the Teacher Training Division of Elementary and Secondary Education Bureau, the Ministry of Education, as a 'Pioneer in Curriculum Development in Teacher Training Courses' of the 'Research Projects for the Development of the Curriculum and Methods of the New Curriculum in the Teacher Training Course'. In this TA Programme, students were assigned to classes to assist English teachers of the school. Most students visited the school once a week.

Through written records and questionnaires we can see the kind of activities the TAs did in the classes. These activities were evaluated in three ways: in written reports by the TAs after each class activity, in notes provided by cooperating teachers at Seiro Middle School and in questionnaires given to both the TAs and Seiro students. The data were collected three times in March 2000, July 2001, and in February 2002.

The results of these surveys showed that about 75% of the TAs gave positive answers. They reported that their main activities were to observe the class and to be aware of pupils who needed assistance and to assist individual pupils. Although at the beginning the TAs did not feel confident enough to help pupils in the class and tended to hesitate in assisting teachers, over time they became more active and enjoyed the role of being a TA. They also learned about teaching techniques and appropriate teaching attitudes not only by observing the lessons but also by taking part in the team teaching.

In order to find out how pupils of Seiro Middle School evaluate the Teaching Assistant Programme and assess the activities of Keiwa students' activities, we administered additional survey questionnaires in October 2000, January and October 2001, and in January 2002. Pupils said that 'it was good because we could ask questions more easily', or 'they taught very kindly, in detail'. Although some gave negative comments such as 'we became nervous with their presence', and 'it was confusing because the TAs' explanations were different from our teachers', as a whole, pupils appreciated the help from the TAs and their friendly manner.

Looking at the survey results, we found the TAs became more positive and confident in their activities. They learned by participating in the programme 'to be acquainted with the atmosphere of English teaching class in secondary schools' and 'to be ready for teaching practice by having a chance to interact with pupils and by learning teaching skills of English teachers'. The teacher trainees highly appreciated this TA Programme. At the same time, they realised they were not yet fully qualified to teach English at secondary schools. They felt that at the college they should have devoted more effort to acquiring English language skills and learning more about developing lesson plans based on teaching methodology. Hopefully the experience at Seiro Middle School provides motivation for our teacher trainees to focus more on the skills they will need to become teachers in the future.

We have found that it has been a very useful strategy to provide teacher trainees with learning opportunities in Seiro Middle School before confronting the actual teaching practice. While teachers of Seiro Middle School evaluated this TA Programme highly as well, they found room for improvement in the management of the programme. The following five points were what should be reconsidered in order to have a more effective system:

(1) Establish a 'follow up' system to improve communication among the parties involved.

(2) Familiarise students with whole contents of English textbooks and have them study how to develop textbook activities according to pupils' progress.
(3) Make TAs understand that it is more important to encourage pupils' motivation toward learning than to help them by simply correcting their mistakes. This should be done through observation of teachers' teaching approaches in the class.
(4) It is necessary to make TAs understand the actual educational environment by interacting with teachers and pupils more often.
(5) Since Seiro Middle School is an 'open plan school', TAs should study its unique school philosophy and organisation. In this way, they will be aware of varying ideals of education before they go to other 'conventional' schools.

Development of the programme

The required units of teaching practice at lower secondary schools have doubled with the new Ministry of Education curriculum standards for teacher training courses: these new standards applied to students who entered colleges and universities in the 2000 academic year. The TA Programme at Seiro Middle School that started as a voluntary programme was included as a required two-credit course called Teaching Practice 1 in 2002. Interestingly enough, the Keiwa programme predates the new standards implemented by the Ministry of Education. Most colleges and universities have been forced to make plans to implement these four weeks of teaching practice into their teacher training curricula. While most universities conduct teaching practice in the students' senior year, we divided the four credits of teaching practice into two parts, that is, Teaching Practice 1 for the Teaching Assistantship at Seiro Middle School in the junior year and Teaching Practice 2 at other schools in the teacher trainee's senior year.

Teaching Practice 1 consists of a one-week orientation programme in which students attend lectures on educational policy and are given an explanation of the unique system at Seiro Middle School. During this week the TAs also begin observation and assisting in language classes. In addition to this initial one-week programme, students are required to continue TA practice for 16 weeks. More than four years have passed since we adopted this scheme; the Teaching Assistant Programme has been well organised and we have continued to develop more opportunities for orientation and reflection. So far, the Seiro schoolteachers' assessment of the TAs has been very positive, although we should continue to evaluate the achievements of this programme. We could say that our system of teaching practice is a pioneering one.

In addition to Teaching Practice 1 at Seiro Middle School, we started teaching assistantships at other lower secondary schools, Higashi Middle School (in 2002), Daiichi Middle School and Saruhashi Middle School (in 2006) in Shibata City. We are sending sophomore students on a weekly basis to help pupils in these schools. These schools are more conventional than Seiro Middle School, so TAs have an opportunity to be involved in, and learn from, different school environments. Recently, the number of lower secondary schools which want to be involved has increased and our local networking is expanding. Through our college's Teacher

Education Course, students have a variety of pre-service experiences. In their second year, they go to lower secondary schools in Shibata City, in their third year, they serve as TAs in the college oral communication classes. In their fourth year, they return to their own secondary schools to finish their required teaching practice. In addition to these, in more informal programmes, volunteers from freshmen to seniors from our college visit nearby elementary schools to introduce children to English.

We administered survey questionnaires to teacher trainees and Higashi Middle School students in November 2005. About 80% of the college students responded positively to the experience in Higashi Middle School saying, 'It was useful as a way of considering a future teaching career'. About 60% replied, 'It influenced my attitude toward studies related to teaching profession'. About 60% of the middle school students said, 'Keiwa students were helpful'. In addition, 80% of the juniors who did Teaching Practice 1 at Seiro Middle School said, 'the teaching assistant experience at Higashi Middle School and Keiwa College had been valuable'.

The Ministry of Education's earlier standards for pre-service training were clearly not most effective for teacher trainees. The students had their teaching practice in their fourth year, and only then, for the first time, did they experience the reality of the teaching environment. The pre-service training was certainly inadequate. It is crucial for the development of student teachers to have practical in-class experience year by year and to understand and verify the educational theories that they learn in academic courses. It should be noted that at an early stage Keiwa College had developed a teacher training programme that supplemented the standards set by the Ministry of Education and that it has worked very well.

Programmes for in-service teachers

Seminars to support secondary school English teachers

Over the years, in order to support local teachers of English, we have offered seminars for secondary school English teachers. We started this seminar in 2001 and hold it once every year. This section reports how we started the seminar, and what we have done in these seminars.

In 2000 through 2001, the Ministry of Education designated Keiwa College to be in charge of a research project for the development of the curriculum and methods for the teacher education course. A research project was conducted under the title of 'Enhancing Practical Competence in Teaching English in the Teacher Education Course: Curriculum Development and the Teaching Assistant Programme on Campus and at Middle School'. In December 2001, we invited local secondary school English teachers to take part and reported on this project. We asked the participants to observe a Level I English oral communication class with a TA, and we also asked them to take part in our English workshops. The purpose of this seminar was to demonstrate the role of our TAs in our oral communication classes and also to highlight communicative language learning activities which are central in our English language programme. In fact, however, we later found out from questionnaire results that the participants made use of this seminar for their own training and were hoping to get some hints to take back to activate their own classes.

There were requests from many of the participants that we offer this type of seminar regularly, so in 2002 we changed the name of the project to the 'Refresh

Seminar for Secondary School English Teachers' and made it an annual seminar. Since then, we have offered various themes for the seminars such as 'Activities for the Learner-Centred Language Class', 'Textbook Plus', and 'Creating Communicative Classes'. As these titles suggest, we have planned to make our seminar as realistic and practical as possible. While we try to meet the needs of the teachers who want more opportunities to brush up their own English, we offer some ideas and hints to activate their classes. In these seminars, the participants do not simply listen to a lecture but they actually take part in various workshop activities. Moreover, the participants use this opportunity not only to improve their English skills but also to learn various teaching methods together. These seminars offer teachers a chance to exchange ideas on English education and education in general, no matter how different their working environments may be. Since the fourth refresh seminar in 2004, we have offered the seminars under the auspices of the Niigata Prefecture Board of Education.

In earlier refresh seminars we had more upper secondary school teachers, but in 2004, there were more lower secondary school teachers and even elementary school teachers because we started an English course for elementary school teachers as a part of our extension programme in this year. This is due to the fact that many elementary schools are beginning to offer English activities as part of the 'Interdisciplinary Studies' required by the Ministry of Education. However, there are very few English specialists assigned at the elementary school level. That is to say, while English is not required in Japanese primary education curriculum, there is immediate need for elementary school teachers to acquire English teaching skills.

We have tried to answer the needs and requests of teachers who teach all age groups in the community. Instead of the usual grammar translation method, participants can experience what a class taught in a communicative approach is like, and learn about various teaching activities and learning styles. This mix of elementary and secondary schoolteachers learning together at the same workshops is unusual as interaction among teachers from such a wide range of teaching environments does not happen often in Japan. The teachers could share and exchange ideas, and in that way, expand their views while 'stepping out', or away from their schools.

Refresh seminars have been rewarding for us as well. By reaching out locally, we can directly exchange ideas with teachers. Through this process we at the college also learn what is happening in English classes at a secondary school level. Although the teachers in public schools must follow the required curriculum, with the college offering an opportunity to learn about teaching theories and methods along with various communicative activities, local English teachers can get broader understanding of what it means to teach and learn English. Teachers are intellectually stimulated and mentally refreshed by regularly attending our seminars.

We are in the process of building up a dynamic 'feedback cycle' in the community by learning together, and understanding the teaching environment. We need to strengthen the links between schools and teachers. In the year 2004, especially, it was significant that a teacher from secondary school offered a workshop in the refresh seminar. We think it important that we have a reciprocal relationship between the local schools and the college. Refresh seminars are invaluable in the process of building up such relationships.

The English course for elementary school teachers

As mentioned earlier, an increasing number of elementary schools have started to include English language in their 'Interdisciplinary Studies' classes. In the meantime, the Ministry of Education has announced a plan to investigate whether it is appropriate to implement English as a subject in the elementary school curriculum. However, at the moment, many elementary schools rely heavily on ALTs (non-Japanese assistant teachers who come to teach in secondary schools) who are assigned to several elementary and secondary schools in a given area and can therefore visit a school only sporadically. As a result, most of the children in public schools may have an English class very infrequently. Therefore, we decided to offer an English course, 'English for Children: Theory and Practice', to meet the needs of elementary school teachers. Recently, many one-day or two-day seminars for teachers of young learners are available, but it still is unusual in Japan for elementary school teachers to take a regular college credited course in English for young learners.

The instructor in charge of this course is a professional teacher trainer in the field of English for young learners. She emphasises that it is meaningful for elementary school homeroom teachers, who know children best, to teach English to these children, and that they should not 'cram' children with English but they should try to create an enjoyable child-centred class.

According to the questionnaire at the end of the semester in 2004, elementary school teachers appreciated this course because they could systematically learn English teaching methodology, and they could experience many fun activities as well as understand the theoretical background. It is important to point out that since there are presently no formal guidelines for English class at elementary schools, it is up to each school to decide what to teach or how to teach. Therefore, we hope that the teachers in Niigata who take this course will play an active part to promote English education that does not depend too much on non-Japanese ALTs.

The year 2006 is the third year to offer this course. Participants increased by 30%. This increase is in response to the announcement of the Ministry of Education in April 2006 that they are considering implementing English curriculum into primary education in a few years. Teachers at the elementary school level may be feeling more acute needs for learning English teaching methods as well as improving their own English proficiency. English education at the elementary school level will invite controversial discussion in Japan. Is English really a must at this level? What is the purpose of requiring English at this point? Who is going to teach English to schoolchildren? Is there any national guideline? What skills should be emphasised? How will this new project be evaluated?

Although the answers to these questions are not clear, we have tried to make the best use of our resources in developing and strengthening the local network of English teachers. The new concerns are right ahead of us, and we hope to keep offering opportunities to think about and discuss the relevance of starting English earlier as well as supporting the teachers in need.

Conclusion

Envisioning the new century, the Ministry of Education had endeavoured to cultivate teachers who have professional competence, responsibility for promoting better education for the next generation, and deep human compassion. As one of the ways to realise this, the Education Personnel Certification Law was revised in 1998. The new Education Personnel Certification Law specifically emphasises practical guidance and teaching competence by increasing the required credits of teaching skills in specified subjects and in teaching practice.

The curriculum of the teacher training course at Keiwa College has been accredited for certification in English for lower and upper secondary schools since 1993. This curriculum was designed to enable the teacher trainees to develop qualities necessary to become teachers who are sensitive to each pupil's needs and who are ready to support each pupil's positive growth.

As we have discussed in the previous sections, we offer various voluntary Teaching Assistant Programmes for students both in the college and in the local schools, which were recognised by the Ministry of Education mentioned earlier. Our programmes have developed into a collaboration with other local lower secondary schools. We now work with four schools. We also provide annual seminars for teachers in the community.

We expect that students can enhance not only their teaching ability of English but also improve their competence as teachers through instructional experiences. These experiences will help to complement and integrate what they have learned in theoretical study in the related teacher training subjects in the college. This paper reports our efforts to set up a sort of a spiral curriculum in order to assist our students to become more confident teachers, and at the same time we envisage creating a 'feedback cycle' between the college and the community.

Gender inequality among Japanese high school teachers: women teachers' resistance to gender bias in occupational culture

Tomomi Miyajima

Human Development Unit, The World Bank, Middle East and North Africa Region, Washington, DC, USA

Introduction

Research focusing on Japanese teachers' gender inequality is scarce. Many researchers have found that as an important agent in students' socialisation, teachers' gender perception significantly affects students (e.g. Bailey 1993; Barrie 1993; Acker 1994; Beyer 1999; Weiss 2001). Parents and teachers alike play an important role in nurturing children's perception of gender because they teach various gender norms both consciously and unconsciously (Acker 1994; Grossman and Grossman 1994; Duffy 2001; Smith 1992). Most previous studies in gender and education have examined students' experience and viewpoints. Similarly, most Japanese studies focus on teacher–student interaction rather than teacher–teacher interaction (Biklen and Pollard 1993; Kameda and Tate 2000; Ogawa and Mori 2001; Arnot 2002; Kimura 2002).

This study focuses on gender inequality among teachers. Feminist theory suggests seeing the world through 'gender-sensitive lens' so that we can illuminate the various forms of gendering practice (Peterson and Runyan 1999; Padavic and Reskin 2002). In observing teachers' daily interactions, critical feminist perspectives are useful in identifying the contexts in which gender-biased practices happen and how women teachers cope with them. By studying gender inequality among Japanese high school teachers, this study aims to provide significant insights into the achievement of gender equality in education and employment.

Research questions and methodologies

Questions explored

1. Some scholars argue that Japanese teachers have unique forms of occupational culture – see the studies on Japanese teachers' occupational culture conducted by DeCoker (2002), Inagaki and Kudomi (1994), Fujii (1998), Shimahara (2002), and Le Tendre (1999). What are the characteristics of the occupational culture of Japanese high school teachers? What factors are involved in shaping this culture?
2. What is the process of teacher occupational socialisation? How does occupational socialisation (which includes daily on-the-job training by peer teachers, mentoring from senior teachers, and official teacher training provided by the local government) help new teachers naturalise and internalise certain norms and values?
3. Is teacher culture male-dominant and reinforcing of gender inequality?
4. What forms of resistance do women teachers develop to cope with gender-biased practices in the workplace?
5. Are the educational policies addressed in the current reform gender-sensitive? Is the formal and informal teacher training programme effective in raising awareness of gender issues?
6. In studying Japanese teachers' gender inequality, what is the implication for gender studies and education as a whole?

Ethnographic case study

This study exploits ethnographic case study methods and intends to prove its relevance and usefulness for obtaining in-depth information about sensitive issues such as gender, discrimination, and many other elements of a person's life story. The intention behind this method is to obtain a wide range of significant findings to account for the state of Japanese gender inequality in employment, with substantial consideration given to cultural factors commonly seen in the workplace. Data were collected at five schools in Gifu and Aichi, Japan, over the five-year period of 2000 to 2005. Fieldwork was conducted through on-site observation and in-depth interviews with 37 teachers, four school principals, and four superintendents in local government. Interviews were conducted in both formal and informal settings. Quantitative data released from government sources and research institutions, as well as journalistic articles, were used to clarify the social and economic status of teachers. Research sites were selected to cover different types of curriculum and locale to identify differences in workplace culture.

I observed teachers basically during normal school hours, but sometimes staying late, until 10 or even 11 pm, to see how teachers spent their extra work hours. I took notes during observation, but occasionally joined in conversation and activities without taking notes. Upon returning home, I would solicit my memory and record in detail what I had observed.

I noticed that some teachers, though not talkative, sent out clear messages in their communication. It was equally clear that they did not necessarily express their true feelings in exact words. Oftentimes, true intention was shown in very subtle or implicit ways, so I needed to guess because the language or verbal part of

Table 1. Profile of selected schools and interviewed teachers.

Schools	Public/private	Number of students/teachers	Curriculum feature	Regional characteristics	Number of interviewed teachers by gender
A	Public	450/38	Vocational, co-ed	Rural	6 female, 9 male
B	Public	720/47	Academic, co-ed	Rural	5 female, 3 male
C	Private	1160/46	Christian, girls only	Urban	2 female, 1 male
D	Private	1040/59	Academic, co-ed	Urban	4 female, 2 male
E	Public	820/59	Mix of academic and vocational	Rural	3 female, 2 male

communication itself was vague or ambiguous. Thus, I found it inadequate merely to record conversation and analyse solely from the transcript. In coding and analysing teachers' interactions, I sought an in-depth analysis, as opposed to a mechanical or superficial reproduction of a verbal exchange, without regard for non-verbal messages and context-embedded meanings.

Keeping these things in mind, I observed teachers in order to grasp their candid opinions and true feelings in their daily communication. I aimed to identify power relations and other dynamics working beneath the conversation. Semi-structured interviews were conducted based on the interview protocols, but I used these flexibly. When teachers began talking eagerly and passionately about other issues or anecdotes, I did not re-direct them to return immediately to the questions at hand. We typically spent one and a half hours for each interview. Essentially, all interviews were recorded and our conversations were transcribed after completing the data collection. The number of interviewed teachers was 37, of which nine were interviewed again, for a total of two to three times each. In addition to scheduled interviews, informal interviews, which mostly consisted of casual conversations at school and outside the school, were also conducted. These conversations were not recorded, but I took notes after each one. Observations and interviews were conducted primarily at school, but I also actively attended teachers' extracurricular socialising, where many teachers tended to open up and freely expressed themselves on many issues. All teachers cited have been anonymised.

Teachers' occupational culture

Being a teacher in Japan has many unique characteristics in its social, economic, and cultural status. Teaching is one of the most respected occupations in the society, and the expected level of accountability to the society is deemed to be almost equal to that of doctors, lawyers, or the police. Social expectations of teachers are both elevated and strict. Parents, community, and media maintain a strict view of teacher conduct (Moricguchi 1999; Kakinuma and Nagano 1998). Mass media heavily criticise teachers if they are ever involved in any unethical, immoral conduct. Parents too will accuse teachers for suspected inappropriate, disreputable behaviour. Teachers in Japanese schools are under ceaseless scrutiny and pressure.

Today, as respected educators and wise leaders, teachers face enormous societal pressure to behave in certain prescribed ways. They feel obliged to take part in the endless pursuit of decent, respectable, and superior character. Other major works on Japanese teachers' workplace culture support this view (e.g. Inagaki and Kudomi 1994; Nagai and Koga 2000; Shimahara 2002). Teachers have often cited the pressure they continually feel to behave correctly.

> Shiraishi: In staff meetings, usually after teacher misconduct has been in the national news, the principal reminds us how we should behave in and outside of school. No teacher actually thinks we'll ever be involved in such an incident, until it actually happens around us. I think most teachers are aware of their social status and don't do anything so stupid as to act indecently. We have been told so often not to engage in any misconduct.

> Nomura: I was taught by a senior social studies teacher the other day how the community sees us, teachers. During official teacher training, we were also told that we should be proud to be teachers and to be responsible at the same time. The leader of the training said we couldn't be too responsible as teachers. In many sessions and workshops, new teachers learn about teachers' heavy responsibilities.

> Higashino: I try to behave even in my private time, especially if I am around town. Lots of parents are watching teachers without your knowing. I go out of town for shopping or anything. I want to feel free. In this neighbourhood, I am a teacher seven days a week.

In addition to these tremendous external pressures, there are strong internal incentives to form a tight community at work. As Shimahara (2002) and Sato (1994) summarise, Japanese teachers are overwhelmingly responsible for all aspects of their students' lives. Teachers are in charge of the totality of their students' personal education, and their responsibilities are so broad that one cannot work alone to cover all aspects of students' development. This increases their incentive to establish 'strong teamwork' in order to work smoothly, and this is one of the major characteristics of the Japanese culture of teaching.

Compared to teachers in the west, Japanese teachers are expected to be more tightly knit, to work closely together, and to systematically collaborate to solve daily problems in the classroom (Kainan 1994; Roehrig, Pressley and Talotta 2002). This teamwork is based upon a strong bond, which sometimes requires the sacrifice of private time. 'Close and tight teamwork', 'mutual cooperation and harmonization', and 'strong bond among colleagues across ages' are considered important values in order to create a pleasant and efficient working environment. Good communication and cooperation is essential to settle daily classroom problems.

> Yamaguchi: I have to do my part, you know? In any case, we cannot do everything all by ourselves. For example, if your homeroom students commit some misdeed, I will ask his or her closest teacher to act as a counsellor, to identify the background of the problem and to understand the student's emotional state. Then, I will ask a teacher in the student guidance section, to determine how to treat the student, and then … So, each teacher has their own role in dealing with a problem. I cannot be objective when it comes to my student, so it is very helpful if other teachers work together and do their own part. This involves role-taking. Some teachers assume the role of gentle listener, another teacher that of a strict preacher; this is all done according to the student's individual circumstances. We need to develop a strategy depending on the case. In solving one problem, many teachers take different roles. I often take multiple roles but other teachers' help is a must.

The teaching community is a cultural circle; not only is this where senior teachers transmit teaching skills and knowledge, but it is also the milieu where values and morals are taught to young teachers (see Nagai and Koga 2001; Nihon Kyoshi Kyoiku Gakkai 2002; Shimahara 2002). Teachers' occupational culture consists of a whole set of explicit and implicit rules and regulations. Not only dress code and language, there are codes and unwritten rules for certain attitudes and behaviour. First-year teachers learn how to speak and behave appropriately as a teacher. By fully acquiring norms and behavioural patterns codified in the pre-existent teachers' community, new teachers learn to become a 'whole' teacher. Daily interaction with fellow teachers and mentoring from senior teachers also contribute to occupational socialisation. In fact, this informal teacher training is crucial to new teachers' occupational socialisation. Through consistent mentoring and close daily teamwork with colleagues, novice teachers acquire and internalise the existing norms of the occupational culture, which gradually become 'habit', so that these new teachers stop questioning many workplace customs.

> Murata: I stopped wearing earrings. I stopped wearing flashy-colour clothes. I remember I was told my first month not to wear these. I think a senior female teacher advised me on what I should wear. I don't remember exactly though. Anyhow, I got too busy and I didn't want to be bothered by these things. So I began to wear grey, black, or white. No pink, no blue, no orange. Now I don't care much about my outfits even in private life (laughs).

> Hattori: I am a first-year teacher at an academic school. I graduated from college and became a teacher, so my behaviour looks 'very studentish' to senior teachers, they said. I was told not to use such casual language with teachers and parents. Needless to say, no overly friendly talk with students. For example, I was having a really girly talk – topics such as fashion, cosmetics, TV drama and film stars – and one girl showed me her beautifully manicured nails. I completely forgot that I was a teacher and commented: 'Wow! You've got a pretty colour! Where did you get your nails done?', with too much excitement showing on my face. Yes, I was alerted afterwards, by senior female teachers that my behaviour was totally inappropriate. I understood that, and since then, I have modified my language and behaviour.

Teachers understand that their attire, language, and attitudes all affect students. It seems a shared understanding that teachers should set a good example for students. Thus, decent, professional, and semi-formal looking wear is preferred and required. PE teachers are told not to go to class in overly casual sports wear. These dress and language codes are part of teachers' workplace culture. As model professionals, teachers have to behave and conduct themselves in a certain way, and they have an entire set of norms and standards which eventually become part of their comportment. Teachers live within this professional community and play by the rules particular to the occupation.

Gender-biased practices and women teachers' resistance

This section explores the kind of gender inequality which exists in teachers' occupational culture. Who defines knowledge, and who controls power in the teaching workplace? Is gender the most powerful determinant in creating inequality among teachers? Previous studies show that the ratio of males to females in the workplace affects the formation of a 'mainstream' workplace culture (Kimura 2002; Jones et al. 2000; Miya 2000). In Japanese schooling, the ratio of women teachers decreases in higher education, and this has not changed for several decades. While the opposite is true at the elementary school level, male teachers are the overwhelming majority at high schools throughout the country (the percentage of female teachers is 93.9% at kindergarten, 62.7% at elementary school, 40.9% at junior high school, and 27.1% at high school level – School Basic Survey 2004). As for women's representation in managerial positions, the number of female school principals is also very small (17.7% at primary school, 4.7% at junior high school, and 4.3% at high school). Given that the national average age of high school teachers is 43.8 years (Statistics Survey on Teachers' Status 2003) the high school teachers' workplace culture could have many andocentric and patriarchal aspects. In some schools, it has been clearly seen that women teachers as a minority feel compelled to act in certain ways. Moreover, not only does the male-dominant occupational culture affect teacher behaviour, but so do students and school culture.

As shown in teachers' narratives, gender code does exist in their occupational culture. Gender code is part of the whole set of codes and rules of workplace norms. It guides and regulates teachers by prescribing the 'appropriate' outfit, language, attitudes, and behaviours for women/men teachers. Gender codes vary across schools where the roles expected of teachers differ. In a large part, school culture defines teachers' expected roles, and gender code is similarly shaped by the entire school culture. Some teachers' narratives reveal that gender code is heavily influenced by overall school culture, which consequently affects workplace culture. For example, at vocational school, where violence is not uncommon, even women teachers are expected to act very manly in an effort to maintain classroom discipline. Compared to that at vocational schools, the workplace gender code of academic school teachers is more closely connected to conventional gender roles widely recognised in the society. At both types of schools, it has been commonly seen that women teachers are basically expected to be soft, gentle, caring and accepting. They are encouraged to take a 'mother's role' while male teachers are expected to act as protector, taking a 'father's role'.

> Nomura: In a vocational school where I work, the great majority are male teachers and conversation topics in the staff room are very guy-favoured ones. Sometimes I have difficulty in relating myself to this manly atmosphere. I also think all teachers have to act very manly, unshakably, or rigorously because some students here act tough and aggressive. If you are not firm, they take you too lightly, discipline collapses and homeroom becomes chaotic. As a young female, I could become a target. I have to behave really manly sometimes. I often envy male teachers since they seem more advantaged in pretending to be 'strong, threatening' figures who can take control in class.

Research has revealed that in these 'women as minority' environments, women teachers are vulnerable and tend to suffer sexual harassment (Kimura 2002 cites a previous study conducted by Nikkyoso [Japan Teachers Union 1993], which shows women teachers at high school reported more sexual harassment incidents than women teachers in elementary school). For example, a woman teacher working in a male predominant school had the experience of being harassed and humiliated. Verbal harassment by male colleagues deeply hurt this teacher, a woman in her late 20s. She confessed that her male colleagues had cruelly berated her:

> You are now 29 years old and unmarried. You look very old, although you were so young when you first got here a few years ago. Look at those first-year teachers over there! They are so young and fresh!

This was not about her job performance or dedication to work, merely rude commentary on her age and appearance. She felt humiliated in that appreciation of her work was totally absent, while she was being judged for youth and physical appearance only. Facing such abuse, she naturally felt offended and harassed. Many women teachers revealed episodes in which gender plays a crucial role in judging and discriminating among teachers. A woman teacher in her late 30s recalls that a male principal suggested that she quit her job and raise children at home when she informed him of her third pregnancy and requested arrangements for before and after her maternity leave. By her account, the male principal implied that she should prioritise raising her own children as a mother's responsibility. He may have considered raising three children and working as a full-time teacher to be too great a burden and was doubtless displeased with the fact that she had already taken two maternity leaves and was planning to take another. He must have thought she was accumulating too many absences to fulfil her commitment as a qualified teacher. However, given that family planning is a solely private matter, and that it was her legally assured personal right to take maternity leave, the pregnant teacher was infuriated by his comment. Similar stories are told by other senior women teachers who have experienced pregnancy and child rearing.

Against these gender-biased treatments, what kind of coping strategies or resistance do women teachers develop? By close observation of teacher interaction, I found certain patterns in women teachers' strategy building. It is not my intention to mould women teachers into rigid categories, and I am aware that each person is different. We cannot oversimplify and generalise people's behaviours and women cannot be labelled as one monolithic group with a few different categories. However, after careful observations and repeated interviews with women teachers, I found commonalities in their forms of resistance and divided these into at least four major categories. The purpose of this categorisation is not to stereotype women teachers. While it is true that coping strategies differ with the individual, I believe it is important to articulate characteristics, trends, and similarities to wholly understand the real life of women teachers.

Reluctant fighter, careful observer

This is seen in many young, beginning teachers in their mid 20s with one to three years of teaching experience. She is in the 'apprenticeship phase'; still trying to see what is acceptable in the workplace culture, carefully observing when and how to speak up. Though highly aware of gender-biased practices at work, she is reluctant to resist. She is afraid of creating a fuss. When frustrated by work-related issues, she utilises her network of friends, cohorts, family, and boyfriend in order to let out her emotions to release stress. She tries to maintain a good relationship with teachers of all age groups, but she is especially close to similarly aged colleagues in similar circumstances.

Burnout or avoiding burnout

This is mainly seen in teachers with 7–12 years of teaching experience and it is often seen among women in their early 30s. She enjoys acquired job responsibilities and has a high level of self-confidence and self-efficacy after passing the 'apprenticeship' phase. Due to the heavy workload, she continually feels distressed but never stops working. She is a near-workaholic and sometimes experiences an 'emotional rebound' and 'apathy' resulting from concentrated work. She is neither neglectful nor careless about gender issues, but tends to avoid confronting any extra conflicts which would entail heavy emotional burden. She wants to focus on her work such as homeroom management, teaching difficult classes, gaining trust from colleagues, parents and students. Sometimes she displays 'burnout' symptoms or narrowly avoids falling into that status. She tends to spend excessive time at work and works harder to accomplish goals, which is one of her ways of easing stress.

Tough fighter

This would be an experienced teacher with more than 15 to 20 years of career. This is frequently seen among women in their 40s. She is very confident and determined, having very strong career aspirations. She possesses aggressive attitudes in general and is not afraid of speaking up or displaying overt forms of resistance. She fights against any unfair practices but this does not always mean for the benefit of women as a whole. She often fights for reasons of self-interest. Her awareness of gender issues is not necessarily high. In most cases, her strengths and determination to build a career are backed up by strong emotional support from her own mother. The mother is a full-time housewife and strongly encourages her daughter to pursue a career to be independent. The mother–daughter tie is very strong and they depend upon one another.

Silent but practical resistance

This is seen in female teachers across all age groups; teachers adopt this strategy depending on individual situation. She does not overlook unfair treatment, but does not immediately speak out forcefully. She carefully examines each case and quietly takes practical means to solve the problems. She does not wish to disturb workplace harmony, but neither does she embrace severe inequalities. She chooses where and how to express her complaints. She has a good network of colleagues from whom to ask for support.

Again, I do not mean to stereotype or categorise all women teachers, but I found it interesting that teachers in the same age group often show similar patterns of resistance. Mainly represented by young, beginning teachers, Type 1 individuals are still not fully confident or fully satisfied with their own work performance. On occasions such as student guidance or homeroom management, they tend to count on advice from senior, experienced teachers. This does not imply they are completely dependent on other teachers; rather, these young teachers are very enthusiastic about self-improvement and have been struggling to develop their own way of settling cases. However, they feel more comfortable reflecting advice and comments provided by experienced teachers in order to strengthen homeroom management skills. Basically they are eager to learn and are seriously working for the well-being of students. The more serious they are, the harder they struggle. Thus, a minor flaw or shortcoming in their own skill will hinder these young teachers and they become trapped by feelings of self-incompetence. Oftentimes they become insecure due to low self-efficacy as a professional; they tend to observe very carefully what other teachers do rather than try to initiate activities. In staff meetings, these teachers tend to be quiet and attentive to others' opinions.

It seems teachers with 7–10 years experience have moved on to another phase after graduating from this first stage. These teachers fall into Type 2: burnout, or avoiding burnout. She has gained confidence after several years of struggle for self-improvement. She has developed her way of teaching and dealing with homeroom problems, and has become aware of her own unique teaching style. Her sincere attitude and high professional standards inspire trust among colleagues, and consequently a lot of job assignments and related responsibilities inundate her every day. Unless controlled carefully, it is easy for her to fall into the 'work-is-everything-life' and to spend extremely long hours at work even over the weekend. Although she enjoys the heavier workload and added responsibilities, stress becomes enormous and sometimes difficult to handle. Some teachers become exhausted and go to 'rebound' of avoiding commitment and responsibilities. These 'avoid-burnout' teachers tend to carefully prioritise things in order to reduce stress and fatigue as much as possible. Some teachers avoid reflecting deeply on gender inequality because thinking about or struggling with such an issue would augment stress and conflict. Thus, they focus exclusively on certain 'selected issues' or 'urgent cases', mainly prioritising homeroom management and student problems. Since their self-efficacy, self-reliance and competence level is not low, gender issues will not hurt or impact them so much.

This attitude of 'avoiding extra cost and sources of stress as much as possible' paralyses incipient and real feelings on the part of the teacher and she gets used to the state of 'not feeling'. Having once acquired and internalised this way of thinking and forgetting feelings, teachers become less preoccupied with gender issues and concentrate more on work. This pattern is commonly seen in women teachers with 7–12 years of experience.

I have also noticed that the women in Type 3 showed strong maternal ties. These teachers recalled that their mothers always supported their education and encouraged them to pursue a 'lifelong, real career' to become financially independent. I found that mothers significantly affect their daughter's educational and occupational choice and success. According to the interviews, these mothers are essentially full-time housewives and are frustrated with their dependence on their husbands. These mothers instructed their daughters to have a 'decent job, stable income, so you have more freedom and choice in your life'.

The effectiveness of formal teacher training in raising gender awareness

In addition to in-house training, Japanese teachers receive substantial amounts of rigorous and systematic teacher training organised by the local government. Yet, is this formal teacher education effective in raising gender awareness among teachers? Voices of both new and experienced teachers suggest that the programmes included in this training are inadequate in some prefectures. Here the feedback from teachers shows how young and experienced teachers perceive the official teacher training.

Each workshop and training session has specific goals and objectives, but teacher comments indicate they are not always effective. The common perception among young teachers was that teacher training is a good place for networking and socialisation. They make friends with cohort teachers in different schools and share information. Getting away from school and having a dedicated time for self-training also provides refreshment. Official teacher training offered by the Education Centre at the local board of education is a good chance to reflect on oneself and one's teaching practices. Getting away from school, stepping back from the hectic work life can give teachers a chance to reflect on their daily schedule; however, some teacher training burdens teachers with extra tasks in addition to regular work. It often deprives them of free time, and the overwhelming amount of paperwork makes them even busier. However, teacher training provides additional communication and mentoring opportunities with senior teachers who have already undergone it. Thus, Education Centre-based teacher training programmes, as well as in-house teacher training, play an important role in socialising and acculturating teachers. Through this mentoring and training, teachers acquire occupational norms and standards.

Training for teachers of managerial positions is also effective in helping them gain knowledge and refine skills in personnel management. However, with regard to raising awareness of gender issues, sufficient training is currently unavailable, and interviewed school principals and superintendents stated that they don't remember taking such gender-oriented training programmes at all. For teachers in managerial positions, it is important to provide gender-sensitive training because its influence on regular teachers is enormous (Gender Equity Bureau, Cabinet Office of Japan, 2004).

Other factors shaping power relations among teachers

Senior teachers seemingly have greater self-confidence and self-efficacy compared to young, beginning teachers. In the course of a teaching career, they confront innumerable difficult problems with students, especially in their homeroom management. Teachers who have worked at several different schools will have experienced diverse educational issues in the community. Time spent working as a teacher is one of the most influential factors in determining one's level of confidence and self-reliance as an educator. I have also noticed that young teachers are full of hope and positive energy; however, they suffer from severe self-doubt and lack of confidence from time to time, especially when they encounter problems of a sort that they have not previously confronted and resolved.

Teachers of all ages often say 'experience is everything' in becoming an '*ichininmae*': a 'whole teacher, a real professional'. This does not mean senior teachers look down on young teachers; they do appreciate each colleague's unique talents and particular contributions to the workplace community regardless of years of service, but there is a fundamental respect for senior teachers. This was commonly seen across schools regardless of differences in school culture.

Teachers' behaviour is deeply affected by the seniority system, and the power dynamics among teachers are significantly based on the seniority-focused hierarchy examined in the previous section. When asked 'Who do you think shapes the mainstream workplace culture in your school?', many young teachers answered 'senior teachers with more than 10 years of experience'. Interestingly, they mentioned length of teaching career, but not gender itself. Regardless of gender, senior teachers' opinions are esteemed. The seniority system is at work in any school. Length of career matters when it comes to who is in power, who is influential among teachers. Some women teachers are actually very powerful – even more so than male teachers.

> Togawa: I think the most powerful people in the teacher group are definitely the experienced female teachers. Everyone is afraid of them. Nobody can rival them. Even

in staff meetings, some powerful female teachers can make senior male teachers shut up. For example, in our school, there is a female teacher, I guess she is 48 years old, who is so powerful, that she explicitly decreed, 'Japanese women's hair must be black!', and she never seems to conform to other opinions. Nobody could oppose her.

Moreover, it was interesting to see that gender does not always matter in determining power relations, especially among the teaching cohort. Age, or teaching experiences, and the authoritative level of the person matters more than gender itself in determining power. It is interesting to see how teachers situate themselves in the whole teachers' group, and oftentimes gender is not the most powerful variable to determine power relations. As a prime example, for beginning teachers, especially among the cohort, gender plays a small role in distributing power, or they do not even care about the 'power game'. They see each other as 'friends' or 'comrades' who share the same concerns and experiences as beginning teachers. Young teachers often get together, go out for a drink, and discuss each other's problems frankly. During the probationary first year, teachers have ample opportunity to meet in workshops and training sessions periodically held in each region. These young teachers enjoy social gatherings and bond strongly with one another. Thus, 'power' is not an issue within the group; rather, they help one another regardless of gender. In addition, one's exact age does not matter either. Some teachers already have several years of experience working as full-time lecturers or in another occupation. The teacher selection exam is highly competitive and it is very difficult to pass it right after graduating from college. Many people work as full-time lecturers while attempting the exam a multiple number of times. Thus within the cohort, though differences in age and occupational background preclude homogeneity, actual age or previous experience does not prevent friendships. On the contrary, diversity enriches and energises the young teachers' community.

Besides the age and length of teaching experience, one's position also plays an important role in power relations. Part-time teachers and language assistants affirm that regular teachers treat them as second-class citizens. Thus, it is equally important to note that not only is there gender inequality in the workplace, but other inequalities exist as well.

Summary and policy implications

In summary, findings suggest these conclusions. Similar to many other case studies, this research is region specific and its focus is limited, thus this conclusion does not constitute a definitive analysis of the complex teaching culture of Japan. Further research will reveal more detailed aspects of gender inequality among teachers.

1. Teachers' workplace culture consists of various norms and standards which define official knowledge: i.e. what is acceptable/unacceptable as a respectable teacher. A whole set of these rules regulate teachers' behaviour.
2. Both external forces (pressure from mass media, societal expectations, etc.) and internal forces (power relations, hierarchy among teachers), and the backgrounds of teachers themselves (age, gender, length of career, teaching beliefs, etc.) all shape the occupational culture in each school.
3. Occupational culture greatly varies across schools and is affected significantly by the characteristics and demands of students, parents, and

community. There is no one single 'mainstream culture' which can explain the whole complex teaching culture of Japan.
4. Through occupational socialisation, beginning teachers assimilate into the workplace culture. In order to work efficiently as a team, teachers closely cooperate and follow group values rather than promote individual beliefs.
5. Not only official teacher training programmes but also informal on-the-job training such as daily mentoring from senior teachers plays a crucial role in beginning teachers' assimilation into mainstream workplace culture.
6. Some workplaces are male-dominant and marked by substantial gender inequality. Once acquired and naturalised by each member, the 'gendered' culture of teachers systematically reproduces itself through 'self-regulated behaviour' and 'habits' of each member.
7. Teachers' perception and attitudes towards gender issues significantly vary depending on each teacher's standpoint, regardless of sex. However, in schools where overt and covert forms of gender-biased practices are often seen, women teachers create various coping strategies and develop implicit and explicit forms of resistance.
8. Workplace culture within the teachers' community is constructed of multilayered power politics. Most importantly, gender is not the only factor which determines power, nor the single absolute source of inequality. Age, or length of career, for example, is another powerful determinant in shaping hierarchy and power politics among teachers.

It is often said that the Japanese teacher training system is well designed and systematically implemented on a nationwide scale. The local government board of education is in charge of designing, developing and providing teacher training, in order to meet specific educational needs in each region. Thus, the contents vary significantly across prefectures. Especially for social issues such as gender equality, many teacher training curricula are not fully incorporated. For example, contents analysis of teacher training programmes shows that Gifu prefecture compares poorly with Edogawa Ward, Tokyo, where training includes detailed sessions about the importance of promoting gender equality in school. In my fieldwork, interviewed school principals, superintendents, and teachers in managerial positions recalled that they had never received gender-oriented training. Improving teacher training curricula to raise teachers' awareness of gender issues is the first step to achieving greater gender equality in Japanese society.

Many elements of informal, casual forms of occupational socialisation are controversial and require immediate attention and change. Oftentimes gender stereotypes are perpetuated through subtle messages or signals within regular conversation. This is worse at social gatherings such as drinking parties, where some young women teachers have become targets of sexual harassment. Such cases are rarely reported in 'serious' fashion to higher authorities because victims are afraid of losing peer support by making a big fuss about things occurring during parties. Therefore, it would also be helpful to establish 'counselling sessions' to let teachers discuss problems. Although school counsellors are becoming more available, teachers often hesitate to reveal their problems to the on-site counsellor, who is part of the workplace human relations. Going to see a doctor is sometimes difficult because of the hectic schedule, and especially if mental issues are involved, teachers will see a therapist only reluctantly. Thus, incorporating these counselling sessions into existing mandatory training for each career stage would be helpful, so that teachers need not take extra leave to obtain counselling. In providing such sessions, anonymity and privacy are essential to ensure that teachers feel free to speak.

It is essential first to ensure teacher well-being in order to provide high-quality education to students. Teachers are important agents in students' socialisation; students absorb values and norms from teachers' words and actions. Thus, teachers' unconscious behaviour affects students' holistic development. If teachers are satisfied with their lives and have fair and just views on gender, they can exercise a positive influence on students. Therefore, we should not merely pressure teachers to become superman-like figures, but rather provide sufficient support for them to enjoy a balanced professional life. To combat teacher burnout and alleviate the struggle to balance work and family, not only local boards of education but other policy institutions should formulate realistic plans to ensure care and support for teacher well-being.

This study suggests that society as a whole sees teachers and their workplace through different lenses, with deeper consideration for teachers' well-being and their quality of life. This would enable teachers to spare more time and energy for gender equality-oriented education, without suffering from burnout or apathy. Creating a gender-sensitive workplace environment is important and raising awareness should be part of any teacher training curriculum, both at formal and informal levels. Well designed teacher training is crucial to delivering high-quality education to students.

References

Acker, S. 1994. *Gendered education: Sociological reflections on women, teaching and feminism.* London: McGraw-Hill, Open University Press.

Arnot, M. 2002. *Reproducing gender?*. New York: Routledge.

Bailey, S.M. 1993. The current status of gender equity research in American schools. *Educational Psychologist* 28: 321–39.

Barrie, T. 1993. *Gender play: Girls and boys in school.* New Brunswick, NJ: Rutgers University Press.

Beyer, S. 1999. Gender differences in causal attributions by college students of performance on course examinations. *Current Psychology* 17: 346–58.

Biklen, S., and D. Pollard. 1993. *Gender and education.* Chicago: University of Chicago Press.

DeCoker, G. ed. 2002. *National standards and school reform in Japan and the United States.* New York: College Press.

Duffy, J. 2001. Classroom interactions: Gender of teacher, gender of student, an classroom subject. *Sex Roles: A Journal of Research* 45: 579–93.

Fujii, S. 1998. *Gakko no Sensei niwa Mienai koto.* Shizuoka: Japan mashinisutosha.

Gender Equity Bureau, Cabinet Office of Japan. 2004. *White paper on gender equality.* Tokyo: Cabinet Office of Japan.

Grossman, H., and S. Grossman. 1994. *Gender issues in education.* Boston, MA: Allyn and Bacon.

Huberman, M. 1993. *The lives of teachers.* New York: Teacher College Press.

Inagaki, T., and Y. Kudomi, ed. 1994. *Nihon no Kyoshi Bunka: The culture of teachers and teaching in Japan.* Tokyo: Tokyo Daigaku Shuppankai.

Jones, K. et al. 2000. Gender equity training and teacher behavior. *Journal of Instructional Psychology* 27, no. 3: 173.

Kainan, A. 1994. *The staffroom: Observing the professional culture of teachers.* Brookfield, VA: Avebury.

Kakinuma, M., and T. Nagano, ed. 1998. *Kyoshi to iu Genso*. Tokyo: Hihyosha.
Kameda, A., and K. Tate. 2000. *Gakko wo Gender-free ni*. Tokyo: Akashi shoten.
Kimura, R. 2002. *Gakko bunka to gender*. Tokyo: Keiso shobo.
Le Tendre, G. 1999. *Competitor or ally?* New York: Falmer Press.
Miya, T. 2000. *Sexual harassment*. Tokyo: Asahi Shimbunsha.
Moriguchi, H., ed. 1999. *Kyoshi*. Tokyo: Shobunsha.
Nagai, S., and M. Koga ed. 2000. *Kyoshi to iu Shigoto=Work*. Tokyo: Gakubunsha.
Nihon Kyoshi Kyoiku Gakkai, ed. 2002. *Kyoshi toshite Ikiru*. Tokyo: Gakubunsha.
Ogawa, M., and Y. Mori. 2001. *Jissen gender free Kyoiku*. Tokyo: Akashi shoten.
Padavic, I., and B. Reskin. 2002. *Women and men at work*. Thousand Oaks, CA: Pine forge Press.
Peterson, V.S., and A.S. Runyan. 1999. *Global gender issues*. Boulder, CO: Westview Press.
Roehrig, A., M. Pressley, and D. Talotta, eds. 2002. *Stories of beginning teachers: First year challenges and beyond*. Notre Dame, ID: University of Notre Dame Press.
Sato, N. 1994. Ethnography of Japanese elementary schools: Quest for equality. In *The culture of teachers and teaching in Japan*, ed. T. Inagaki and Y. Kudomi, 125–39. Tokyo: Tokyo Daigaku Shuppankai.
School Basic Survey. 2004. Japanese Ministry of Education, Culture, Sports, Science and Technology.
Shimahara, N. 2002. *Teaching in Japan: A cultural perspective*. New York: Routledge Falmer.
Smith, D. 1992. A description of classroom interaction and gender disparity in secondary business education instruction. *Delta Pi Epsilon Journal* 34: 183–93.
Statistics Survey on Teachers' Status. 2003. Ministry of Education, Culture, Sports, Science and Technology.
Weiss, R.P. 2001. Gender-biased learning. In *Training and development*, vol. 55, no. 1. Alexandria, VA: American Society for Training and Development.

Teacher induction across the Pacific: a comparative study of Canada and Japan

Edward R. Howe

Utsunomiya University, Japan

Introduction

Educational practices should be shared among educators globally. As an expatriate Canadian secondary teacher working in the school of education within a Japanese university, I have just such an opportunity. Here, I offer my first-hand experience and research to describe and to critically analyse strengths and weaknesses of teacher education in Canada and Japan (see also Howe 2003, 2005, 2006). In this comparative and evaluative study, an attempt is made to generalise findings across the boundaries of two distinct cultures, while taking into account the context in which information is gathered. Teacher education occurs within different political, social, economic and cultural realities. Nevertheless, while differences in educational milieu exist, there are commonalities relevant to education across the Pacific and everywhere.

The rationale for this study is perhaps not immediately obvious. Cultural relativists may suggest the two educational systems embedded within each cultural context are so dissimilar there is little to be gained from studying the other in any detail. However, many educators argue to the contrary, that there is much to be learned from such cross-cultural international studies (Stevenson and Stigler 1992; Shimahara and Sakai 1995; Rohlen and LeTendre 1996; Cummings and Altbach 1997). Nevertheless, comparisons have led to an international economic competitive agenda and distortions of education in East Asia. Rohlen (1995, 104) adds:

> Portraits emphasizing 'exam hells', authoritarian teachers, student malaise, lack of creativity, and excessive conformity are common. These portraits raise doubts that there is anything to be learned from school systems with such a seemingly alien character. Success at such a price, we say to ourselves, is actually no success at all. I cannot agree. I

think I speak for most of my colleagues who study Asian education in asserting that there is much to learn.

Over 3000 Japanese teachers are sent to Canada and the US every year to study the education systems (Kobayashi 1993, 11). Since 1993, over 600 Canadians per year have taken part in the Japan Exchange and Teaching Programme (JET) to enhance international education and the exchange of ideas (Monbukagakusho 1996, 30). To further this notion, I focus on aspects of teacher education in Japan and Canada that are most successful in training pre-service teachers and in providing professional development for in-service teachers. However, in order to fully appreciate teacher induction within the each cultural context, it is necessary to first provide some background information. Thus, what follows is an overview of education, higher education and teacher education in each region.

Education in Japan

Japanese culture and tradition have played an important role in shaping the education system. Since the Meiji restoration in 1868, Japan has looked beyond her shores for ideas and more efficient or better ways of accomplishing things. The Japanese are remarkable in the way they have been able to take good ideas from abroad, perfecting and adapting them for their own purposes, while maintaining their culture and traditions. Education is a prime example of this. By learning Western methods of production and adapting the Western model of capitalism to suit Japan's unique culture, Japan evolved from a feudal state to a modern industrial nation in a very short period of time. To be globally competitive, Japan had to learn to be modern, so scholars were sent to Europe, North America and Asia to study education systems. This was a significant event influencing Japanese education for years to come.

After WWII, Japanese education was modelled after the American 6-3-3-4 system. In 1947, the Fundamental Law of Education and the School Education Law were enacted, establishing a formal educational system on the principle of equal educational opportunity. Yet, curriculum, teaching and learning underwent little change as a direct result (Rohlen 1983; Shields 1993; Beauchamp and Vardman 1994; Takakura and Murata 1998). Japanese secondary schools have long been characterised by didactic teaching and rote memory learning. However, Japanese education is poised to undergo a major paradigm shift from rote learning to critical thinking (Takakura and Murata 1998). During the past decade, the Japanese Ministry of Education, Science, Sports and Culture (MEXT or Monbukagakusho) initiated significant far-reaching reforms to ensure students have the necessary thinking skills to be successful in the global economy of the twenty-first century. The Law of School Education was revised in 1998 and 1999, and the New Course of Studies came into effect in 2002. Highly controversial reforms included more flexible school curricula, giving children more free time to enrich their school lives and cross-curricular 'integrated learning', which teachers had difficulty implementing (see Namimoto 2001; Suzuki 2007). Other significant changes are a shortened school week (from six to five days) and new assessment methods.

North American education is often compared with education in European countries, but Japan is a better comparison with regard to educational selection. First, both Japan and Canada have reached the 'universal' stage of secondary education and the 'mass' stage of higher education: in 2000, the total enrolment rate in senior high school was estimated to be 88.0% in Canada and 97.0% in Japan, while the advancement rate to higher education (which includes technical and vocational institutes) was estimated at 62.0% in Canada and 70.6% in Japan (Bowlby and McMullen 2002; Monbukagakusho 2002a). In contrast, many European countries have lower enrolment rates in secondary and post-secondary education. Second, both Japan and Canada have comprehensive public elementary and junior high schools offering a broad-based liberal education, in contrast with Europe's selective system. Despite these similarities, Japan's national system is a striking contrast to the pluralistic Canadian provincial system.

In Japan, the responsibility for engendering the healthy development of young people is more diffusely shared by family, school, and the workplace (White 1987). High schools and colleges take active roles in finding employment for graduates. Japan's high schools provide a broad academic foundation and the opportunity for students to be selective in their choice of career path. Upon graduation from junior high (grade 9), students take various entrance exams to determine which high school they will attend. High school entrance exams then sort each age cohort into what amounts to an eight-to-ten tier high school ranking system (Rohlen 1983, 308). Future occupational and status levels (elite, managerial, blue-collar, and so forth) are closely equated to this ranking. Further, at the point of high school entrance the entire age cohort is divided into three largely immutable classificatory distinctions: those leaving school, those entering vocational ranks, and those going on to academic high schools. The ratio of students attending academic high schools has been steadily increasing from 60% in 1965 to over 74% in 2000 (Monbukagakusho 2002b). Others attend specialised vocational schools in agriculture, industry, commerce, fishery, home economics, nursing and other fields. But since 1994, the Monbukagakusho has introduced comprehensive schools, so there is a trend toward all high schools offering a more liberal education with significantly more choices for students.

Higher education in Japan

Traditionally, higher education in Japan functioned as a selection process used to maintain an elitist hierarchical structure. Through strict entrance quotas and competitive entrance examinations, admission to the top universities was limited. Nationwide, in 1980 about 40% of all graduates were advancing to higher education, but from public academic high schools the rate was approximately 70% (Rohlen 1983, 85). University enrolments increased dramatically during the 1960s and 1970s and continued in the 1980s and 1990s with increased competition for entrance to the most prestigious institutions. Higher education enrolment increased from 10.2% in 1960, and 18.7% in 1970, to 33.5% in 1980 (Monbukagakusho 1996). At that time, although over 80% of high school freshmen aimed at higher education there was insufficient space for all applicants (Rohlen 1983, 82). However, private universities and special training schools absorbed much of the increased numbers of upper secondary school graduates wishing to continue their studies. Since the population 'bulge' of the 1992 cohort of graduates, there has been no need for further quantitative expansions in universities (Takakura and Murata 1998, 33). For individuals not going to college it has meant beginning work with a major disadvantage. Until very recently, going back to school has not been an option and rarely have the most talented high school graduates gained promotion above the university-educated employees. However, those individuals that were fortunate enough to be admitted into the best national universities such as Tokyo University or the exceptional private universities such as Waseda were assured a promising career in government or in business.

During the past decade, the Monbukagakusho has attempted to change the elitist structure of higher education, to reform the exam-based admissions to universities, and to eliminate the government and business links to the most prestigious institutions. However, the critical determining factor for Japanese post-secondary students is still the university entrance examinations rather than what is actually studied during the undergraduate degree. Japanese people fondly reminisce about the freedom from study, work and adult responsibilities they experienced as carefree university students. While North American higher education demands hard work and intense study, Japanese higher education is widely recognised and accepted as a place of rest and relaxation before facing the rigors of the workplace.

Japan's private sector has responded to the demand for more higher education, resulting in an abundance of institutions but a lower quality of instruction and a significant imbalance of male to female students in universities and colleges (Fujimura-Fanselow 1993, 163–165). Only recently has progress toward full equality of participation for women in higher education been realised (Takakura and Murata 1998, 34). However, a disproportionate number of women continue to attend junior colleges and most will not go on to university. Japan's junior colleges do not serve the same role as colleges in Canada. University transfer is not an option nor is it a goal for most college graduates who will enter the work force directly in positions such as secretaries and junior employees. While the percentage of women in universities increased from 2.5% in 1960 to 12.3% in 1980 and 36.2% in 2000, as of May 2000, women's participation rates were 89.6% for junior colleges and only 18.7% for technical colleges (Monbukagakusho 2002c). Although the ratio of women enrolled in university and technical institutes has increased, there is a need for further reforms to Japan's higher education in order to accommodate greater diversity in students. Furthermore, a paltry 16.7% of Japan's post-secondary teachers are women. This is the lowest participation rate among all developed nations (Monbukagakusho 2005). However, this is typical of Japanese workplaces, as Japan remains a highly gendered society.

While the Japanese education system is among the best in the world, higher education has been considered inadequate by international standards. Thus, in 1988 the University Council was established and issued 28 reports recommending vast improvements in the quality of teaching and research, in order to bring Japanese universities to the international academic level (Kotokyoiku kenkyukai 2002). Consequently, most of the University Council's policy recommendations were implemented into practical reforms. One of the most significant changes occurred in April 2004, when the administration of all national universities was reformed to make them semi-independent institutions and thus more competitive. The rationale for these reforms was: (1) freedom of choice; (2) diversification; (3) accountability; and (4) international competitiveness in light of globalisation of education. Ironically, these reforms have resulted in tremendous budget cuts, pay cuts, layoffs, increased workloads for professors and a lowering in the quality of education at national universities.

Japan's graduate programmes are underdeveloped and widely recognised as an area where improvements must be made. As of 1995, about two-thirds of Japan's universities had a graduate school and less than half offered doctoral courses (Monbukagakusho 1996, 29). By 2005, 78% of the 726 universities had a graduate school but just over half offered doctoral courses (Monbukagakusho 2005). While the number of universities having a graduate school in education increased from only three in 1985 to more than 43 presently, demands still exist for both qualitative and quantitative improvements at graduate schools. Reform proposals have attempted to make graduate study in many fields more accessible, but systematic strategies for achieving this goal have been slow to develop. This remains an ongoing problem; however, recently there is some evidence of reforms taking effect to make universities more flexible in admissions and to accommodate lifelong learning.

Thus in 1999, the central government invited an independent critical assessment of compulsory and higher education (Kyoiku kaikaku kokumin kaigi 2000). This forum dealt with some urgent issues including enhancing and strengthening research and education in universities and graduate schools. Education and training of teachers were also debated (Suzuki 2007). Subsequently, several American colleges and universities including MIT, Harvard and UCLA have opened branches in Japan. Through such attempts at internationalisation, bureaucrats see a means by which Japan can compete in the global economy. But while politicians have recognised 'internationalisation of education' as an important area of reform, this requires further scrutiny to ensure the needs of students are at the forefront rather than neoliberal agendas (Howe 2008).

Teacher education in Japan

Japanese teacher education is regulated by national laws established by the central government. The most important statute regulating the Japanese national system of teacher education is the Law for Certification of Educational Personnel. This law in conjunction with other laws set forth the basic characteristics of Japanese teacher education. Certification and teacher training is the primary responsibility of the Monbukagakusho but each of the 47 prefectures has some autonomy with their own boards of education, which issue renewable teaching certificates. New teachers are recruited by the prefectural boards of education annually from qualified teachers and teachers in training through competitive screening tests. First-year teachers have a one-year probationary period before becoming permanent employees. During this time they must receive significant initial service training. The planning of all initial and in-service training is the prefectural board of education's responsibility.

Teacher education in Japan takes the form of a united pattern. The curriculum for pre-service education at each university and college is developed within the framework of the Law for Certification of Educational Personnel. Since education is valued by Japanese society, teachers have traditionally been highly regarded, and well paid. However, the working conditions of teachers have been steadily eroding with increasing incidents of school refusal, classroom chaos, violence and other serious problems. Teachers are often blamed for the ills of society. With the changing population demographics of fewer and fewer children, accompanied by further socio-cultural changes, there has been a public outcry for better schooling. Moreover, it is extremely competitive to become a teacher and the exams to obtain a teacher's licence are difficult.

The job of teachers is becoming more challenging. Most graduates don't get a full-time teaching position immediately. Many teachers find their way into the system first through part-time work. So, the vast majority of beginning teachers are in effect 'second-class citizens' as they don't receive formal initial teacher training unless they are later hired as full-time employees. Thus, it creates a 'two-tiered system of teachers' – those full-time with comprehensive initial teacher training and those part-time, with significantly less formal training. This remains a serious flaw with Japanese teacher induction.

To become a teacher, one must obtain a teacher's certificate by completing the subjects in a university programme for teacher education. Candidates complete teacher training curricula at a Monbukagakusho authorised university or junior college. But programmes vary widely as there are nearly 1000 institutions offering teacher training throughout Japan. Advanced, first-class, and second-class certificates are awarded for completion of Master's degrees, four-year Bachelor's degrees and two–three-year Associate degrees, respectively. In order to teach elementary or lower secondary school a second-class certificate is required. There is no second-class certificate for upper secondary school teachers. To teach in upper secondary schools a first-class certificate is required. As a result of recent reforms to teacher education, teachers holding a second-class certificate must make an effort to obtain a first-class certificate by taking 45 university credits upon completion of five years of teaching. The number of credits can be reduced according to the number of years of teaching experience. Currently, due to increasing competition for teaching positions, most new teachers obtain a four-year Bachelor's degree and first-class certificate, yet only one-fourth of all graduates receive teaching appointments (Shimahara and Sakai 1995). Consequently, there is a trend for teachers to attain higher degrees. According to Takakura and Murata (1998), more than 90% of the teachers from primary school to upper secondary school have graduated from institutions of higher education (university or junior college). Shimahara and Sakai (1995, 234) add:

> The flaw of postwar teacher preparation was evident especially in the certification requirements at the secondary level that were in force until 1990: merely 14 credits of professional studies, including two credits in student teaching, equivalent to two weeks of clinical experience. Students seeking teacher certification at institutions whose primary mission was not teacher education tended to meet only the minimum requirements. These were the students who, of late, filled two-thirds of the lower secondary positions and nine-tenths of the upper secondary positions in the public school system.

However, since 1990 improvements have been made in the number of professional credits necessary for certification. Upper secondary teachers must now obtain 25 credits in professional subjects including: essence and goals of education; teaching methods; educational guidance and counselling; and a teaching practicum. Nevertheless, teacher education programmes are still poorly coordinated and the practicum continues to be an area where vast improvements are necessary. In the following section, I contrast the rather uniform national Japanese case with the Canadian province of British Columbia (BC) as a salient example. Education is under the jurisdiction of each province of Canada and thus varies from province to province. For brevity, BC is used as an exemplary Canadian case. BC was the first province to establish a college of teachers. Ontario and other provinces have used the BC College of Teachers (BCCT) as a model.

Education in British Columbia

Education in BC has evolved from the one-roomed rural schools of the late 1800s to the present complex system of rural and urban schools within large school districts. During the 1990s, nearly half the 75 school districts went through a process of amalgamation and centralisation. Furthermore, due to an unprecedented population increase and an explosion of English as a second language (ESL) students, especially in urban areas like Vancouver, schools remain overcrowded and under-funded. Education spending barely kept pace with this growth but now the political climate has changed. Budgets have been slashed. Teacher unions are in conflict with school boards and the government. These factors combine to produce a difficult and changing environment for education in BC.

Significant changes to the curriculum have been initiated in order to reflect the changing needs of the society. In 1988, the Eighth BC Royal Commission on Education reported on the state of education in BC. As a result, many reforms have taken place (see: http://www.bced.gov.bc.ca/grad_req_rev/research/history.htm#sullivan). Currently, the curriculum is divided into three programmes: primary (K–3), intermediate (4–7), and secondary (8–12). Curricular decisions are made by the BC Ministry of Education while the responsibility for teacher training and certification is left to the BCCT. The BCCT is comprised of 15 teachers, two cabinet appointees, two Minister of Education appointees and one representative from the Deans of the Faculties of Education. Prior to 1988, there was little accountability and standards for teachers. Since the BCCT was established however, teacher qualifications and teacher education programmes have improved commensurately.

Higher education in British Columbia

Until the mid-1960s, higher education in BC was provided almost exclusively by the University of British Columbia (UBC). However, as the demand for greater variety in post-secondary education rose sharply and enrolment expanded, systems of publicly operated post-secondary non-university institutions began to develop throughout the province (see http://www.mala.bc.ca/homeroom/).

The first of these colleges included Vancouver Community College and Selkirk established in 1965; followed by Okanagan Regional in 1966; Capilano in 1968; Malispina and New Caledonia in 1969; Douglas in 1970; and Camosun in 1971. During the 1970s community colleges assumed responsibility for many night school programmes and adult basic education including ESL, advanced technical education, certificate programmes, short courses and special interest classes. In 1977, BC's pioneering Open Learning Agency and its on-air division, the Knowledge Network, began to play an important role in making adult education even more accessible to remote rural areas. Enrolments in higher education steadily increased during the 1960s and 1970s with the expansion of the economy. Two other major institutions responsible for teacher training were also established at this time: the University of Victoria (UVic) in 1963 and Simon Fraser University (SFU) in 1965. In addition, BC founded the British Columbia Institute of Technology (BCIT) in 1964, which became a well-respected model for advanced technical and vocational education. During the 1990s, the expansion of post-secondary institutions continued with the addition of the University of Northern British Columbia (UNBC). In addition, since 1995 several institutions have been designated University Colleges, gaining degree-granting status. The newest, with a teacher education programme is UBC Okanagan, in the interior of the province, reflecting the trend for many colleges to become degree-granting institutions. In April 2008 the BC Government announced that these three University Colleges and two more institutions would become full 'universities' (see http://www.universityaffairs.ca/issues/2008/june-july/new-universities_bc_01.html). There are now 28 post-secondary institutions throughout the province. Furthermore, BC has become a pioneer in establishing satellite campuses around the province, making university more accessible for people in rural areas and providing distant learning around the globe.

Since 1991, and coincident with rising tuition fees, enrolments in Canadian universities have reached a plateau (discounting Ontario's double-cohort of 2003) and part-time participation rates have fallen dramatically (Statistics Canada 2000). However, college enrolments continue to increase, reflecting the trend for the participation of more women in higher education. In 1998–1999 college students accounted for 41% of all full-time post-secondary enrolment in Canada (Statistics Canada 2001).

BC's adult education participation rate at 30.1% is among the highest in Canada (Statistics Canada 2001). Moreover, BC has developed a highly successful, efficient and seamless system to accommodate college–university transfer. Over half the college students in BC are enrolled in university transfer courses (Statistics Canada 2001). Virtually, all post-secondary institutions in Canada offer both full and part-time adult education. Over the past three decades, with the emphasis on lifelong learning, there has been a marked increase in the number of students from outside the usual 18- to 24-year-old age group. In 1990, nearly one quarter of Canada's university students were over the age of 24 (Statistics Canada 2001). This is in stark contrast to Japan where nearly all university students are under age 24.

Canada has achieved considerable gender equity in post-secondary participation rates. Currently over 55% of the university students are women, and more women than men receive university degrees. Moreover, over 53% of full-time and nearly 60% of part-time college students are women (Statistics Canada 2001). Canadian post-secondary institutions have developed comprehensive, diversified systems of education, designed to be universally accessible, responding to the diverse needs of its residents.

Teacher education in British Columbia

Teacher education in BC has progressed substantially since the Normal schools of the early 1900s. Even as recently as the 1960s it was possible to teach in BC's public schools with little or no formal teacher training. However, since 1988, all teachers must have obtained the equivalent of at least five years of university training in an approved post-secondary programme leading to a Bachelor of Education degree. Upon completion of an elementary, middle or secondary programme, graduates then apply to the Teachers' Qualification Service and the BCCT to have their academic credentials assessed. The BC Professional Teaching Certificate issued is valid indefinitely for as long as the individual continues to remain a member of the college in good standing.

The Normal schools were a precursor to the first university teacher education programme in the province, established in 1956 at UBC. Presently, the Two-Year

Elementary Teacher Education Programme at UBC is open to applicants who have completed a minimum of 90 credits in Arts, Science or Human Kinetics, including relevant pre-admission studies. The 12-Month Elementary Teacher Programme, the Middle School Teacher Education Programme, and the Secondary Teacher Education Programme are open to applicants who have completed a four-year Bachelor's degree including relevant pre-admission studies. Admission to teacher education is limited by the available spaces in each programme and employment prospects. Because of competition for admission, students are often required to have a grade point average well above the 65% minimum. Initially, candidates develop a foundation of teaching through courses designed to provide a balance of general and specialised knowledge about curriculum and instruction, including pedagogical knowledge, educational psychology and special education. In addition, students have a two-week practicum for observations and orientation to the school in which they will be doing the extended practicum. After the first semester of study, students enter a 13-week extended practicum consisting of a 20–30% teaching assignment, which is gradually increased to 80% for the final four weeks. By the time they successfully complete the extended practicum, students should have demonstrated they can plan, implement and evaluate instruction at a standard expected of a beginning teacher. After the practicum, students return to campus to engage in studies designed to put their teaching experiences in a broader context.

It is interesting to note that SFU's programme varies somewhat from UBC's. SFU has students take two practica. One is a four-week practicum, done at the beginning of the programme, before any significant course work has been completed. The other is a 10-week intensive practicum that demands that the student must teach a full course load over at least a six-week period. SFU's programme attempts to place more emphasis on a variety of practicum experiences and on the beginning teacher as a reflective practitioner. There is decidedly less emphasis on pedagogical theory and teacher education courses. In either case, there are few bridges between the practicum and the first year. Thus, in the following section, I assess the strengths and weaknesses of Canada's approach to teacher education in comparison to Japan's comprehensive yearlong teacher internship.

Assessment of teacher education in Japan and Canada

While Japanese teachers are expected to address all aspects of children's lives, BC's teachers tend to be primarily concerned with the development of cognitive competence (Howe 2002/2003, 2004). However, the role of teachers is quite different in each educational system and culture. In North America, teaching is considered to be a highly idiosyncratic profession and the common lore is that teachers can't be taught how to teach because they are born not made (Rohlen and LeTendre 1996; cf. Stevenson and Stigler 1992). In contrast, the view of 'teaching as a profession' is a relatively new concept in Japan (Takakura and Murata 1998). Teaching is considered a craft, perfected through practice and learned through the shared wisdom of experienced teachers.

In Japanese schools, beginning teachers learn a great deal from experienced teachers through informal contact. This is often a one-way pedagogical exchange however, with little offered from neophytes to veteran teachers. Therefore, it is difficult for new teaching strategies to be disseminated from universities through student teachers and eventually to become accepted by the mainstream, since it is assumed more experienced teachers must pass down all the lessons to be learned. In BC, frequently just the opposite is true. Often experienced teachers learn a great deal from their student teachers – it is widely recognised as one of the best forms of professional development, since teachers do not have many opportunities for collaboration and peer consultation.

Teachers in both BC and Japan tend to view learning to teach as an apprenticeship where practical knowledge learned while teaching takes precedence over theory learned in university. The Japanese in-service training of teachers serves as a model for the enculturation of beginning teachers and has been recognised as one of the lessons that could be learned from the Japanese educational system (Stevenson and Stigler 1992; Shimahara and Sakai 1995; Rohlen and LeTendre 1996). Newly appointed teachers undergo 20 days of intensive training at a prefectural education centre. Teachers are provided with significant professional development during their first year under the tutelage of senior teachers. Professional development in teaching is further enhanced by ongoing in-service training and 'hands on' experiences. Like many Japanese professions, most of the training occurs in the workplace.

While Japan's pre-service training of teachers includes general education with professional courses in pedagogical theory, educational psychology, and teaching methods as well as specialised subjects, teacher education programmes are characterised by courses that have little relevance to classroom teaching (Howe 2005). Many graduates of BC's teacher education programmes lament similar weaknesses but Japanese professional development and in-service training far surpass their 'sink or swim' first-year teaching experiences.

During my first stay in Japan (1990–1992), I was an assistant English teacher in several different junior secondary schools in Tokyo. I observed a student teacher as he was being evaluated by his faculty advisor. He taught the same lesson, in exactly the same way and style as his sponsor teacher. The entire lesson had been rehearsed previously for the benefit of the student teacher and the faculty advisor. The 'performance' however, was abysmal. The student teacher appeared very anxious and uncomfortable in his role as a teacher. He refused to face the students. Instead he talked to the board while moving around nervously. This was the first and last time he taught this class. Perhaps it is not surprising that most sponsor teachers would rather not have a student teacher, and that this one class was done merely as a show to appease the faculty advisor (Howe 2005).

In September 2007, I had the opportunity to observe some of my students at the end of their three-week practicum at the attached junior high school. Their lessons, while rather didactic, were well planned and they appeared more confident than the student teacher I observed 15 years ago. It was encouraging. Furthermore, students' lessons were observed by peers and videotaped. At the end of the day, there was a reflection period, chaired by a fourth-year student, where everyone critically discussed the lessons. It was attended by students (from freshmen to graduate students) and some faculty. Conspicuously missing however, were the classroom teachers. Their feedback was only to be shared in private with individuals.

Japanese teacher education programmes continue to suffer from poor linkages between coursework and classrooms. The practicum is an area that requires substantial changes in order to provide a necessary bridge between universities and schools. Generally, the tradition of student teaching in one's alma mater continues (noteworthy exceptions include attached junior high schools). The advantages of letting students do practica in schools familiar to them, with teachers of their choosing seems obvious. However, this arrangement is fraught with uncertainty, complications and serious drawbacks. Student teachers are tolerated in schools but they are not active participants in the day-to-day routines of classroom teaching. A brief stint in a school does not facilitate that. Student teachers aren't included in all the activities of teachers and teaching. Furthermore, rarely can faculty participate fully or make connections to sponsor teachers. The practicum, while a potentially meaningful experience, along the road to becoming a teacher, remains a haphazard and stressful experience for many individuals.

Students' practica can occur at various times throughout the year without any formal break from university courses. Most students leave for three to four weeks during their third or fourth year, in September or June, often missing university classes. Thus, faculty advisors have few opportunities to visit students during their practicum. Furthermore, with students all over Japan, from as far away as Okinawa to Hokkaido, it can be challenging.

Teacher educators must work harder at articulation and dialogue between student teachers, faculty and classroom teachers. Japan needs an improved pre-service programme to foster a more gradual acculturation into the profession of teaching. While Monbukagakusho mandates curriculum, it remains largely at the discretion of individual teacher educators. My teaching methods class provides a salient example. In a recent survey of my class of 40 students, everyone indicated a need for more practical advice and lessons focused on classroom management. More support is needed for student teachers from faculty and sponsor teachers.

Japan's teachers claim the university does little to prepare student teachers for the profession of teaching but classroom teachers do little to change the status quo.

> The real training of Asian teachers occurs in their on-the-job experience *after* graduation from college ... graduates of teacher training programmes are still considered novices who need the guidance and support of their experienced colleagues ... the system of teacher training is much like an apprenticeship. (Stevenson and Stigler 1992, 159)

This is in direct contrast to the experience of BC's teachers, who complain that most of what they know had to be learned by them, alone, in isolation, while on the job. There is a serious deficiency in Canadian public education since there is little provision made for mentorship and there is insufficient time to reflect on teaching practices. It is well understood by leading educators and teachers alike that this situation is less than ideal. What is needed is a system that supports mentorship, collaboration and peer consultation among teachers.

Canadian teacher education is focused on pre-service education at the expense of in-service training. In the Canadian context, the practicum is the most important component allowing novice teachers to start with a new class on the first day, to learn how to develop routines and rapport, to teach right through a full term, including writing report cards, participating in parent–teacher interviews and so on. This allows student teachers to experience a complete cycle of planning and teaching an entire unit – often practicing it with various learners – not just a lesson or two. On the other hand, in Japan, novice teachers have the opportunity to learn how to teach during their year of induction. So, it might sound like an overly simplistic solution but if you could combine the strengths of a Canadian pre-service education and extended practicum with the Japanese yearlong induction programme, you'd have a winning combination!

Conclusion

Ironically, while Western countries are attempting educational reforms to promote national standards and a centralised uniform system, Japan is attempting educational reforms in order to decentralise their education and to make it more comprehensive rather than more focused. Japanese and Canadian school reforms are now evolving in opposite directions. Japan is slowly diversifying its schools while Canada is trying to promote new national academic standards. In Japan, where the central government plays a decisive role in determining policy, two diverse trends in teacher education have emerged. While the professionalisation of teachers has improved due to the increasing requirements for professional training, liberalisation has taken place through the addition of programmes in non-teaching areas.

BC's reforms to teacher education have been predominately influenced by university schools of education. Despite much progress in professional teacher training, criticism of faculties of education has remained quite strong. University schools of education have tended to distance themselves from the concerns of classroom teachers, and the research agenda has not often produced knowledge useful to the practitioner. Also, there are no permanent, durable models of teacher training (Barman, Sutherland, and Wilson 1995, 313).

Perkins (1992) makes some very convincing arguments for reforms to pre-service and in-service teacher education. He suggests that Japan's educational system offers a model for the professional development of teachers and the promotion of potent teaching practices. The key successful elements of Japan's model include: time to think, a shared culture of the craft of teaching, and an apprenticeship model of teacher development. Japanese teachers spend fewer hours per day actually teaching classes. More time is devoted to thinking and reflecting about their teaching. 'They plan lessons, share plans with one another, get critiques, attend workshops, observe other teachers teaching, [and] watch videotapes of teaching practices ... Through organized time and commitment, teachers can learn to teach much better than native ingenuity alone could allow' (Perkins 1992, 225). Rather than working in isolation, Japan's teachers recognise the power of collaboration. This is even evident in the very physical structure of the schools. For example, the staff room is arranged with teachers of each grade level seated at desks grouped together, in order to promote daily exchanges. This is where all the teachers plan their lessons during several hours of the working day when they are not in front of the classroom. This is in direct contrast to BC teachers, who do most of their lesson planning at home or in the isolation of their own classroom.

Many of Japan's practices are complimentary or similar to current suggested reforms to teacher education in BC. However, the Japanese model is far from perfect. Improvements must be made to the teacher education programmes of Japan's universities and to the pedagogical training of pre-service teachers. This fact is widely recognised by educators in Japan: 'We must pay more attention to student teaching through which a sense of mission as a teacher might arise. If the transition from pre-service preparation is not attended to, the effects of teacher improvements in education may have little influence on the quality of teaching in Japan' (Mizoue and Inoue 1993, 28). Through further international comparative studies in teacher education, the Japanese teacher education programmes can be improved. Much can be learned from BC's teacher education programmes. Likewise, BC's training of teachers can be improved by studying Japan's apprenticeship model of in-service training and professional development. Teachers must be given opportunities to learn from one another and to benefit from the accumulated wisdom of generations of skilled practitioners. In addition, teachers must be given adequate time for collaboration, planning and reflection. The reforms of education in both BC and Japan require a rethinking of the profession of teaching, for any effort to reform the structure or organisation of education ultimately depends on the effectiveness of the teacher.

References

Barman, J., N. Sutherland, and J.D. Wilson, eds. 1995. *Children, teachers & schools in the history of British Columbia.* Calgary: Detselig Enterprises.
Beauchamp, E., and J. Vardman, eds. 1994. *Japanese education since 1945: A documentary study.* New York: M.E. Sharpe.
Bowlby, J.W., and K. McMullen. 2002. *At a crossroads – first results for the 18 to 20-year-old cohort of the Youth in Transition Survey.* http://www.statcan.ca80/english/freepub/81-591-XIE0001.pdf (accessed 7 June).
Cummings, W.K., and P.G. Altbach, eds. 1997. *The challenge of Eastern Asian education – implications for America.* Albany: State University of New York.
Fujimura-Fanselow, K. 1993. Women's participation in higher education in Japan. In *Japanese schooling: Patterns of socialization, equality, and political control,* ed. J.J. Shields Jr, 163–175, University Park, PA: Pennsylvania State University Press.
Howe, E.R. 2002/2003. Canadian and Japanese secondary teachers' values: A cross-cultural comparative study. *Japanese Society* 6: 115–43.
Howe, E.R. 2003. Curriculum studies within the context of comparative, international and development education. *Canadian and International Education Journal* 32, no. 2: 1–14.
Howe, E.R. 2004. Secondary teachers' conceptions of critical thinking in Canada and Japan – a comparative study. *Teachers and Teaching: Theory and Practice* 10, no. 5: 505–25.
Howe, E.R. 2005. Japan's teacher acculturation: Critical analysis through comparative ethnographic narrative. *Journal of Education for Teaching: International Research and Pedagogy* 31, no. 2: 121–13.
Howe, E.R. 2006. Effective teacher induction: An international review. *Educational Philosophy and Theory* 38, no. 3: 287–97.
Howe, E.R. 2008. Internationalization of Japanese higher education – a critical study through comparative ethnographic narrative. Paper presented at the 52nd annual conference of the Comparative and International Education Society, New York.
Kobayashi, T. 1993. Japan's teacher education in comparative perspectives. *Peabody Journal of Education* 68, no. 3: 4–15.
Kotokyoiku kenkyu kai [Higher Education Study Group]. 2002 *Daigakushingikai Zen Toshin-Hokokushu* [Collected reports and recommendations from the University Council]. Yokyo: Gyosei.
Kyoiku kaikaku kokumin kaigi [National Forum on Educational Reform]. 2000. *Hokokusho* [Report]. Tokyo: Monbukagakusho.
Mizoue, Y., and W. Inoue. 1993. Reforming teacher education to increase teacher competence and improve entry to the profession. *Peabody Journal of Education* 68, no. 3: 21–37.

Monbukagakusho, Ministry of Education, Science, Sports and Culture, Government of Japan. 1996. *The current main activities of the Monbusho.* Tokyo: Monbukagakusho.

Monbukagakusho, Ministry of Education, Science, Sports and Culture, Government of Japan. 2002a. *Advancement rates to institutions of higher education 1960–2000.* http://www.mext.go.jp/english/org/formal/05e.htm.

Monbukagakusho, Ministry of Education, Science, Sports and Culture, Government of Japan. 2002b. *Upper secondary school enrollment by school type.* http://www.mext.go.jp/english/statist/gif/58-59b.gif.

Monbukagakusho, Ministry of Education, Science, Sports and Culture, Government of Japan. 2002c. *School education (summary tables) school, students, teachers and non-teaching staff, 2000.* http://www.mext.go.jp/ehglish/statist/gif/02-09a.gif.

Monbukagakusho, Ministry of Education, Science, Sports and Culture, Government of Japan. 2005. *Education at a glance.* http://www.mext.go.jp/english/statist/05101901/005.pdf (accessed 9 February 2007).

Namimoto, K. 2000. On authenticity of the ad hoc national council on educational reform. *SEKAI,* February, no. 681. Tokyo: Iwanami (Japanese version).

Perkins, D. 1992. *Smart schools: From training memories to educating minds.* New York: The Free Press.

Rohlen, T.P. 1983. *Japan's high schools.* Berkeley: University of California Press.

Rohlen, T.P. 1995. Differences that make a difference: Explaining Japan's success. *Educational Policy* 9, no. 2: 103–28.

Rohlen, T.P., and G.K. LeTendre, eds. 1996. *Teaching and learning in Japan.* New York: Cambridge University Press.

Shields, J.J., Jr., ed. 1993. *Japanese schooling: Patterns of socialization, equality, and political control.* University Park, PA: Pennsylvania State University Press.

Shimahara, N.K., and A. Sakai. 1995. *Learning to teach in two cultures: Japan and the United States.* New York: Garland.

Statistics Canada. 2000. University education: Recent trends in participation, accessibility and returns. *Education Quarterly Review 2000* 6, no. 4: 24–32.

Statistics Canada. 2001. *Education in Canada, 2000.* http://www.statscan.ca.

Stevenson, H., and J. Stigler. 1992. *The learning gap: Why our schools are failing and what we can learn from Japanese and Chinese education.* New York: Summit Books.

Suzuki, S. 2007. *Higher education reforms in Japan: Backgrounds of reform policies and the new scheme of university management.* Unpublished paper.

Takakura, S., and Y. Murata, eds. 1998. *Education in Japan – a bilingual text: Present System and Tasks/Curriculum and Instruction.* Tokyo: Gakken.

White, M. 1987. *The Japanese educational challenge: A commitment to children.* New York: The Free Press.

Reform of teacher education in China

Xiaoguang Shi[a] and Peter A.J. Englert[b]

[a]*Graduate School of Education/Institute for Higher Education Studies, Peking University, Beijing, PR China;* [b]*Center for Chinese Studies, University of Hawaii at Mānoa, Honolulu, HI, USA*

Introduction

Over the past two decades, teacher education in China has witnessed unprecedented changes occurring throughout the entire higher education system, including rapid expansion of enrolment, innovation and structural system reorganisation, mergers between institutions of higher learning, and teaching quality improvement. As an important part of the system of higher education, teacher education cannot escape facing the formidable challenges of change. A few facts and other evidence demonstrate that significant development of teacher education has taken place in this environment. It is confirmed that the past two decades have been the fastest and most interesting period for developing teacher education in China (Ma 1998). Achievements of Chinese governments in promoting changes in the teacher education system, and how institutions at different levels and of different types responded to the changing circumstances will be reported and analysed in the paper.

The purpose of describing and analysing the extent and effects of all the changes on Chinese teacher education is to assist those who care about the success of the reforms. The paper should provide insight into and understanding of what has occurred in Chinese teacher education reform including its current direction and future trends.

The changing environment and responses of institutions

Government policy

Although many reforms of teacher education have taken place at various times in the history of Chinese higher education for a century and more, the new round of changes may be traced back to the early 1980s when China began to welcome a new era of reform and openness to the outside world. Since then, in terms of teacher education, a series of initiatives undertaken by the Central Government have been implemented. For instance, it was at the Fourth National Conference on Teacher Education convened in 1980 that the government placed the development and reform of teacher education at the top of its agenda, and defined the targets and tasks of teacher education in the new era for the first time.

The second hallmark was the historic document *Decision on the reform of the education system*, published in 1985 by the Ministry of Education (MOE), which indicated that the development of teacher education should be regarded as a key strategic measure in developing education (MOE 2000).

The third hallmark impacting on teacher education was the National Meeting on Secondary and Primary School Teachers held in the same year, where targets, policies and procedures for building a contingent of teachers for basic education were further emphasised. In 1993, another important document, the *Outline for reform and development of education in China*, was officially issued. It declared that governments at all levels would increase their financial input to improve teacher education (MOE 2000).

In 1996, at the Fifth National Conference on Teacher Education, it was further emphasised that teacher education should be regarded as a strategic priority for the development of education. In 1999, the Third National Conference of Education promulgated a new document, *Decision about deepening the reform of education and boosting the quality of education*, which officially encouraged those competent, non-normal, i.e. non-teacher education and comprehensive, institutions, to engage in teacher education. In 2001, the State Council delivered an Executive Circular, *Decision about reform and development of basic education*, where the concept of 'Teacher Education' was adopted for the first time to replace the previous term of 'Normal Education'.

This change meant that the traditional institutions of teacher education would no longer be the only legal organisations to prepare and train teachers. It indicated a significant transformation, from a system of teacher education in China which was independent and separate from other institutions and forms of higher education for almost half century, into one operating within an open and multi-institutional framework (Yuan 2004).

Response at institutional level

Teacher education in China generally means pre-service education and in-service education for those who are preparing to be teachers (Yang, Lin, and Su 1989). The respective education activities, until the early 1990s, were provided separately by two independent systems of institutions. The system of pre-service teacher education was composed of four types of institutions[1] at three tiers while the system of in-service teacher education consisted of training in a three-level organisation.[2] Historically, as the systems were separated thoroughly, teachers' preparation and training was implemented by institutions of the two systems, respectively. All of the institutions together constituted a huge, independent and closed system in charge of preparing or training teachers at different levels, and meeting the education needs of different school tiers.

However, along with a rapid shift of the country's economic system from a planned to a socialist market one, and a dramatic transition of social power from bureaucratic control to market forces, the system of higher education (including teacher education) as it existed for at least half a century commenced meeting both internal and external challenges and pressures, and needed to address or overcome them inevitably in the 1990s. As a response to the changing environment, a dramatic movement towards institutional amalgamation and upgrades continued to proceed during the period from 1992 to 2005. Consequently, at present, the monopoly institutions of teacher education used to have in the past half century has been replaced and is gone forever.

Currently there are 475 institutions involved in teacher education, among them, 183 so-called normal (teacher) colleges and universities, 34 independent educational (training) institutes, and 258 general comprehensive colleges and universities. Based on Ministry of Education (MOE) statistics, about 1083 institutions had been merged by a series of different processes into 431 new entities by the end of May 2006. Among them, 293 different types of teacher education institutions at different tiers were involved in the wave of amalgamations (MOE 2006).

Two modes of adjustment

The mode of 'merger and upgrade' is one of the regularly applied processes for institutions of the same type. With regard to teacher education, institutions and systems used to be independent organisations and communities without bridges between them, barely connected and coordinated. In order to turn this situation around, about 132 teacher education institutions have been merged into 74 new entities under the leadership of governments at all levels. Of the 74 merged institutions, half were independent normal/teachers' institutions or secondary teacher schools with the task of preparing pre-service teachers, and the other half were independent educational institutes or teacher training schools, with the mission of continuing education for in-service teachers.

In merged institutions, naming was addressed as follows. The guiding principle was that the level of the original institutions should generally be considered. The basic rule of naming a new merged entity therefore was that the original name of the larger, more prestigious institution of higher level should be kept, while the previous names of smaller, less-renowned institutions at a lower tier would be replaced by that of the former, or by new ones. For instance, when the majority of educational institutes at provincial levels had been merged to form provincial normal universities, their previous institutional names were renounced. The names of these new institutions still refer to their tradition of normal/teacher education, such as Shenyang Normal University which is the result of a merger between Shenyang Teacher's College and Liaoning Teacher Training Institute. The former used to prepare future teachers, and the latter to provide in-service training. In the example, the chosen name for the new entity indicates one of a higher tier than their original ones, reflecting the additional strength gained through combination of resources and teaching capacity. The name of Shenyang Normal University has more prestige than either name of the merged institutions.

The mode of 'transformation and upgrading through amalgamation' is a different process, referring to mergers between institutions of different types. According to statistics (MOE 2006), about 91 former teacher education institutions, such as NN [local or regional name] teachers' college, or NN teacher school, were merged with 136 institutions including general universities, professional colleges and vocational schools, which previously had no relationship with teacher education (MOE 2006). Their merger resulted in the establishment of 53 new entities which are comprehensive or polytechnic institutions. About 17% of these new institutions still carry the original name inherited from one of involved institutions, generally that of the predecessor with the higher academic reputation. The other 83% have newly created names such as 'NN University' or 'NN College'. Since the majority of the institutions involved in the mergers were smaller in size and less well known or of lower reputation, each of them was hopeful to be upgraded and be given a better-sounding name. Consequently, for outsiders it is hard to judge where some new universities or colleges come from and what type of institutions they used to be. Internal change processes and quality assurance processes will be able to evaluate their academic standing in the future. Although some amalgamated entities still retain a certain number of functions of preparing and training teachers through their schools of education, teacher education has not become their priority. Some of the newly amalgamated institutions have completely given up their previous mission of preparing and training teachers.

There are several additional driving forces for the merger of teacher education institutions and their incorporation and assimilation into general comprehensive institutions of higher learning. One reason is that based on demographic developments enrolment at primary and secondary schools will decrease, and that in line with these developments, the teacher workforce, especially for those prepared to teach in lower school tiers, will have to be adjusted in the near future. According to MOE statistics, enrolment at primary schools will decrease from 120 million to 105 million by the end of 2010, leading to a workforce oversupply of one million primary school teachers (Huang and Wu 2006). Under these circumstances it would have been impossible for small primary teacher education institutions to survive independently, making merger or incorporation a preferable option in managing supply and demand.

Second, because of the anticipated limitations in availability of positions for new teachers, career entrance barriers are expected to be elevated and more competition will occur. It is therefore highly likely that general undergraduate education of prospective teachers will become a new passport for career entrance, following international trends. This education can be provided in normal and comprehensive universities.

Third, the influence of governments at different levels was an additional factor in promoting and implementing the incorporation and assimilation of teacher education institutions. For instance, in the year 1999 or even before, the MOE permitted and encouraged some comprehensive universities or other general colleges to participate in the preparation and training of teachers in order to break the monopoly of normal universities and colleges.

Recent priorities and developments

Professional development

Improving teachers' professional development is not only a major international trend but also a new national orientation and direction, integrated into the development and reform of teacher education in China (Chen 2003). The former director general of the Department of Teacher Education (DTE) in the MOE pointed out that accelerating the process of professionalising teaching work of primary and secondary teachers is an important measure for improving teaching quality (DTE 2001). The Teachers' Law enacted in 1993 stipulates that teachers are specialists whose duties are educating and teaching, but the reality and practice of teachers' professional development still offers significant room for improvement. To address these issues and to improve teachers' professional development and teachers' working conditions a set of solutions was adopted by the Chinese government.

First, there is significant concern about the social and economic condition of the teaching community. One of the main problems is the low social status and income of teachers resulting in low attractiveness of teaching positions and instability of teacher appointments, particularly at primary and secondary schools. In China teachers have traditionally been accorded the highest esteem, but the esteem is not matched by commensurate economic rewards. In a recent survey covering 'satisfaction of status', based on an available sample of 424 primary teachers, 49.76% responded that there is a significant discrepancy between their workloads and their remuneration; 23.82% of the primary teachers asked do not consider their teaching career as a desirable profession; and 71.93% of the respondents do believe that their status may be improved but still not receive more recognition (Du 2004). Many primary schools can barely recruit the talents they need to supplement their teaching staff (Sun 2004). Meanwhile, having to endure relatively low salaries and associated standards of living, and lacking opportunities for professional development, many qualified and competent in-service teachers are dissatisfied with their positions and tend to leave soon after their initial appointment, creating instability.

As a reflection, the eulogistic description of teaching careers as the 'noble profession' has become conspicuous by its absence in the current discourse on the subject. One main reason why teachers at primary and secondary schools have low salaries is the comparatively low and possibly inadequate financial input into compulsory education. In the past two decades, the Chinese government has increased spending on higher education faster than for primary and secondary education, according to the Annual Chinese Statistic of Educational Expenditure (Statistical Yearbook 2001). From 1996 to 2001 the total investment in higher education has increased by a factor of three, while that in compulsory education has increased only by a factor of 0.6 (Wang 2006). To improve teachers' living conditions and social status, an adjustment of education investment policies may perhaps be the best solution. Governments at all levels are in the process of addressing these issues and are making efforts to improve the situation in the coming years.

Second, with the demographic decrease of children of school age and primary school graduates combined with an increase of student enrolment in high schools, staffing issues have become a major concern. The relationship of demand and supply of teachers at primary and secondary schools has undergone great changes, from an overall lack in quantity to a structural imbalance (Yuan 2003). This means that overstaffing is occurring at primary schools but not at middle and high schools. In high schools teachers are in short overall supply. In addition, overstaffing does not mean that there is a sufficient supply of qualified and competent teachers for primary and secondary education. By the end of 2003, about 2.15% of teachers at primary schools, 8.02% at secondary schools, and 24.29% at high schools had not achieved the standard provided for by the *Teacher' Law* of 1993 and other regulations. Even for those teachers in compliance with requirements, the standard achieved is below that of developed industrial nations (Sun 2004). Under these circumstances, advancing professional development, i.e. turning from meeting need in quantity to improving levels in quality for all school tiers, is an opportunity for Chinese teacher education, which will move teaching to a new stage (Yuan 2003).

The *Suggestions on reform and development of teacher education* during the 11th Five-Year Plan made by the MOE in 2002 proposed new goals and efforts to be realised in large and medium-sized cities and economically developed regions in the following two years: new teachers with associate and bachelor degrees will make up over 80% of teaching staff at primary schools and middle schools, respectively. Among the new teachers in high schools those with masters' or doctoral degrees should become an increasingly larger fraction of the teaching staff (Chen 2003). By now theses goals have basically been achieved. But the degree requirements for teachers in China are still below those in developed countries where most new teachers should at least have a bachelor or masters' degree to be appointed by primary and secondary schools (Chen 1999).

To achieve these outcomes and to improve the quality of teaching staff many plans of action have been adopted and implemented. One such action plan is the establishment of projects for continuing education for different types of educators in schools. Other projects address the continuing education of in-service administrators such as principals and the training of leading teachers, such as the in-service or future heads of subject areas, and the training and upgrading of degrees of general in-service teachers. Continuing education complements other programmes established to improve standards for entering a primary and secondary school teaching career. An MOE officer in charge of teacher education noted that in the near future a bachelor degree would become the universal requirement for most of those intending to enter a teaching career. This goal will likely be achieved between about 2015 and 2020 (Anon. 2005). It is expected that many in-service teachers of primary and secondary schools will enter Master of Arts in Education (MAE) programmes, actively or passively, in order to advance their degrees and professional capabilities.

Third, in addition to a basic qualification through an academic degree, systems of certification for teaching are recognised and accepted for the qualification of teachers in many countries, frequently governed by laws or regulations of the respective polities. In China, a system of certification has been introduced in 1993, when the Teachers' Law was enacted, which clearly provided for the implementation of a teacher certification system. In 2001, the National Meeting on Operating the System of Teacher Certification convened by MOE highlighted that the operation of the certification system in China had entered a new phase (Chen 2003). According to laws and statutes in China, teacher certification is based on five core elements and conditions: (1) Chinese nationality; (2) good personality and morality, professional spirit, and attitude of serving education; (3) diplomas or degrees in line with education at a given level; (4) ability and skill of educating and teaching; (5) the process of recruitment and appointment (MOE 2000). The implementation of the teacher certification system is difficult to achieve evenly across the entire country.

This is partly due to the many imbalances between the urban and the rural domains, the economically developed eastern and the economically underdeveloped western areas. Another reason is that there is still language, definitions or provisions in the Regulations for Teachers' Qualification and the Teachers' Law on the length of time a teaching certificate is valid once obtained, resulting in an understanding or interpretation that it may be a lifelong certificate. However, under the auspices of improved professional development teaching certification should be renewed periodically. For instance, in the United States the criteria of certification are redefined every five years (Sun 2004). In comparison with this case it is obvious that professionalising teachers' work in China still has room for improvement.

Application of information technology (IT)

Advancement in information and communication technology has enabled new approaches to teaching, learning and research that were previously unimaginable (Gumport and Chun 2005). Application of IT to teacher education has been wholeheartedly embraced in China as a valuable educational innovation. In recent years relevant administrations in MOE have been conscious that issues of application of IT to education must be paid attention to at both national and institutional levels, and the governments at different levels have placed it at the top of their agendas. In particular, in November 2000, MOE delivered two notifications: the first was on making education in IT at secondary and primary schools universally available and the other was on implementing a project called 'Connection between Schools' for secondary and primary schools. The notifications outlined that it would take the ministry five to ten years to provide education in IT at the basic education level, including the distribution of hardware and software, such as the design of Computer Aided Instruction (CAI), opening IT curriculum and courses and training teachers in different IT related subjects. As a result, many measures have been adopted and are currently implemented, including: (1) build-up of national networks such as the China Education and Research Network (http/www.edu.cn), the China Computer Instruction Network (http://www.yzcc.com), and institutional networks such as a continuing education network or primary and secondary teachers network built at Northeast Normal University, as well as individual campus networks at different levels; (2) build-up of many centres for distance education based on the internet in universities and colleges; and (3) the establishment and formation of a consultative committee by MOE with the purpose of advancing application of IT in education, including teacher education.

Contemporary advancements in IT have the potential to influence four broad areas of teacher education and education: (1) teacher knowledge or certification requirements; (2) teacher education curriculum; (3) the process of teaching and learning; and (4) the social organisation of teaching and learning.

To obtain universal availability of information technology the teachers' quality of knowledge and information has been regarded as the most important tasks for improving teaching through new requirements for teachers in the information literacy. In the Chinese context, so-called teachers' quality of information or information literacy refers to the ability or practical skills of obtaining teaching resources efficiently from the internet, and of using them creatively, which includes in detail: (1) searching Google/Baidu.com; (2) presentation skills based on Power Point; (3) communication or feedback by email or web log; and (4) teaching with Web Quest (Jiao 2007).

However, it is not sufficient for teachers to just be users of information technology as tools for instruction. Naturally, the application of IT to teacher education means that new models of curriculum and instruction based on IT and the Internet are developed, aiming at revolutionising the traditional modes of teaching and learning. For instance, while IT has given teachers across all disciplines the opportunity to shift the focus and orientation of their courses, the ability of integrating and reorganising content of instruction is required in the process of preparing and training teachers. To meet the need, almost all institutions related to teacher education have established schools of IT education, where both theory and practical skills for IT based instruction are developed and taught (Chen 2003). IT has affected teaching and learning processes in institutions of teacher education.

In traditional teacher education settings, faculty and students come together in the same classes at the same time, largely communicating face to face with the spoken word and using basic tools such as chalk, blackboard, and textbooks. However, the introduction of IT can bring about a transformation of instruction as IT alters substantially how knowledge is obtained, classified, used and represented. Such changes may reshape both the delivery of education and mode of instruction in universities and colleges of teacher education. In China, IT has also affected teaching and learning processes in training teachers in-service. Traditionally, those who are willing to receive training had to attend certain institutions in charge of training programmes. Traditional delivery of education to in-service teachers is very costly, disruptive of the teaching engagement, and creates significant obstacles and difficulties for those who live in less developed rural areas far away from teacher education institutions. IT and the internet may help them to further their professional development as it provides opportunities through distance learning in the location of employment.

Along with the shift in education from a lecturer-dominated mode to a more learner-centred one, the teachers' new social role as guide and facilitator has taken the place of the traditional instructor role. Teachers are encouraged to guide learners through information resources rather than to disseminate the content of textbooks. It will be more important to help learners to learn in educational settings than to teach content. The new effort of changing the teachers' knowledge about their old social role into a modern one has been a challenge to institutions of teacher education. Faculty in charge of teaching theoretical and practical knowledge, such as modern pedagogy, psychology, history of education, philosophy of education, are responsible for renewing teachers' concepts of education desired and required in the IT age, i.e. to fulfil a role as guide and facilitator in the process of instruction. While current teachers are expected to adapt far beyond what they were trained for, institutions of teacher education have the obligation to define the new functions in order to meet the needs and requirements for teachers in times of significant knowledge and information potential growth (Ye and Liu 2005).

Models of teachers' cultivation

As discussed before, the traditional model of preparing and training teachers began to face many challenges after the radical shift of China's social system and the transformation and amalgamation of institutions of teacher education. The challenges and pressures can be summarised as follows: (1) knowledge growth and knowledge economy; (2) economic globalisation; (3) information technology and communication technology; (4) international trends; and (5) reform of teacher education (Wang 2004). In order to adapt to these challenges and pressures most institutions, particularly normal universities and colleges, responded promptly. An important outcome of their response is a reform of the model of 'teachers' cultivation'. Several models have been created by universities and colleges.

The first is called the model of 'three plus one', which is suitable for the four-year local universities and colleges at which 'teachers' cultivation' or teacher education can be divided into two stages. The first stage refers to a period of three years, from the freshmen to junior year, when all students are taught under the context of their chosen discipline, independent of whether they are oriented towards becoming teachers or not after their graduation. The second stage refers to the period of the last or senior year, when educational courses will be offered to those who are willing to become teachers at primary and middle schools after completion of the teacher training programme, receiving a bachelor's degree or certificate.

The second is called the model of 'two plus one plus one', which is also suitable for four-year institutions of undergraduate education at which teacher education can be completed in three phases. In the first two years, students are classified by disciplines into two categories, one of which includes those who are studying in the disciplines of science, such as physics, chemistry, math, biology, computer science, etc., and the other those who are studying in the disciplines of liberal arts such as philosophy, sociology, economic, history, education, public administration, etc. In both categories students receive education in areas common across their disciplines, similar to general education. In the junior year, predominantly courses specialising on in-depth content in the chosen discipline are taught. In the last year, those who are willing to become teachers after completion of college can be provided with educational courses, while other students will continue to study in their chosen specialty.

The third is called the model of 'two plus two'. It is similar to the second model, but somewhat different in that there are only two phases: general education in science or liberal arts in the first two years and specialty education in the last two years. When students have completed the required first two years, they can choose to continue with programmes covering teaching knowledge and skills offered to those who are preparing to enter a teaching career, or to select programmes provided in a discipline. The model is very popular in general undergraduate institutions of higher education such as Ningbo University at Zhejiang province and Sichuan Normal University.

The fourth is called the model of 'four plus X', which will be the future trend of teacher preparation and training in China. In the model, X can refer to one or two years. Students who are pursuing and completing bachelor degrees in specific disciplines at schools or departments of four-year institutions can obtain additional credits provided by schools of education at the same institutions. Students may obtain these credits in parallel to their subject area education. Students who have completed all requirements of their specific disciplines and have received a bachelor's degree can continue for one year with educational courses. Upon completion they may be awarded a double-diploma/degree, such as the bachelor degrees of science and the certificates of education. In this case, the model is called 'four plus one'.

Students who have completed their college degree, and are willing to continue their education, have the opportunity to sit an entrance examination for a Master of Arts in Education programme (MAE). These programmes are frequently offered by schools of education at the same institutions or different institutions. In these programmes students are required to take MAE courses, conduct independent research, write a dissertation and successfully complete a public defence, over a time frame of two years. A professional degree or certificate of MEA will be awarded upon completion. This pattern is typical for a 'four plus two' model. The model of 'four plus X' is gradually becoming popular in some large and prestigious institutions of teacher education, such as Beijing Normal University, East China Normal University, and Central China Normal University.

Conclusion

The reform of teacher education in China over the last two decades has many complex and multidimensional implications for the change of the higher education system, as well as for education at all levels. The reforms indicate the end of traditional ideas and models of teacher education and the beginning of new ones. Chinese teacher education has parted with a closed independently built system of preparing and training teachers for primary and secondary schools, and moved towards a new open system of diversified models of teacher education. In the new system, 70% of the effort that prepares and trains teachers is undertaken by normal (teacher) institutions of higher education, while the other 30% of effort is contributed by general comprehensive institutions of higher education which became involved in teacher education through establishing schools of education on their campuses.

It is clear that Chinese teacher education is at a crossroads, stretched by old and new forces, shifting from a planned environment or orientation towards an environment influenced by market drivers. As a result, the system of Chinese teacher education is no longer what it used to be.

For a start, systematic reforms and institutional mergers have been reconstructing the framework of the teacher education system as well as redefining institutional functions. For instance, some traditional institutions previously renowned for their teacher education have not limited themselves any more to an exclusive mission of educating teachers for primary and secondary schools. Of course, they continue having an advantage in terms of teacher education, over other institutions of higher education, but there is no difference in basic university functions such as teaching, research, and social service between the former and the latter. On the contrary, other institutions including both old and new comprehensive and general universities and colleges have also enlarged their education portfolio by becoming involved in teacher preparation and training since they incorporated or merged with smaller and less-renowned normal institutions and teacher schools.

The reform of the teacher education system in China has been characterised by two achievements. One is that standards and conditions of teacher education have moved and continue to advance from a lower level toward higher levels of accomplishment. For example, the numbers of three-year teacher schools at secondary education level have decreased from above 800 to below 400, the number of three-year teacher schools awarding associate degrees and diplomas have decreased from 160 to 70, while the numbers of institutions of teacher education awarding a bachelor degree and above have increased from 80 to 100, not including those incorporated into larger comprehensive institutions. In addition, teacher education and training resources have been diversified. By now more than 270 institutions of higher education are engaged in the task of training teachers for primary and secondary schools through the establishment of new schools or departments of education (Yuan 2004).

Second, the fact that teachers' professional development is emphasised is an outcome of the transition from pursuing quantity over quality in teacher education. It represents an alternative to the reflection of the old orientation of teacher education toward the new one, and delivers an expression of teachers' new social role in the era of information, globalisation and internationalisation. As Professor Yuan Zhenguo, a deputy director of DTE in MOE, pointed out: professionalising teacher education has been a new trend of guaranteeing the quality of teacher education (Yuan 2004). This has several implications for development of new concepts in reconsidering the importance of teacher education, including: (1) being a first-class scholar doesn't mean being an excellent teacher from a professional perspective; just like a doctor or a lawyer, a teacher also needs to gain more specific training including knowledge of theory and practice as well as teaching abilities and skills; (2) the recruitment of new teachers has been transformed from the old pattern of appointment into the new one of certification. An important outcome is that the higher a teacher's qualification, the better are their opportunities of obtaining teaching appointments. It is confirmed that many people have devoted themselves to continuously pursuing higher degrees or diplomas; (3) the concern for teacher quality and social role has moved to the forefront of institutional management and evaluation. What are the criteria and standards for 'good teaching'? What defines a teacher of 'qualified teachers'? Questions of this kind are being discussed inside and beyond academia and government offices nationwide.

Third, the reform of teacher training has led to a diversity of models and a new reality in Chinese teacher education. The situation that several models co-exist in the same system at the same time will continue far into the future. The diversity of models can meet the different needs of schools at different levels, also providing opportunities for flexibility in response to labour market demands. Notably, innovative models of teacher education of some institutions are not mature yet. One reason may be that they are not recognised and accepted by all institutions of teacher education; another is that many institutions of higher education are still in a state of adjustment after institutional amalgamation or incorporation, having to address issues of experience and quality.

Altogether, many changes in teacher education have taken place in China in the past two decades, along with changes of the country's environment. Many activities at government organisations and academic institutions, including policy decisions, development of mission statements, strategy development, and design and development of curricula, show that the reform of Chinese teacher education is making great strides in catching up to the standard and direction of teacher education worldwide. Especially in comparison with developed Western countries the distance between Chinese teacher education and their standards is diminishing rapidly. Provided that in the coming years China remains socially and economically stable, reforms and developments in teacher education, as in other areas of the country, will progress steadily with incremental results, which will benefit not only Chinese education at all levels, but also the development of the country and its people.

Notes

1. Historically, the four types of institutions of Chinese pre-service teacher education were: (1) top-level normal (teacher) universities with postgraduate education such as Beijing Normal University, East China Normal University, etc., preparing faculty members for other teacher institutions of higher education at lower levels; (2) four-year undergraduate normal (teacher) universities and colleges, preparing teachers for high schools; (3) two- to three-year professional teacher colleges preparing teachers for middle schools; (4) normal (teacher) schools at secondary education level, preparing teachers for primary schools and kindergarten.
2. Historically, the three-level institutions of in-service education were: (1) provincial institutes of education or teacher colleges of continued education for high school teachers; (2) regional and municipal institutes of education or teacher colleges of continued education for middle school teachers; and (3) county teacher continued education schools for primary and kindergarten teachers.

References

Anon. 2005. Teacher education institutions have never again had privilege to enroll newcomers, and general institutions will be involved in teacher education. *Educator* 5.
Chen, Y.M. 1999. *On modern teachers*, 35–36. Shanghai: Shanghai Education Press.
Chen, Y.M. 2003. *Studies on teacher education*, 107–16. Shanghai: East China Normal University Press.
Department of Teacher Education (DTE) of the Ministry of Education. 2001. *Theories and practices on professionalizing teacher education*. Beijing: People's Education Press.
Du, L.J. 2004. How career satisfaction of primary and secondary teacher in Henan Province is impacting SCL-90 score. *Chinese Journal of School Health* 25, no. 2: 246–7.
Gumport, P.J., and M. Chun. 2005. Technology and higher education. In *American Higher Education*, ed. P.G. Altbach, R.O. Berdahl, and P. J. Gumport, 394. London, Baltimore: Johns Hopkins University Press.
Huang, Y.Y., and Y.M. Wu. 2006. Discussion on models of preparing primary teachers in China in the new era. *Modern Education Science* 2: 17–9.
Jiao, J.L. 2007. Eight types of teacher's competences required in the internet era. *IT Education* 1: 54–7.
Ma, L. 1998. Bringing an active and dynamic Chinese teacher education into twenty-first century. *China Higher Education Research* 6: 19–23.
Ministry of Education (MOE). 2000. *Decision on the reform of educational system, Outline for reform and development of education in china, Decision about deepening the reform of education and boosting the education of quality,* Teachers' Law. In *Foundation of educational law*, ed. W.P. Zhang, 632–33, 643, 666, 722. Shenyang: Liaoning University Press.
Ministry of Education (MOE). 2006. A list of merged institutions of higher education since 1990. http://moe.edu.cn/edoas/website18/info19558.htm.
Statistical Yearbook. 2001. *Annual Chinese statistic of educational expenditure*. Beijing: Chinese Statistics Press.
Sun, J.H. 2004. Teacher professional development facing challenges and responses. *Contemporary Education Science* 24: 19–20.

Wang, X.L. 2006. Analysis of and proposal for the investment of rural elementary education. *Journal of Tianjin Normal University* (Elementary Education Edition) 7, no. 3: 15–7.
Wang, Z.H. 2004. Constructing the opinion of the new-type training mode of Normal universities and colleges' personnel. *Curriculum Teaching Material and Method* 24: 75–9.
Yang, Z.L., B. Lin, and W.C. Su. 1989. *Teacher education in the People's Republic of China.* Beijing: Beijing Normal University Press.
Ye, J.H., and X.W. Liu. 2005. The interaction and development of teacher cultivation model and higher teacher education. *Curriculum Teaching Material and Method* 26, no. 5: 77–82.
Yuan, Z.G. 2003. Professionalizing teachers: A new stage of building faculty teams. *Beijing Educational Science Research* 11: 19–22.
Yuan, Z.G. 2004. On the transition from 'normal education' toward 'teacher education'. *China Higher Education* 5, 29–31.

Early childhood teacher education in China

Jiaxiong Zhu

Department of Early Childhood Education, East China Normal University, Shanghai, People's Republic of China

Introduction

Early childhood education in China refers to education for children from birth to the age of six. The educational institutions for children of three to six years old are called kindergartens; for children younger than three years they are called nurseries. In recent years, the effort to emphasise both care and education has created a trend to integrate nurseries with kindergartens (Zhu 2001). In most rural areas, counties, towns and some cities, many pre-primary classes in primary schools or kindergartens offer early education for children aged five to six for one or more years. Otherwise, these children may never have a chance to attend kindergartens. In comparison with kindergartens, pre-primary classes usually place greater emphasis on academics and use teaching methods similar to those in primary classrooms (Zhu and Wang 2005).

Overview

In China, education resources are generally scarce at the local and state level. The government pays attention to the nine-year compulsory education (six-year primary education and three-year middle school education) when allocating the education budget. Early childhood education is non-compulsory. For more than 10 years, the government has given only 1.3% of the total education budget to preschool education. There are two large categories of ownership among preschools: one is non-governmental including collectively owned, and privately owned preschools and the other is owned by various education bureaus of the government.

By 2005, China had 124,402 kindergartens, 774,859 classes, of which 303,243 were preschool classes for five-year-olds. Education bureaus were in charge of 25,688 kindergartens and 395,038 classes, of which 248,811 were preschool classes for five-year-olds. These figures comprised 20.65% of total kindergartens, 50.98% of total classes and 62.98% of total preschool classes, respectively (Ministry of Education 2005). The total number of children served by kindergartens is 21,790,290, including 8,554,212 five-year-olds in preschool classes. The total number of children in preschools run by various education bureaus was 11,475,425, including preschool classes for five-year-olds, 52.66% of the total kindergartens (classes), but 80.79% of the total preschool classes for five-year-olds (Ministry of Education 2005).

The above numbers show that kindergartens supported by education bureaus at various governmental levels are clustered in cities, counties and towns, and most preschool classes for five-year-olds are in rural areas. The recent national census also shows about 70 million children aged three to six (Cai 2005), which means about two-thirds of this age group are not served by preschools.

The nature of non-compulsory education for young children in many areas places teachers in a low social and economical status. The preservice teacher education and in-service training present many problems. For example, regarding kindergartens in China, there are 721,609 full time kindergarten teachers and 114,511 directors, making a total of 836,120. Among these teachers and directors, 51,219 people or 6.13% have a bachelor degree and 359,773 people or 43.02% had a two- or three-year college education. And yet, more than one half of these teachers and directors have no professional training (Ministry of Education 2005).

For four decades after 1950, Chinese kindergarten teachers were trained mainly in normal schools, vocational schools that admitted graduates from the junior middle schools. These students would study for three more years to become kindergarten teachers. At that time, China had more than 60 normal schools to train kindergarten teachers. Kindergarten teacher education programmes could also be found in other types of normal and professional schools.

In the recent decade, the older Chinese system of kindergarten teacher education has been transformed from a system with three tiers (vocational normal school, junior college, and four-year college) to two tiers (junior college and four-year college). But this transformation is not a uniform change. Some normal schools have become three-year vocational colleges while others have been incorporated into nearby teachers' colleges or normal universities that offer bachelor degrees. In addition to formal education, state and local governments also provide education for pre-service and in-service teachers through distance education, self-teaching, and internet education programmes. As a result, a large number of teachers have had three or more years of college education. In some well-to-do regions, almost all kindergarten teachers have such a diploma or degree.

Problems of current early childhood teacher education in China: conflict between the traditional pre-service/in-service teacher education and the early childhood education reform

Since the late 1980s, the Chinese government has promoted early childhood education reform throughout the country, focusing its efforts on curriculum reform. The early childhood curriculum has shifted from an emphasis on teaching knowledge and skills to an emphasis on the development of children and the acquisition of abilities, from an emphasis on the result of educational activity to an emphasis on the process of activity, from an emphasis on the uniform curriculum standards to an emphasis on diversified and autonomous curriculum development and implementation (Zhu 2004).

Before the onset of the reform, curriculum implementation was in the hands of those specialised curriculum designers and administrators who effectively controlled those who implemented the prescribed curriculum. Therefore, the paradigm for teacher education was to train faithful executors of the blueprint for early education. This paradigm presumed the so-called 'technical rationality' with which kindergarten teacher education is a process of transmitting knowledge and providing drill exercises.

Recently, the curriculum reform has been the core of the overall reform in early childhood education. It has shaken the foundation of the traditional teacher education paradigm. A host of national and local policies, laws and regulations, demand that early curriculum should be the centre of all activities in kindergartens. It requires early educators to examine children's experiences, interests and needs, engaging children in the activities that teachers and children collaboratively initiate and select to carry out. In this situation, the old teacher education paradigm that required teachers to be 'faithful technical executors' has met profound challenges.

Teachers play a central role in the curriculum reform which requires them to study the educational processes and the experiences of children. To implement a new curriculum, teachers must perform at a much higher level than executing a standardised curriculum because the new curriculum places teachers in a decision-making position in both curriculum design and implementation.

Through decades of living and learning in the traditional teacher education system, many teachers and teacher educators have been resistant to change. Teacher educators have been accustomed to training 'faithful technical executors'. Those who teach early childhood teachers, found their traditional ideas very hard to change.

Unevenness in development: urban vs. rural areas, developing vs. developed regions

In China, differences are great between urban and rural areas, developing and developed regions in terms of economical, cultural and educational resources. In the 20 years following the open-door policy and economic reform, these differences have become even greater.

This uneven development of urban vs. rural areas and developing vs. developed regions has certainly been reflected in early childhood teacher education. Many east coastal mid-sized cities and metropolitan areas have a disproportionally large share of teacher education programmes with better quality and more resources. In inland regions, such as the rural areas in the west, resources for teacher education are scarce. Even within the same district, great gaps exist between rural and urban areas.

Take Shanghai, for example. Ten years ago, there were three normal schools for training kindergarten teachers. In order to improve kindergarten teacher education, one of them was incorporated into East China Normal University which is directly supervised by the Ministry of Education. The other two normal schools were eliminated. East China Normal University created a College of Early Childhood Education and developed a complex system to offer a variety of degrees in early childhood education such as PhDs, Master's, bachelors, and three-year college diploma.

The consolidated teacher education programmes are of pre-service, in-service, and professional development. In recent years, to meet the needs of further development, Shanghai has taken advantage of its municipal resources to establish an early childhood education department in Shanghai Normal University and three other colleges, offering three-year diplomas or more advanced degrees. In addition, the opportunities and resources in Shanghai have attracted kindergarten teachers with higher degrees and richer experiences from many other parts of China.

In comparison, western regions, especially the rural areas, suffer from lack of resources and are unable to improve their kindergarten teacher education programme at a fast pace. Most kindergarten teachers have only high school diplomas or lower education. They hardly have a chance to obtain specialised professional training. Usually, they cannot even find the kind of teacher education in vocational schools that used to be common and fundamental in coastal cities.

Disparity in resources and programming among teacher education programmes at different levels

The nationally mandated transition from three-tier to two-tier teacher education systems (the original vocational normal schools, which produced all the early childhood education teachers) was transformed in three ways: being incorporated into a university, being eliminated completely, or moving up to become a college. But in this process reformers do not have any explicit guidance and directions from the state government, nor do they have any prior experiences to refer to. In most circumstances, the success of such transition depends on the local economy, education, and the whims of local government officials. Sometimes, chaos results.

During this transition period, many normal schools for early childhood teachers undergo some painful and even traumatic changes, including ownership, the length of semester, programmes, personnel, location, and facilities. The changes involve the qualifications and abilities of administrators, and the qualifications and stakes of teachers. Up to now, those normal schools that have already completed this transformation, those that are in transformation, and those that will transform, are all faced with significant costs.

In response to this situation, on 14 March 2005, the Ministry of Education issued 'Notice regarding the regulation of primary school and kindergarten teacher education'. This document requires that education departments at all the governmental levels must take seriously the problems that appeared in the process of moving from the three-tier to the two-tier teacher education. Following the general strategy of the education reform, the document also requires a series of focused endeavours on the part of the various government levels: the active restructuring and allocation of teacher education programmes; long-term development for teacher education; the integration of kindergarten teacher education in the local economic development; the provision of thoughtful approaches in teacher education; the ensuring of the quality of kindergarten teacher education programmes; the gradual establishment of early childhood teacher education programmes in the higher education system. The document mandates that all the kindergarten teachers education programmes must meet basic requirements issued by the education departments of the state or provincial government before the programmes are allowed to operate.

Orientation toward a future: trends in early childhood teacher education

Teacher education is an endeavour aimed at the future. The future orientation in early childhood teacher education in China has a dove-tailed perspective. On the one hand, the teacher education programmes must adapt to the rapid economic development, meet the demands for educating citizens who will be capable, innovative and worldly. On the other hand, early childhood teacher education in China should be in line with the Chinese culture and national conditions to create a 'harmonious society' under the principles of justice and equality.

For a decade or so, Chinese kindergarten teachers enjoyed better education with higher degrees than they did in the past. Opportunities for in-service professional development have multiplied significantly. However, as teachers created and implemented their curricula, they ran into many issues that prevented them from following the requirements the government has outlined for early childhood education curriculum reform. The curriculum reform has indeed challenged the traditional paradigm of teacher education and has frequently and strongly called for a paradigm shift (Zhu 2002).

In the twentieth century, industrialisation and post-industrialisation impacted the whole world which experienced great technology advancement and knowledge explosion. The twenty-first century as an information era sees knowledge development as the centre of the educational mission. This context requires the educators to change their role of knowledge transmitters.

The traditional understanding of what constitutes knowledge underlies both the traditional paradigm of curriculum design and implementation, and the traditional paradigm of teacher education. This traditional view regards knowledge as being objective, universal and value-neutral, but neglected the contextual difference and cultural diversity. Teachers not only used this kind of knowledge in their teaching practice smoothly, but also dealt with all kinds of teaching needs with the prescribed methods once they grasped the knowledge.

Today, in the knowledge economy era, teachers have to help young children acquire the knowledge that could make them competent in their future life. And teachers need to facilitate in children knowledge growth that may motivate children, induce their innovation, develop their observation skills, obtain useable knowledge. At the same time, children are expected to ask questions until they can propose new method to answer their own questions independently, and obtain critiques and verifications.

The world is changing rapidly. Globalisation and the interaction of different ideologies confront researchers and practitioners in early childhood education with many new problems and challenges such as diverse cultures, multiple languages, methodology of de-colonisation and localised knowledge. In China, the society is developing in the direction of multiculturalism as people flow from rural areas into cities, from developing to developed regions, and from other countries to China. This trend is also reflected in the social interpersonal relationships, people's life style, local and national politics, economical operations, and cultural ideology. All these affect early childhood education directly or indirectly.

The traditional curriculum paradigm and the traditional teacher education paradigm are centred on structuralisation, systematisation, centralisation, uniformity, standardisation, but they ignore complexity, contradiction, multiplicity, historical and contextual peculiarity, especially cultural appropriateness. The standardised curriculum with universal principles in child development and education ignore children's family backgrounds, personal history, social relations, and cultural origins. It is not only unfair, but also inefficient. The teachers need to put themselves and their children into various complex ecological relations. The teachers need to help children accept, identify with, respect and develop their own culture. Altogether they construct knowledge and culture through cooperation, exchange, deliberation and sharing with other people in complex ecological relations.

With this understanding of what teaching will be about in the future, it is clear that early childhood teacher education should prepare future teachers to teach in rather unique situations on a daily basis. Although explicit and definite theoretical knowledge may be used to guide teachers' curriculum activities, there are few teaching models and skills that teachers can use in their actual teaching. They must rely on their own experiences and pedagogical wisdom to make independent judgments and choices in varied contexts in teaching.

However, the economic development in China is extremely uneven. This imbalance inevitably affects early childhood teacher education. In many areas, especially in those developing areas, early childhood teacher education programmes need to prioritise the basic provision and distribution of trained teachers instead of trying to raise the bar. Excessive expectation of the teachers will render teaching impractical and may bring about many problems. Thus, early childhood teacher education programmes in China should take into account the need to:

1. mobilise their available resources for early childhood teacher education to build a support network for pre-service and in-service development at various levels (state, local) and of various types (within school and distance education);
2. develop an effective mechanism for early childhood teacher education, which could support diverse, flexible and context-sensitive practice; and
3. prioritise in-service professional development and promoting teachers' engagement in critically reflective activities that help to shape innovative and supportive environments for early childhood care and education.

Countermeasures and strategies to deal with the current problems of early childhood teacher education

The transformation and improvement of early childhood teacher education in China is an ongoing process. Organisations for pre-service and in-service professional development at different government levels have been established as required. Formal and informal education for teachers has been made available. Kindergarten teacher education programmes in China also have generally taken the following specific types of measures and strategies:

- Establishing 'bases for autonomous research programmes' within early childhood education organisations and implementing 'kindergarten-based professional development through examination of teachers' actions'.
- 'Helping teachers become researchers' has been a slogan in teacher professional development in the developed regions; the '*kindergarten-based* professional development through teachers' examination of their own actions' is widely held as an effective approach to fostering teacher researchers.

'Helping teachers become researchers' is a strategy not meant to make teachers act like professional researchers in the university, but rather to help teachers do research which grows from their own interests. It is a reflective examination of their own practices in their daily contexts. The *'kindergarten-based* professional development through examination of teachers' actions' is aimed at supporting teachers in becoming action researchers as a way to foster professional growth. It rejects the notion that teachers should obtain objective and technical knowledge from outside their daily environment, but it encourages them to conduct research in their practice, and practise while conducting research. Teachers can reflect on, and improve, their practice through studying their own experiences in professional settings.

Such research facilitates teachers' understandings of themselves and their professional activities. As a new paradigm for teacher development, it requires teachers to make sense of their own teaching experiences and contexts. It is recommended that teachers frequently reflect on their professional life, constantly explore their contexts, and make effective decisions for their curriculum needs and implementation. As mentioned earlier, this paradigm for teachers' professional development respects teachers as decision-makers who don't always have clear solutions to any educational problems. They will plan and act with great uncertainty, multiple possibilities, and a variety of choices in their awareness and decision-making processes. In their educational practice, the complexity and uncertainty foster their ability to deal with continuous and frequent change.

'Kindergarten-based training' is a process of group professional development in an evolving context. In this sense, creating and sustaining teacher group collaboration are essential to effective professional development. The mechanism for teachers to co-construct their meanings and collaborate in the research is the 'discourse' process. Each participant in the discourse can understand and share their ideas and thought process with one another. They can value, tolerate, inspire, counter and interact with each other's ideas. The converging point of different perspectives may eventually improve teachers' professional ideas.

To amplify the significance of 'kindergarten-based training', the members of these teachers' research communities come together to reflect on their experiences and research. In doing so, they record their reflections and discussion through narrative, resulting in what is called 'documentation' that summarises and generalises their practice. A valuable documentation is practically a research report that demonstrates the events and processes in teaching. It captures the teaching and learning in the classroom, and delves into different factors that have entered the educational and teaching processes. And it allows those who were described in the documentation to think back and further about 'how to make their teaching meaningful'; it inspires and enlightens those who are merely audiences and outsiders to the classroom. For years, kindergarten-based training has unfolded in many parts of China and this approach has already produced very good effects in kindergarten teachers' professional growth.

Professional development for rural teachers through distance education and other means

In comparison with urban areas, teacher education in rural areas is in desperate need of more resources and professional development opportunities are scanty. In order to alleviate this situation, some rural governments already set aside funds to purchase distance education services and other means for providing professional development and improving the quality of rural kindergarten teachers. Some education agencies assume the responsibility for providing such services. This kind of professional development sometimes is carried out on a large scale.

For example, the Shanghai government initiated a project called 'Shanghai "New Village" Teachers Professional Development'. It has involved all the kindergarten teachers in Shanghai rural areas surrounding the city. This project has these features:

- It is a parallel effort to the curriculum reform in the early childhood education in Shanghai.
- It presents concrete cases in curriculum and it focuses on a special topic at a time. The goal is to help teachers solve real problems in teacher education and teaching practice – starting from teaching and returning to teaching.
- It highlights the theory–practice connection, offers easy-to-use interpretations for practitioners, and provides cases for teachers to examine.
- It provides teachers with full freedom to choose a curriculum.

Creating useful resources for curriculum development

The rural government makes the purchase of commercially available curriculum development packages for kindergarten teacher education. This provision gives teachers accessible multidimensional curriculum resources and encourages them to apply these to their own teaching. Consequently the quality of the curriculum improves with enhanced flexibility and reduced workload. Such curriculum resources should be easy to access and use, of high quality and multidimensional, including books, the Internet, and multimedia.

Conclusion

It is clear that early childhood education, including teacher education, in China is strongly influenced by social cultural changes and influences the harmony of society. Early childhood teacher education is crucial to the success of the early childhood education reform, which aims to modify curricula to be diversified and flexible to suit local and individual programmes' needs (Zhu and Wang 2005). New policies and teacher education programmes have to be concerned with how to make improvements including changing teacher qualifications, pre-service and in-service training. With rethinking about early childhood education politically, culturally, economically, socially and practically, teacher education in China is confronted with a series of major challenges.

References

Cai, F. 2005. *2005 yearbook of China's population*. Beijing: Chinese Academy of Social Science Press.
Ministry of Education in Peoples Republic of China. 2005. *China education yearbook (volume 2005)*. Beijing: People Education Press.
Zhu, J. 2001. *Introduction and reflection on staff training in China*. Paper presented at the International Conference on Teacher Education, Shanghai, China.
Zhu, J. 2002. Early childhood care and education in P.R. of China. In *2002 KEDI–UNESCO Bangkok Joint Seminar and Study Tour on Early Childhood Care and Education*. Seoul: Korean Educational Development Institute Press.

Zhu, J. 2004. Reflection on the two-decade reform in early childhood curriculum in Mainland China. *Hong Kong Journal of Early Childhood* 3, no. 2: 5–8.
Zhu, J., and X.C. Wang. 2005. Contemporary early childhood education and research in China. In *International perspectives on research in early childhood education*, ed. B. Spodek and O. Saracho. New York: Information Age.

English education and teacher education in South Korea

Seongja Jo

Graduate School of Education, Waseda University, Tokyo, Japan; Taerang Middle School, Seoul, South Korea

Introduction

Nowadays, the world is becoming more globalised and internationalised. English is used not only in English-speaking countries but in many other countries. In this sense English is an international common language. We often call such variations of English 'World Englishes'. A rough estimation of the number of native English speakers in the world is about 350 million and that of non-native English speakers is about 1.2 billion, or four times the number of native speakers (Crystal 1995, 107). Thus, it has been argued that English is no longer the language of native speakers alone and that non-native speakers could have linguistic identities of their own in their versions of English (Yano 2001). English is used in various settings around the world. In such situations, English cannot be limited only to British or American culture, but can be the means of expressing the speaker's culture (Crystal 2003, 145). Thus, many countries where English is not used as a mother tongue strive to improve English education through educational reforms. Consequently, the roles of English teachers have become increasingly important in school education. Training English teachers becomes more important and training programmes are increasingly required to become innovative enough to cope with the new tasks of teachers in English.

The use of English is second only to Korean in South Korea. Owing to the swift development of the national economy and the overwhelming stream of globalisation, people are in favour of promoting the use of English. South Korea is also making efforts to enhance English education within its school system.

The purpose of this study is to investigate South Korea's English education by clarifying the kinds of practical issues in the field of English teacher education, and exploring policy perspectives to prepare for the twenty-first century.

School articulations in South Korea

Korea, a country in northeastern Asia, has been divided into two countries, South Korea and North Korea, since 1953 due to the Korean War. Originally Korea was one nation consisting of a unitary race of Koreans. South Korea is a democratic country, while North Korea is a communist state. The common language of Korea is Korean, which uses a *Hangeul*, a unique writing system originally developed in the fifteenth century.

The school system of South Korea is a so-called 6-3-3-4 system of institutions which covers elementary school, middle school, high school and college or university. Compulsory education extends from age 6–14, or the nine years before high school. With the newest educational reforms beginning in 1997, English education starts in the third grade of elementary school. Many pupils are interested in English and study hard. One school year is divided into two semesters. The first semester lasts for six months from 1 March to the end of August, and the second from 1 September to the end of the next February.

Pre-school education

Kindergarten is not compulsory but is provided for children from the age of three until their admission to elementary school. The aim is to promote the psychological and physical development of children through suitable educational environments and diverse educational activities centred on play. The kindergarten curriculum developed by the state is composed of the five life fields: healthy life, social life, expressive life, language life (Korean and English), and inquiry life. In Seoul (the capital of South Korea), there are 90,000 children being educated at over 900 kindergartens (as of 2005). Public kindergartens have increased in number to improve the pre-school attendance ratio, while pre-school educational materials have been developed and distributed to institutions in order to enhance the quality of education. Kindergartens aim at realising the ideal of a happy kindergarten with which more parents can be satisfied. Children are provided with various types of systems, such as a half-day system, an extension system, and an all-day system for working parents called 'educare'.

Primary education

Primary education, starting at the age of six, is free and compulsory. The average enrolment ratio is 99.9%. Such quantitative expansion of primary education is the outcome of a public zeal for education and the educational policies of the government. The sudden growth in the number of students and the migration of the rural population into cities gave the government the incentive to introduce an education tax in 1982, by which it financed the expansion and modernisation of physical facilities and improved the socio-economic status of teachers. As a result, the number of students per class dropped to 34.8 in 1990. Overcrowded schools have been divided into smaller ones and the dual scheme of morning and afternoon schooling terminated. The government continues to strive toward improving primary education.

The objectives of the curriculum are implemented practically in the very basic levels of elementary education, which are indispensable for citizens' lives. Schools run for more than 220 days a year with the course of study consisting of Korean ethics, social studies, mathematics, science, practices, gymnastics, music, arts, foreign language (English), and optional extracurricular activities. The lesson hours, however, can be appropriately adjusted (shortened or lengthened) to the weather conditions, seasonal conditions, academic achievement level of pupils/students, and the quality of learning.

Moreover, with the revision of the regulations that once prohibited children under six from attending elementary school, some five-year-olds have been allowed to register at elementary schools when they are assessed to have the abilities to enter school as long as there is space. From 1997, in order to offer children more opportunities to learn foreign languages, 1 to 2 hours of English lessons a week were introduced from the third grade of elementary school except in special education classes or schools.

Middle school education

The purposes of middle school education are twofold: to develop students' and pupils' basic abilities for everyday life and to cultivate attitudes appropriate to democratic citizens, based upon what they achieved during elementary schooling. Entrance examinations to middle schools were abolished in 1969. Subsequently, all elementary school students continued to middle schools within their residential districts. These three years of free, compulsory, middle school education began in 1985 in rural areas first. Between 1992 and 1994, the scheme was expanded to the rest of the country except for highly urbanised areas. In 2002 the principle became standard throughout all regions of South Korea. The curriculum is composed of 10 nationally standardised subjects, extracurricular and optional activities with an emphasis on developing students' various abilities and aptitudes.

High school education

High school education is aimed at providing secondary basic but advanced education based on middle school education. Three-year high schools are divided into general high schools, vocational (technical) high schools and others (foreign language, art, science and physical high schools). School fees vary from school to school due to the particulars of each school. However, in order to support families and students with financial difficulties, there are provisions which grant subsidies for school fees as well as various scholarships.

The aims of general high schools are broad but specific: to foster the qualities of international citizens who can appropriately develop their respective careers based on their aptitudes and abilities. In general high schools this system is composed of (1) a course of the national common subjects in the first year and (2) a course of studies planned with optional subjects for students to choose from according to their needs and career plans in the second and third years.

At vocational (technical) high schools students choose courses from a professional curriculum leading to various careers. Students choose their subjects by identifying their individual goals and needs in order to realise their ideals in adulthood. At all high schools, whether academic or vocational, some subjects in the humanities like foreign languages, music, and fine arts are provided. Science and physical education are optional subjects, which gifted students can learn at the advanced level.

Higher education

Institutions of higher education in South Korea are divided into seven categories: (1) colleges and universities, (2) industrial universities, (3) universities of education, (4) junior colleges, (5) broadcast/correspondence universities, (6) technical universities, and (7) miscellaneous institutions. The aims of higher education are threefold: (a) to advance academic and professional education required for the development of humanity, (b) to apply research findings to enhancing human well-being, and (c) to educate national and international citizens who are capable of contributing to human culture and civilisation worldwide.

In South Korea the reputed high competition levels of university entrance examinations have been a serious policy issue, prompting the government to improve matriculation systems for university entrance. Generally speaking, the applicant selection scheme is institutionalised into three types: 'regular', 'specific' and 'supplementary'. The government has issued a code requiring all higher educational institutions, particularly universities, to offer fair opportunities for all applicants by developing the best measures of selecting appropriate candidates. This includes making student selection scientifically accountable to the public, and not the least, establishing academic independence. As a result, new measures for testing academic achievement and practical skills are at present partly still on the table and partly already in practice. More objective tests have been suggested and introduced. Such innovation in university entrance examinations is expected in turn to reform school education along more 'normal' lines and to alleviate the economic burden of private tutoring which has already reached notorious levels. To expand the entrance opportunities for students, higher education institutions are being required to develop more flexible procedures for assessing candidates records and achievements. Such requirements resulted in the development of comprehensive measures for examination which not only rely on written tests, but also on student profile records compiled by high school teachers. Other innovative schemes to moderate competition have also been adopted.

Policies on other topics
Special education
Special education is provided at kindergarten, elementary, middle, and high school. About 5300 disabled children are studying at 29 special schools, while at 750 special education classes in general schools there are about 4900 disabled children and students. Free special education is compulsory at elementary and middle school. No fee is required at either kindergarten or high school.

Lifelong education
Lifelong education has diverse forms and characteristics. Seoul Lifelong Education Center, which is open to the public, is the core institution with more than 600 affiliated public groups. Lifelong educational groups such as lifelong education centres attached to colleges, libraries, museums, and schools are administering various lifelong education programmes. Under the constitution, the government is responsible for promoting lifelong education and instilling the importance of education and learning throughout society. The government strives to provide the general public with the opportunity to receive continuing education and to engage in ongoing enhancement of their potential. The Lifelong Education Law, established in August 1999 under the Social Education Promotion Law, provides strong support for related education institutes.

Gifted education

A gifted education programme was set up in 2001 to develop the special abilities and creativity of gifted students in various fields early in life and help them contribute to society. From 2002, the programme was expanded to various fields on the basis of lawful and systematic rules, so that there are now a total of 2000 students at 26 institutions, including 18 educational institutions for gifted students and eight gifted schools in 2004 in Seoul. The field of gifted education has expanded to include information technology, music, art, math and science. Currently the programme targets students from fourth grade of elementary school to the second year of high school. By 2007, the programme is scheduled to increase the number of students to 8000 (0.5% of the total student numbers). Gifted education operates outside of regular classes through special programmes after school or during vacation periods.

English education in South Korea

English education as a foreign language was first provided at middle school. However, recognising the importance and effectiveness of English education at earlier stages, the Ministry of Education introduced English into elementary schools in 1997. According to the plan, learning English was scheduled to start in the third grade of elementary school. Thus, many elementary school pupils are now learning English through chants, games, and other activities. However, elementary school English is only an hour or 2-hour lesson a week, a total of only 34–68 hours a year. The lessons in middle and high school consume 3–5 hours a week (102–170 a year). Compared with lesson hours in middle and high school then, elementary school pupils just get a taste of what English looks or sounds like. Time in English lessons is too short for pupils and students to be fully acquainted with English. As a result, they cannot actually use English after finishing schooling. Therefore, many students learn English in private tutoring institutions, increasing the economic burden upon parents and becoming an educational problem.

With the increasing need to improve the English curriculum, the Seoul Metropolitan Office of Education (SMOE) has announced that SMOE would gradually invite more native speakers of English to every elementary and middle school in Seoul by 2010. As a way of improving communication skills in English, in 2005, SMOE recruited and placed Native Speaker English Teachers (NSET) at 100 elementary and middle schools in Seoul. Currently, the number of NSETs is increasing annually. As of September 2006, 214 NSETs had been placed in public elementary or middle schools.

NSETs manage English classes jointly with Korean homeroom teachers or Korean English language teachers and teach English conversation. Such a co-teaching system gives students many opportunities to talk with native speakers of English, helping them psychologically overcome their personal fear of foreign languages.

In addition, young students become motivated to study English while engaging in various activities. NSETs assist pupils and students not only in activities related to English language education but in other extracurricular activities in and out of school provided by the Education Offices of different regions.

According to surveys conducted in 2005, Korean teachers, students, and their parents are satisfied with the NSET–Korean teacher co-teaching system. With such positive outcomes, SMOE plans to place more NSETs in more schools. Moreover, some school districts individually employ native English speakers and make efforts to provide better English education. Consequently, SMOE and school districts in Seoul are in need of more qualified native English speaking teachers. With the expanding English programmes and co-teaching system, it is expected that English education may take a step forward.

Learning English is an essential skill that enables Koreans to be more competitive in the global market. Recognising the importance and effectiveness of English education at an early stage of development, the Ministry of Education plans to introduce English into the first grade, two years earlier than the present third grade, and has carried out a pilot programme from the latter half of 2006 through 2007, with the intention of full, nationwide implementation by 2008. The ministry also conducted a pilot 'English immersion education' programme which will tentatively start, in 2008, teaching mathematics and science in English both in primary and secondary schools located in the country's special economic zones and *Jeju* Free International City.

However, linguistic difficulties in foreign language education occur when English is taught in the Korean context. Although Korean people have learned English for a quite long time (at least more than six years), few of them manage English well. The reasons are twofold. First, English is not a second language but a foreign language for Koreans. That is, there are few chances to speak English because English is not used frequently in daily life. Second, English as a language is linguistically distant from Korean. Korean belongs to the Ural-Altaic language family, and is similar to Japanese in grammar, word order, phrasing, and sentence composition. In contrast, Ural-Altaic is not related to the English family (Indo-European) at all. English and Korean have different semantic and syntactic features. Therefore, there are many barriers to Koreans or Japanese mastering English. Despite this fact, English has been the most popular foreign language among Koreans and it is increasingly necessary to be acquainted with it.

Korean teacher policies and teacher education

The Ministry of Education holds the belief that 'the quality of education can not exceed the quality of teachers', thus it implements various policies to improve teacher quality and capacity. Moreover, as Korea lacks natural resources, the Ministry has set the national motto as 'Education is the nation's strength to compete' and is eager to develop student competence as human capital at the national level. This emphasis is evident in the 1995 Educational Reformation Plan, the 2001 Comprehensive Plan for Teachers' Professional Development, and the current decision to establish a total innovation plan covering all teacher policies. Primary and secondary teachers in Korea enjoy a relatively stable social status as professionals with correspondingly appropriate incomes because they are civil servants. This is why the teaching profession is favoured by talented and competent people. At present there are about 380,000 teachers (as of 1 April 2004) in South Korea.

In order to become a teacher, applicants need to attend education courses run and managed by teacher education institutes, and acquire a teaching certificate relevant to a given category. Teachers are classified into several categories, for example teachers (Grade 1 and Grade 2), assistant teachers, professional counsellors, librarians, training teachers and nursing teachers. They are required to meet the specific qualification criteria for each category and to be licensed by the Deputy Prime Minister of Education and Human Resource Development Department as stipulated by presidential decree.

Kindergarten teacher certification

Kindergarten teacher certification requires all candidates to hold a first degree from a university or diploma from a college. Nowadays many future kindergarten teachers are trained at universities, although most teachers have graduated from college or junior college. Those who major in early childhood studies or nursery education either at universities or colleges can be exempted from teacher qualifying exams. To be exempt from the qualifying exams, applicants are required to obtain 42 credits related to early childhood education. These must include nine basic credit modules from authorised credit issuing universities and colleges accredited in advance which control the procedures for exemption from qualifying exams.

Second grade kindergarten teacher certification does exist. However, the exams are held only when there is a real lack of kindergarten teachers, despite the prescription that second grade kindergarten teacher certificates can be nominally obtained when the candidates pass the exams.

Elementary school teacher certification

To be certified as an elementary school teacher, applicants should graduate from the National Teacher Education University or finish courses from a university department of education. According to the Teacher Qualification Act, an applicant can apply for exemption from the teacher qualifying exam. Those who major in elementary education at a graduate school of education can also obtain an elementary school teaching certificate. However, if they do not major in elementary education at a university, they cannot acquire teaching qualifications due to lack of credits. There are 11 Korean National Universities of Education, and Ewha Women's University which has a Department of Elementary Education. In 1984, all teachers colleges were upgraded to four-year universities. The Korean National University of Education was founded in 1985 as an experimental institution to foster teacher education. From 1990, all teacher candidates have been obligated to take aptitude and personality tests to raise the quality of teacher education and by extension, the quality of education as a whole.

Second grade elementary school teacher certification also exists. Applicants can receive this certificate after successfully passing the national qualifying exams or graduating from Hankook Broadcasting University. However, nowadays in practice there is no policy for issuing the second grade certificate to elementary school teachers. No explanation of the course can be found in the handbook of the University on Air.

Middle and high school teacher certification

Open but intentional policies to recruit middle and high school teachers from several sectors of society differ from elementary school teacher recruiting. Therefore, there are various routes into the profession for those intending to become middle and high school teachers. One way to be certified as an authentic middle or high school teacher is to graduate from a teacher's university or to major in education at another university. However, another way to become a middle school or high school teacher is to obtain an MA degree from graduate school. Those who major in education at a university or graduate school are required to accumulate 42 credits for exemption from teacher qualifying exams. These major 42 credits have to be related to one's major, including foundation course work. A second grade certificate for middle and high school teachers also exists. When there is intense need for teachers, potential applicants can sit for the national exams. However, currently no exam is planned.

Professional counselling teacher certification

Certified elementary, secondary (including middle school) and special education teachers, with more than three years of teaching experience, can obtain the certificate of a professional counselling teacher after completing counselling teacher training at a graduate school of education. All applicants are required to complete six courses and 14 credits as well as psychological testing, character testing, special child counselling, group counselling, family counselling, vocational counselling, theory and practices of counselling, counselling practicum and case study work, etc. Two different courses for training counselling teachers have been opened at the graduate schools of education.

Teacher appointment examination in Korea

The purpose of examinations is to recruit and select fully qualified and able teachers by objective and fair measures. City or provincial authorities invite and select competent teachers for all schools from kindergarten to high school from those who hold teaching certificates every December by way of open competition. Each local authority has a selection management committee supported by an advisory committee and organised under the authority of the local board of education. The whole processes of recruiting able candidates is tightly controlled by the selection criteria. All of the examining institutes have to follow the decisions of the National Management Committee but may adjust them to regional and district recruitment needs. Generally speaking, teaching posts at any level are very competitive. For example, a ratio of over 20 to 1 for posts in secondary schools occurs every year. There are also a number of additional factors which influence de-facto teacher recruitment in Korea, with an age limit of 40 occasionally being used and English proficiency being significant.

The various in-service training programmes of teachers

In order to improve the quality of professionalism in teaching, the Ministry of Education organises local education committees into a network through which it intends to offer more opportunities for teachers to make much use of in-service training programmes. Universities are also required to take an active role. This kind of training scheme is expected to assure quality in the teaching profession. The objective of this in-service teacher's training programme is to establish a new system for teachers to train themselves according to their professional needs. These needs should vary by career development and life stages. The system also aims to develop not only professional teachers but also socially and politically mature citizens. Teachers should be supported with training programmes and lessened workloads so that they may develop expert teaching skills. The Ministry will select successful teaching models and disseminate them widely. These efforts should come together in enhancing expertise in the teaching profession.

This course is very meaningful in the sense that it gives various training opportunities to teachers and administrators. It can be operated as trainee-oriented courses. It can support the spontaneous participation of teachers and others concerned with training and research. Recently, the Ministry has also included the distance training programmes into the ground plan.

Several institutions are clustered together as training centres under the auspices of city or provincial education committees. Other university-affiliated education centres and private training centres come under the umbrella of the scheme. As of July 2004, there were 11 primary education training institutes, 67 secondary education training institutes, one educational administration training institute, 18 comprehensive education training institutes and 55 distance education training institutes providing training services. Among them, Seoul Education Training Center was equipped with the latest facilities for development and application of specified training programmes. The total number of trainees between March 2003 and February 2005 was approximately 454,050 (http://english.moe.go.kr, Teacher Education and Qualification, 15 December 2006).

Teacher performance is assessed and quantified. These scores or indices can be used to build a more generative framework in order to rationalise the promotion of teachers together with wage scales. An assessment was carried out for participants who spent a full 60 hours or more in training programmes. The distribution curve has a range of 80 to 100 and reflects the performance of teachers with 60 points or more out of a total of 100 points.

To become a vice principal, excellent teachers are retrained and selectively promoted. Likewise, vice principals with leadership and management skills are trained and selectively promoted to principal. To be nominated an educational expert, acting teachers can apply for public tests open to them.

Voluntary professional teacher training

There are various subjects available to teachers for further training. Subjects are basically related to the general objectives of the school curriculum. Teachers applying to these voluntary programmes may not require any certification, but may wish to obtain more professional knowledge in their respective fields. In particular, English teachers in voluntary programmes of 18–60 hours are required to develop and present teaching materials for practical teaching. All English language teachers in Seoul are required to be trained in English conversation (basic and intensive courses) at least once every three years.

Teacher evaluation system

The performance of teachers and vice principals is evaluated every year, but this system has several problems. First, assessments are made only by the principals and the vice principals who manage the schools where teachers being assessed work under their supervision. Second, only performance outcomes are assessed. In order to strengthen teachers' educational capacity, the Ministry of Education is preparing a new scheme for assessing teachers in more objective and formative ways than at present. The scheme may include a system which also assesses school management by the principal. As mentioned above, under the current scheme, assessment reports affect promotion of teachers. The proposed new schemes should more effectively enhance the professional capabilities of teachers and motivate them to undertake training spontaneously. Any evaluation system should work to enrich the expertise of all teachers.

The general background of the new schemes was the recognition shared by the Minister of Education and the general public that enormous demands are emerging for a higher quality of teaching and professionalism of teachers, who must be accountable to the growing interest of people in the contributions education makes to society. This realisation is related to general aspirations for trust in teaching and teacher culture, which people believe should be realised through stable evaluations already tested impartially and appropriately in practical settings of society.

In a survey conducted in 2005, 77.4% of the Korean people agreed on the necessity for developing a teacher evaluation system. The Ministry of Education also found it necessary to provide teachers with self-led retraining opportunities, to enhance the expertise of teachers and to strengthen public education, ultimately improving the educational quality of schools.

It is important to recognise that students and parents should be able to voice their opinions in the process of teacher evaluation. How highly or how much they are satisfied with teaching and teachers' performance can and should be reflected in the assessing processes. In addition to teachers, all principals and vice principals should be assessed so that their sense of professional responsibility is also ensured and enhanced.

As of January 2007, a number of trial evaluations were conducted at a number of schools selected prior to the full implementation of the plan. These trials enabled the Ministry to collect diverse opinions and suggestions for improvement, and consequently to adjust the system to best suit the practical demands of schools. There should be more opportunities for students and parents who offer teachers feedback information from their own perspective on the education they received to appeal to the assessment bodies. In that way, people's expectations for access to high-quality education should grow. By making use of multifaceted peer evaluations and parent–student satisfaction surveys, teachers may be able to create self-led opportunities for capacity building aimed at enhancing their profession.

Conclusion

Nowadays, English plays an important role in the fields of politics, economics, trade, commerce, sightseeing, study abroad and other activities. It is a common language in Asia. English is the first foreign language in South Korea. Due to the development of the economy and globalisation, the emphasis on English is increasing and so many students in South Korea make considerable effort to study English.

As concern with English education becomes more intense, many Asian countries are making an effort to improve nation-centred English education. Many Asian people are using English as an additional language. Asian English has various regional gradations which are not the same as for British or American English.

People are speaking English affected by the culture of their mother tongues. English education in the elementary school curriculum has started already in most Asian countries and regions. From now on, English for specific purposes will be more essential in Asia. Spreading English in Asia does not, however, indicate accepting British or American English as it is, but rearranging English and using it uniquely in different ways. Thus, many countries in which English is not used as a mother tongue are making efforts to improve English education through educational reform.

The roles of English teachers are increasing in importance in school education, also strengthening the value of programmes for English teachers. Although difficulties in English education and teacher education exist, South Korea is trying to improve English education. The importance that the Ministry places on introducing English education at an early age can be seen in their plan to introduce English education in the first grade, two years earlier than originally intended with a pilot programme in the latter half of 2006 through 2007, leading to a full nationwide implementation in 2008. The Korean Education Ministry bases its actions on the belief that 'the quality of education can not exceed the quality of teachers' (2007). Consequently, it implements various policies to improve the quality and capacity of teachers. In order to improve the quality and professionalism of teachers, the Education Ministry is providing training programmes through education offices and universities and is working for quality assurance of the training system which provides various training opportunities. To heighten teachers' educational capacity, the Education Ministry is preparing a new teacher evaluation system that will include principals in the evaluation subject, yet another example of the importance that education and teacher education has for the state.

References

Crystal, D. 1995. *Cambridge encyclopaedia of the English language.* Cambridge: Cambridge University Press.
Crystal, D. 2003. *English as a global language.* Cambridge: Cambridge University Press.
Korean Ministry of Education and Human Resources. 2007. 3 January. http://English.moe.go.kr.
Yano, Y. 2001. World Englishes in 2000 and beyond. *World Englishes, Journal of English as an International and Intranational Language* 20, no. 2: 119–31.

Development of primary English education and teacher training in Korea

Shiga Mikio

Center for International Programme and Exchange, University of Electro-Communications, Tokyo, Japan

Introduction

Introducing English instruction to children as early as elementary school is becoming common in the world today. For example, East Asian countries like Korea and China are teaching English in public elementary schools. In Japan, English is not a compulsory subject in elementary school, but this has always been one of the issues of curriculum reform.

Apart from Hong Kong, most people in East Asia do not use English as their main language in daily life. Though international commercial and other economic activities are increasing in East Asian countries, and though people are travelling internationally and getting accustomed to using English as a communication tool, it still cannot be said that English plays a large role in the daily life of East Asian societies.

Korea, Japan and China have their own language: Korean, Japanese and Chinese, respectively. In each country, it is possible to complete the education system from primary education up to higher education in the host language. These three languages and some ethnic languages in China continue to play the main role in the public education systems of each country as the language of instruction. English has been merely one of the foreign languages which most students learn from secondary school.

A consistent criticism has long existed concerning the outcomes of public English education. It touches upon the fact that the students do not become fluent in English after learning English at school for six or more years. However, in an environment where a language is not used frequently, it is evidently very difficult to become fluent in that language, a fact that has led to an acceptance of the problem. But now, the situation has changed. East Asian countries have started to strive to enhance the students' communication ability in English. The levelling up of their English proficiency is now a national demand. Korea has been advancing along this path with a strong will. How it seeks to build up new English teaching staff should be of interest to the people concerned with language education.

This paper investigates the swift development and implementation of the English education system in Korean elementary schools from the standpoint of Japan, where such progress does not exist. Japanese tend to find the development of English education in Korea astonishing, while Koreans may feel suspicious about the tardy progress in Japan.

I should emphasise that the difference in progress of the education of English between these two countries is not unusual because they have their own history of national education and are also in different circumstances socio-culturally and socio-economically. It is quite normal for them not to have a common curriculum.

However, it is still worthwhile to compare these two countries' educational policies on foreign languages. EU countries have already started discussions to find common guidelines concerning the teaching of foreign languages (Truchot 1994). It will be significant also for East Asian countries to find guidelines, if possible, especially for both Korea and Japan; if international cooperation based on their regional proximity is put into action, they will need each other as counterparts. The important task is to understand how these two countries seek to find a common vision on foreign language education, or even to know whether there is any possibility for a common vision or not.

The actual situation of early English education in Korea is continually reported in the Japanese media as an example which Japan should follow. In this paper, I do not take the same approach. It is not essential to look at linear differences of the development of English education between the two countries. It should be pointed out that grasping the situation without neglecting the social and historical backgrounds is important. Each society has its own background, and the actual situation of English education primarily depends on it. As a result I will introduce the actual situation of English education in Korean elementary schools, focusing mainly on the training of education staff, and analyse it qualitatively.

In 1997, English became a compulsory subject in Korean elementary schools. Therefore, the education of English teachers at the elementary level was accelerated. The training curriculum has been reformed according to the educational objective to enhance the students' oral communication skills in English. In the first section, an outline of the Korean education system and the actual situation of English education in Korea, both public and private, will be introduced. In the second section, the recent reform of the education of English teachers will be explained.

In Korea, coupled with the enhancement of the training of elementary school English teachers, the introduction of English Teacher Assistants is also being reinforced to stimulate lively classroom discussions in English. Similar programmes that invite native English speakers to support classroom activities in language classes are generally seen in other countries, which are intended to raise the children's communicative competence (APLV 2000). The Korean case seems to be under full-scale development now. In the third section, the English Teacher Assistants project in Korea will be described, as well as the other big project, English Learning

Facilities. They both have an important role that complements public English education.

Following the three sections which mainly describe the reinforcement of English teachers, including English Teacher Assistants in Korea, the final section will examine the characteristics of English education in Korean elementary schools *vis-à-vis* the Japanese situation, which is said to lag behind Korea's. As mentioned above, the focus is not on the degree of progress of English education, but on what public schools are actually doing to enhance the students' communicative competence where English is not a vehicle of language in daily life and also on how teachers are preparing for this situation. In this sense the paper is related to a matter of policy on language teacher education (Christ 1997).

English education in Korea

The Korean school system is 6-3-3-4. Compulsory education is nine years from the age of six. Therefore, many students enter high school. The current seventh National Curriculum divided 12 years into two periods according to the arrangement of subjects. Elementary school up to the first year of high school was named 'National Common Basic Curriculum', and the second and third years of high school were named 'Elective Curriculum', which provides students with diverse subjects. In the 'National Common Basic Curriculum', the flexible design of curricula corresponding to the ability of each student is encouraged. This curriculum is also called 'Flexible Level-Differentiated Curriculum' as a whole. The design of different types of flexible curricula is promoted according to the subject and level. As for English, there is the 'Step-by-Step Curriculum' for secondary-level English and the 'In-depth and Supplementary Curriculum' for elementary schools to help promote outstanding students and also help lagging students catch up.

Concerning higher education, the stage of 'universal access' has already passed (see Table 1). It is now the so-called 'post-universal access' stage in an age of declining birth rate. Universities are working toward the reorganisation and innovation of learning contents to compete for more students. Enrolment rates are very high in every stage of the school system. Schools are competing with each other by improving their quality of education.

An important characteristic of Korean education lies in the idea and policy of equalisation. Traditionally, the academic background, including graduating from specific famous schools, plays a big role in Korean society. They have determined quite considerably people's social status or position in companies. Such social structure and the elective function of schools have already been recognised and egalitarian educational reforms have been carried out. One of the most remarkable

Table 1. Enrolment rate in Korea.

Year	1985	1990	1995	2000	2005
Advancement rate of middle school graduates	90.7	95.7	98.5	99.5	99.7
Advancement rate of high school graduates	36.4	33.2	69.3	68.0	82.1

Source: MOE&HRD (2005a).

reforms is the 'no exam entry system' for high schools called Equalisation. But there is criticism levelled against it, in that it causes intense competition at the time of university examinations. Newly established high schools for specific purposes, such as Science High Schools and Foreign Language High Schools, have become elitist institutions, and young people are very busy attending private 'prep' school lessons in order to enter these high schools or to enter good universities.

It is English that most Korean students learn, remarkably, outside of school. We must take English study outside of the public school system into account, but first an outline of the English education in schools will be presented.

As was mentioned previously, English was made a compulsory subject in elementary schools from 1997. Two periods (40 min. per period) per week are allotted for fifth and sixth graders, and one period for third and fourth graders. A policy to make English a compulsory subject for the first and second grades of elementary school from 2008 was announced in 2006 by the Ministry of Education and Human Resource Development (MOE&HRD) (2006a). One of the reasons for this extension was to fill the two-year gap with English and thereby students would be able to continue learning English from the age of kindergarten.

English education in elementary school is comprised of mainly communication-oriented activities, and a set of textbooks and teaching materials is well equipped at schools. As well as regular classes, extracurricular classes are held early in the morning and after class hours under the name of 'Education to Help Nurture Special Abilities and Aptitudes'. These are optional classes and students take them voluntarily. English is arranged quite often.

The students have three English classes (45 min. per period) in a week in the first and second years of middle school and four classes in the third year of middle school and first year of high school (50 min. per period). For the second and third years of high school, the number of lesson hours is not decided based on the 'Elective Curriculum'. It seems that second foreign language education characterises linguistic education in Korean secondary education. It began in high school in 1963 (German, French and Chinese). It became a compulsory subject in 1973 with the expansion of languages offered (German, French, Chinese, Spanish and Japanese). Now it is possible for schools to offer even Russian and Arabic classes, but Japanese, Chinese, German and French are the popular languages (only seven schools offer Arabic classes, 2004). Among them, Japanese classes are the greatest in number, both in terms of students and schools. It is worth noting that Chinese classes are becoming popular while German and French classes are not.

From 2002, middle school students have had the opportunity to take a second foreign language if the school chooses it among the four contemporary subjects (second foreign language, information (computer studies), environment and Chinese letters) as an 'Independent Activity'. These subjects are implemented for the modernisation of the curriculum. Besides regular classes, extracurricular classes for second foreign languages exist.

One cannot find a similar example elsewhere in East Asia where second foreign language education is offered in secondary public schools like this. Many children study English outside of public school. They may take lessons at a language school. Language teachers may visit students' houses. The children may learn English by themselves with some teaching materials. Moreover, it is becoming more common for children to study abroad at a very young age. Children in elementary school or middle school go to English-speaking countries to study English for long or short periods of time.

In many cases, the high expense is placing a severe burden on the family budget. Serious concern exists that intense education which continues even after school is affecting children's healthy progress, physically and mentally. Intense extracurricular education is one of the most serious social problems in Korea right now, with English as the subject occupying the biggest portion of extracurricular education.

Underlying such enthusiasm for English learning is a utilitarian or realistic way of thinking. English ability is connected directly to good jobs and good universities. It is not uncommon for the score of English tests, such as TOEIC, to play a crucial role at the time of a student entering a company. The trend to attach greater importance to English in Korean society advanced with the development of globalisation. In particular, the IMF economic order that was introduced from the end of 1997 with the Asian economic crisis greatly influenced the heightening of the social and psychological status of English. Many Korean companies were reorganised and changed their business customs. The social gap between the rich and poor increased while the Korean economy recovered its vitality as a whole. There is also an economic gap between regions. The rich families in Seoul, especially in the Gangnam district or Seocho district, for example, are able to invest in extracurricular activities for their children far more than other families. The regional gap between cities and villages is also big. English is seen as a very effective means to progress to the upper societal status. There is no sign that the enthusiasm for English learning is fading.

Against this background, the MOE&HRD announced 'Measures to Decrease Private Education Expenses through the Normalisation of Public Education' in February 2004 which stated clearly a policy to undertake educational reforms such as the reform of English education. The gist of the reform can be divided into two: one is expansion of English learning opportunity, and the other is improvement of the quality of English teachers. Reducing excessive expenditures for extracurricular learning lies at the heart of the reform.

In addition, the reform plans for English education were announced in sequence. Following the 'Increasing English Classes Taught in English' that was unveiled in 2000, the MOE&HRD announced the *Comprehensive Five-Year English Education Innovation Plan* in 2005, which would be applied from 2006 to 2010 to further promote communication-oriented English education. It contained the five most important tasks, which are: (i) construction of level-differentiated curriculum for English; (ii) education and control of excellent teaching staff; (iii) reform of classroom activities and evaluation; (iv) reinforcement of the supporting system to activate English education; and (v) expansion of opportunities to speak English.

The situation of English education in Korea has been outlined above. In the following section, an overview of the teacher training system is given, and thereafter, attention is focused on the education of English teachers. They are increasingly requested to have high communication skills in English under these circumstances.

Initial and in-service training of English teachers

Primary teachers are trained in the 11 National Universities of Education, the Korea National University of Education established in 1985 and an eminent private university, Ewha Womans University. Almost all the teachers are graduates of the 11 National Universities of Education.

When English became compulsory in elementary schools, many incumbent teachers were rapidly trained. Since 1996, one year before English became compulsory, some 25,000 teachers have received training in English skills and English teaching methods for about 120 hours every year (cf. the total number of primary teachers is about 157,000, 2004). About 70% of the time in the programme is for the increasing of English skills.

The training programmes are carried out by the local education bureau (Office of Education). Decentralisation is being implemented also in the area of education, accelerated by the reform of the Local Government Act in 1990. Historically, the central government exclusively made the decisions on educational reforms (Kang 2002). A kind of democratisation is in progress and the Office of Education in each metropolitan city and province plays an important role in the management of the school and teacher education.

We can see the importance of English teacher training in all the training programmes by representing the subject's uptake in a ratio, in comparison to other subjects. If we take the example of the Seoul Metropolitan City in 2004 (Figure 1), the ratio of English teacher training is 32% for primary teachers and 41% for secondary teachers (excluding office work training).

The MOE&HRD also implements a long-term English teacher training programme at the national level. A six-month programme is offered to both primary and secondary English teachers. The number of trainees in a year is increasing. There were 200 in 2003 and 2004, 333 in 2005, 406 in 2006 and about 1000 are expected from 2007 to 2015 each year. This means that by 2015 10,000 teachers will be trained under this programme.

However, English training programmes are presumed not to realise what is to be done for communication-oriented English education. Thus, other measures such as the reinforcement of English in university training courses, the introduction and spread of primary English teachers, the employment of English Teacher Assistants and so on have been planned and are being put into practice at present.

As for the training course in the universities, the class hours to enhance students' English ability have increased. Two more native English instructors are assigned to each National University of Education (four native English instructors in total in each university).

Reinforcement of English in the training course may have negative influences on future teachers. Because primary teachers have to teach various subjects with respect to children's overall growth, mastering English is, in a sense, a burden. Besides, primary teachers are the models for the children who use the Korean language. The Korean language is the basis of learning and social life for them. The *raison d'être* of primary teachers might lose significance both practically and symbolically by the inclination to English. Based on this concern, it has been argued that it is the primary English teachers that should be trained instead of English teaching classroom teachers (Chung 2007).

In fact, the number of primary English teachers is actually increasing. They are the teachers who have been trained specially for English education. One-third of the public elementary schools leave all their English classes to English teachers.

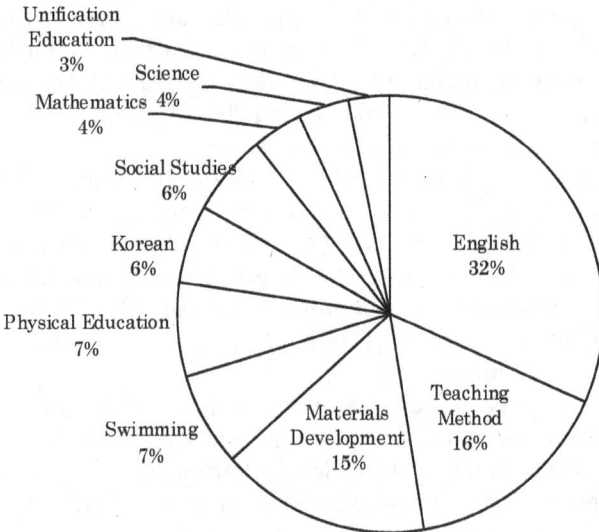

For Elementary School Teachers

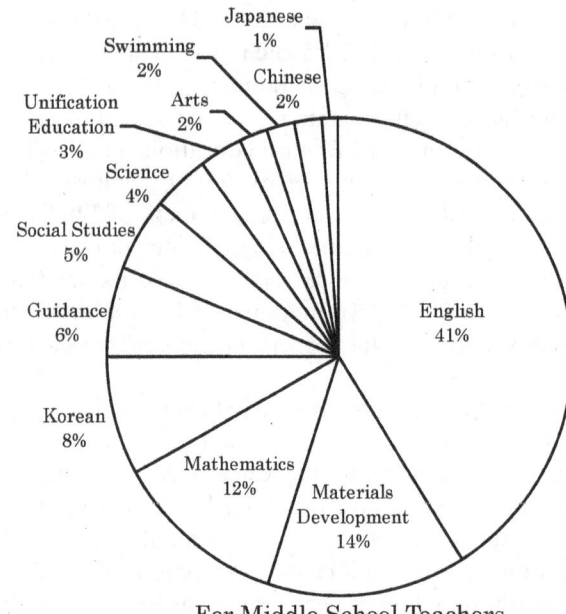

For Middle School Teachers

Figure 1. The content of in-service training programme in Seoul Metropolitan City (2004).

Including them, the percentage of English classes taught by English teachers is 58%, while the classroom teacher teaches English in 41% of elementary schools (2005).

In elementary school, the classroom teacher teaches many subjects, while there are some teachers for specific subjects in each school. The ratio of English teachers among these teachers for specific subjects is high. The total number of teachers for specific subjects is about 12,000, and 4600 are English teachers. This kind of data also show the rapidly growing presence of English in elementary schools.

Recent developments

Along with the measures for developing the teachers' English ability, the system of English Teacher Assistants has been planned and implemented.

There are some programmes being undertaken, such as the nationwide English Programme in Korea (EPIK) and programmes planned and managed by the local Office of Education or local government. The data (MOE&HRD 2006b) show that 1909 English Teacher Assistants were employed as of April 2006. The local programmes (of the Office of Education or local government) invite half of them, the school programme invites one-third and EPIK invites 10% approximately.

The recruitment policy of the EPIK programme, which is seen as a model of other programmes, is as follows. It recruits English Teacher Assistants from six English-speaking countries (USA, Canada, UK, Australia, New Zealand, Ireland). A Bachelor's degree is the minimum requirement for becoming a teacher. The payment system is threefold, ranging from the basic 1.8 million Won (third-level monthly salary) to 2.3 million Won (first-level) for teachers with a teacher's licence, certificate of English ability, experience teaching English or a Master's degree. Once a first-level teacher has worked for the Office of Education for two successive years, s/he will be upgraded to +1 level and be remunerated 2.5 million Won a month.

As a whole, three-fourths are invited from the USA and Canada. As for the ratio of teachers with qualifications, 168 had teacher's licences and 558 had certificates of English ability (TESOL, TEFL) out of 1657 English Teacher Assistants (2006). Regional differences are becoming striking with the advancement of the decentralisation of recruitment of English Teacher Assistants. The average ratio of allocation of English Teacher Assistants is 18.3%, including elementary and secondary schools. Inchon, Seoul, Gyeonggi Do exceed 30% while Ulsan, Jeolla-Buk Do, Gyeongsang-Buk Do do not reach 5% (2006). English Teacher Assistants are placed in schools or public institutions for education. Among the 1909 English Teacher Assistants in April 2006, 781 were in elementary schools, 631 in middle schools, 398 in high schools, 53 in local governments or the Office of Education and 56 in institutions for training. MOE&HRD plans gradually to expand the number of English Teacher Assistants to be able to post them in all middle schools (about 2900) by 2010. MOE&HRD (2005b, 2006c).

Other than the measures to enhance the English ability of teachers and the expansion of English Teacher Assistants mentioned above, measures to place more native English speakers in the English Experience Facilities which are financed and supported by the public sector have not been overlooked.

In Korea, some local governments establish English Experience Facilities where students can visit and use English with native English speakers. Among them, there are extensive constructions on large sites with many buildings. It is a kind of comprehensive holiday area, with the concept of learning English as its main function. These facilities are called 'English Village' and are expected to play a complementary role to public English education. Some facilities were established by a local government and managed by a foundation or the private sector, while others were established and managed by the Office of Education in each metropolitan city and region.

These 'Villages' offer various kinds of programmes such as five-day programmes, holiday programmes and long-term programmes in the summer or winter holidays. They employ English-speaking staff to develop smoothly English experience activities. The biggest 'English Village' is the institution of Paju in Gyeonggi-Do, and about 100 foreign English-speaking people are employed as lecturers or facilitators now. The number is about double the number of Korean teaching staff.

Discussion

As described in the previous three sections, English teachers or teaching staff with higher English ability are more and more needed for public English education in Korea. First, serious consideration is being given to English ability in regard to teacher training. In addition to a focus on primary and secondary English teachers, the policy is one of improving English ability even for other teachers, and the teacher training system is shifting to an English-oriented one.

Second, in-service training for English teachers is also being pushed forward at a fast pace. With the expansion of English education in elementary schools in particular, the ability of primary English teachers has improved as a result of training.

Third, the number of English Teacher Assistants is increasing rapidly in schools, mainly to support classroom activities related to communication in English. Furthermore, they are employed in institutions such as the 'English Village' which are planned and administrated for English experience programmes to complement public English education.

These are the facts that show the Korean characteristics. The three points below are underlined in comparing Korea and Japan.

Social background differences affecting the value of English

English learning fervour, which is sometimes seen as 'excessive', is more intense in Korea than in Japan. The influence of early study abroad is discussed both in terms of national and household economy levels in Korea. In this social situation, the educational policy to meet such a demand for English skills by public education is being planned and advanced. English ability is required of teaching staff and it is being enhanced.

In the larger context, there is a tendency to place importance on English in Korean society. At the time of employment or promotion in companies, English ability is requested or sometimes it is compulsory. Education of English focused on the improvement of communication skills is being advanced under this social background.

On the other hand, there is certainly a tendency to consider English important also in Japan, but it still has not taken concrete form. It does not seem to cover the society as a whole, as is the case in Korea, but functions partially on the part of the people who are pro-English. There are many students who study English after school individually, but not many students go abroad to study English. The situation is not one where the expenditures on English learning impacts on the national budget or even family finances as compared with Korea.

In Japan, a foreign language (in effect English) is a compulsory subject in secondary school, but unlike Korea and many other countries, Japan does not have regular English classes in elementary school excluding private schools. Many elementary schools attempt to organise English experience activities utilising a 'comprehensive learning hour' implemented in 2002, but they are not systematised for raising the English ability over a span of years. In this way, though a plan to make English compulsory in elementary school is discussed here and there, and some public elementary schools in the 'Special Zones for Structural Reform' have started offering regular English classes, profiting from decentralisation and flexible curriculum reform, English education in public elementary schools appears to be 'getting off to a bad start' in Japan on the whole. The social background and the people's attitude toward English vary between the two countries, and consequently there is a difference in their attitude and approach to English education.

The historical background should be noted. Korean people have a close relationship with English-speaking countries such as the US, Canada and Australia through immigration and study abroad programmes. In particular, the influence of the USA has been significant politically and economically since the Liberation in 1945. More than two million Koreans live in the US now, which is more than the number of Koreans living in China or in Japan. As for Japan, its ties with countries through immigration were more divergent. The history of immigration tells us that there are more Japanese immigrants in Brazil than in the US. The Immigration Law in Japan was reformed in 1990 and the Japanese labour market opened up to the descendants of immigrants. There are many Japanese Brazilians and Peruvians in Japan. Its vicinity to English seems to be different also in these respects.

Whether or not the view that 'English is important' in people's social and economic life is accepted might well control the fundamental motive for the promotion of public English education.

Same objective but different educational structures

Though there are differences in their development of primary English education, both countries have the same objective, which is to raise the English communication ability of the students. As mentioned before, conventional English education from the secondary school has failed to produce students who are fluent in English in both Korea and Japan. Speaking and listening are considered to be the most difficult skills to make progress in because of the lack of opportunities to practice in a non-English-speaking society. It is rare in both countries for a student to need to communicate in English in their daily life. Therefore, the low English competence of students is a structural problem rather than a pedagogical problem. When we consider such circumstances, it will be epoch-making for the improvement of students' English communication skills to be considered a sustainable objective of public English education. In this sense, the development of English education in Korea is viewed as a structural change of the English teaching system.

For example, an English Teacher Assistant will be assigned to each Korean middle school by 2010. At first sight this policy is concerned with the pedagogy of English in the sense that classroom work will be invigorated. However, the introduction of English Teacher Assistants to every public middle school is not merely a matter of pedagogy, but a systematic change of the public educational system by way of employing personnel who may not be Korean or speak Korean fluently. In order to enhance the students' English communication skills, the structure of the English teaching system is being revised.

The objective is the same also in Japan, but its system is still stable and Japan seems reluctant to change the structure. The system of English Teacher Assistants started in Japan as a main part of the JET Programme (the Japan Exchange and Teaching Programme) in 1987. Some five thousand English Teacher Assistants are now working in Japan. Without a total plan for English education from elementary to secondary schools, these English Teacher Assistants play a kind of symbolic role for practicing English communication.

Besides the system of English Teacher Assistants, the initial and in-service training system in Korea can also be taken up as examples of structural change. The purpose is to make (future) teachers capable of managing English classes in English. To build up the students' English competence, Korea seeks to change the surroundings of English learning students into an English-speaking environment as much as possible. If the word 'pedagogy' implies the educational power of environment, we may say this change is pedagogical. If 'pedagogy' tends to make us think about the method of teaching, we should say this change is structural.

In Japan, some public schools authorised by the 'Special Zones for Structural Reform' have regular communicative English classes. Official reform plans to invigorate English education have been announced, with even an English immersion school opened in 2005. Although these movements exist, the structural change has not occurred nationally as in Korea.

Strategy for equality of learning opportunity: actively in Korea, passively in Japan

It is clear that the Korean English education policy aims to minimise the gap in English learning opportunity. English experience facilities are developed as part of this egalitarian policy. We can see here an idealistic vision of a policy of equality of opportunity. English is seen as a vitally necessary condition in the prevailing social context of Korea. It could even be said that it is officially recognised. So, the public education system has to guarantee education. However, this aim has not yet been realised and it seems difficult to realise this fully even in the future. The recruitment of English Teacher Assistants and the creation of English Villages are expansion plans of English education opportunity, which are advanced by local educational administration. Decentralising education expands various possibilities for public English education plans while regional differences are produced. Furthermore, the rich will not stop the expansion of their own learning opportunities. It may pour money more and more into extracurricular lessons. The prospect of seeing the difference minimise is slim. On the wave of economic liberalisation and administrative decentralisation, it is difficult to find equal opportunity in society.

There are a few English experience learning institutions similar to the 'English Village' in Japan. They were not founded by the public sector. Private enterprises own them and offer English learning opportunities in the ambiance of authenticity. It is, so to speak, an aristocratic institution to offer an English experience opportunity of scarce value rather than an institution for the common people to spread English experience opportunities.

The difference of opportunities for English study is expanding also in Japan under the trend of the privatisation of education. Some students study English eagerly in private, while others neglect learning in and of itself. This difference is not clearly recognised as a serious social matter in Japan. This is a private matter after all. Unlike Korea, where they address the issue by public education measures, Japan seems to avoid the issue of the growing inequalities and differences by hesitating to implement English in primary education.

If English education is introduced into public elementary school, and its target is the improvement of English conversation skills, it is expected that the struggle for resources (to provide the opportunity to practice English, lessons with English-speaking partner or lecturer, learning materials for self-learning, etc.) will be intensified. The introduction of English into elementary school will lead not only to the expansion of English learning opportunities but also to the expansion of inequality of English learning opportunities. In passing it is worth noting that though the structure is different, this is also a problem to overcome for the English education policy in China (Hu 2003).

Conclusion

The classroom teacher has mainly assumed the responsibility for educational practice in school systems traditionally. This principle does not change fundamentally, but there is certainly expansion in the scene of English education in Korea. Team-teaching with English Teacher Assistants and learning in the English experience facilities are changing the traditional way of education. The English teacher training system is also changing. Attaching greater importance to the ability of English use, initial and in-service training programmes are being developed.

As discussed above, the social backgrounds differ from each other in Korea and Japan. Each country takes different approaches to strive towards developing equal opportunities. In spite of these differences, both countries take a common approach toward the development of the English education system by attaching greater importance to English ability. This is related to the basic common social background that both countries do not use English in daily life. Both countries have to prepare English communication settings in order for students to be able to practice their English fully so as to enhance their communication skills.

In the wider context of primary education, the development of English education seems to be creating two problems. One concerns the basis of primary education that is in charge of basic national education. The development of English education focuses on the specific skill of English while primary education is basically created as an all-round education. As to what part of primary education should be occupied by English education is up for discussion. Actually, as soon as the plan to start English education from the first grade was announced, quite a few opponents appeared and lodged criticisms. English is just a subject among other subjects, so it needs to be balanced with others.

The other concerns literacy education in the broader sense. This point is to be considered from two viewpoints: the viewpoint of balance with other languages and the viewpoint of legitimacy of skill training.

First, a concern exists that English education will influence the main language (Korean and Japanese). When debates concerning English as a public language or the early start of English education in elementary school occurred journalistically or academically in Korea, some argued that early English education would worsen the condition of Korean language education (Kim et al. 1998). In Japan, comments in favour of 'Japanese first' restrain the English compulsory movement in elementary school.

Second, there is the issue of balance with the languages of the countries nearby or of immigrants. Neither Korea nor Japan is an English-speaking country. This does not mean these are monolingual societies. Inner regional differences exist. The fact is that the society and schools are becoming more multi-linguistic with the increase of new residents. The international movement of the labour force and international marriages are changing the society. It is possible to argue that such languages should be taken preference in literacy education based upon the educational methodology which seeks the theme to teach in the real context of students.

Another viewpoint is legitimacy of skill training. In Japan, the Ministry of Education, Culture, Sports, Science and Technology (MEXT) has taken a comprehensive approach to English learning in elementary school that does not pursue English skill training and attach greater importance to understanding internationalisation. Because of this, insufficient time for English skill training in elementary school is leading to the accumulation of practices of language awareness education. Furthermore, it has been claimed that actual English activity would change the rigid school culture in Japan (Matsukawa 2004). It seems important to reconsider how early English education is organised from the viewpoint of English skill training and language awareness education. It must reflect the policy of the training of teachers. The necessity of teaching staff with high English competence is just the consequence of the respect for skill training. We have another choice of promoting language awareness education. Then, the English teacher training system would be reconsidered comprehensively together with the teacher training systems of other subjects in order to build a balanced primary language education.

In East Asian countries, the reforms of English education were centred on how to raise students' communication skills in English. With this common single purpose, they are able to share the common language vision. Starting from this restricted collaboration or competitiveness, East Asian countries may try to seek a common guideline on foreign language education.

References

APLV (l'Association des Professeurs de Langues Vivantes de l'Enseignement Public). 2000. *Les Langues Modernes*, 4. Strasbourg: NATHAN.
Christ, H. 1997. Language policy in teacher education. In *Encyclopedia of language and education*, ed. R. Wodak and D. Corson. Netherlands: Kluwer Academic.
Chung, K.Y. 2007. English education and teacher training in elementary school in Korea. In *Comparative study on early start of English and second language education in Japan and Korea*, ed. Shiga. Tokyo: Seiko-sya.

Hu, G. 2003. English language teaching in China: Regional differences and contributing factors. *Journal of Multilingual and Multicultural Development* 24, no. 4: 290–318.

Kang, S.W. 2002. Democracy and human rights education in South Korea. *Comparative Education* 38, no. 3: 315–25.

Kim, M.S. et al. 1998. 초등학교 영어교육과 민족어의 장래 [Future of primary English education and national language]. Seoul: Korea University Press.

Matsukawa, R. 2004. 小学校英語活動の現在から考える[Thinking from the present English activity in elementary school]. In 小学校での英語教育は必要か. [English education in elementary school: Necessary or not?], ed. Otsu. Tokyo: Keio University Press.

MOE&HRD. 2005a. *Brief statistics on Korean education.* Seoul: Korean Government.

MOE&HRD. 2005b. 영어교육활성화 5개년 종합대책 [Comprehensive five-year plan for the activation of English education] (2006–2010). Seoul: Korean Government.

MOE&HRD. 2006a. Second five-year national human resource development plan (2006–2010). Seoul: Korean Government.

MOE&HRD. 2006b. 영어교육 혁신방안 정책참고자료 (Policy information on innovation strategy for the English education). Seoul: Korean Government.

MOE&HRD. 2006c. 원어민 영어보조교사 관련 자료 (Documents on English teacher assistants) (1–3). Seoul: Korean Government.

Truchot, C. ed. 1994. *Le Plurilinguisme Européen: Théories et Pratiques en Politique Linguistique.* Paris: Editions Champion.

Educational reform and teacher education in Vietnam

Takashi Hamano

Ochanomizu University, Tokyo, Japan

Given the influence of the international movement to promote 'Education for All', the qualitative improvement of basic education has become a critical issue in Vietnam. The country already achieved a net enrolment ratio of 95% in primary education in 2000 and 97.5% in 2005, signalling that it has virtually attained universal primary education. With the quantitative expansion accomplished, and with the attainment of universal primary education in its final stage, the improvement of quality has become the country's key policy challenge.

The central issue for improving the quality of education in Vietnam is the effective implementation of the new curriculum introduced in 2002. Teacher education is the key in accomplishing this task. Teachers must learn new teaching content and methods so that they can grow out of the conventional type of teaching, and 'teacher education' needs to be upgraded so that they can acquire such new teaching methods.

Primary education is the focus of this paper. After reviewing the situation of primary school teachers in Vietnam, I describe the challenges faced by teacher education in the area of primary education as well as the policy of the Vietnamese government. This is followed by an analysis of the type of international assistance that is given in terms of the challenges faced by teacher education in Vietnam. Lastly, the future tasks of international assistance are discussed.

Teachers in Vietnam

Before discussing teacher education, let us first explain the situation of Vietnamese teachers. Table 1 shows enrolment, number of teachers, and the pupil–teacher ratio (PTR) by region. The table shows no significant differences among regions in terms of the PTR, though it tends to be lower in regions such as the North East and North West, where there are many mountainous and remote areas.

As seen in Table 1, while PTR is currently at a level of about 28, from a time-series perspective it has declined in the past 20 or so years. Table 2 shows changes in enrolment, number of teachers, and PTR from 1981 to 1999. PTR, which was 39.6 in 1981–1982, declined gradually, and fell sharply particularly in the latter half of the 1990s. The reason for this, among other factors, is that the number of children began to decline in the latter half of the 1990s, while the number of teachers grew dramatically, at least during the past 20 years. Looking merely at the PTR, we may well be able to say that the education environment has improved.

Let us now focus our attention on the internal composition of the teaching profession. Table 3 shows the ratios of female, ethnic minority, and government-funded teachers (whose salaries are paid by the government) at the national level.

First, the ratio of female teachers is 78.3%. I have visited numerous primary schools since 2000 and found that in most primary schools, the majority of teachers were women and that, in some cases, all were women, except the principal. Therefore, the statistics showing that female teachers account for nearly 80% of all Vietnamese teachers accords with what I saw during the field survey. The reasons given for the high ratio of female teachers include men who do not find teaching attractive due to the low salaries of primary school teachers, and that teaching offers women jobs they can continue in their own communities, as there is virtually no rotation. However, looking more closely at the regional distribution, the ratios of female teachers are higher in the Red River Delta and other areas, which are relatively urbanised and have higher economic standards, while in North West and Mekong River Delta, where harsh living conditions persist, the ratio is lower. The ratio of female teachers in Mekong River Delta is just 57.4%, a remarkably low figure compared to the national level.

The ratio of minority teachers is about 10% at the national level, but the figure varies greatly among regions. In North West, which has the highest ratio of minority teachers, it is 43.5% as opposed to just 0.2% in Red River Delta. Although this certainly reflects the ethnic makeup of the respective regions, the table, coupled with Table 1, indicates that PTR is also lower in areas where the ratio of minority teachers is high. This can be explained by the geographical reality that ethnic minorities live primarily in mountainous and/or remote areas.

The far right column of Table 3 shows the ratio of government-funded teachers. In primary education, most teachers receive salaries from the government, but when the government's funding is too scarce to employ a sufficient number of teachers, some teachers receive salaries from local finance (IIEP 2001). The ratio of government-funded teachers is 94.1%, indicating that nearly all teachers are paid by the government, but there are areas, such as the Central Highlands region, where the ratio of government-funded teachers is below 90%. A number of factors are important for understanding why the ratio of government-funded teachers varies among regions. First, the region's ability or lack of ability to locally finance the employment of teachers is important. In other words, when the region's economic standards are low, or the local population is unwilling to pay teachers' salaries, it is

Table 1. Enrolment, number of teachers, PTR by region (2001).

	Enrolment	Number of teachers	PTR
Whole country	9,751,431	347,833	28.0
Red River Delta	1,790,735	63,926	28.0
North East	1,224,560	52,272	23.4
North West	342,342	16,049	21.3
North Central Coast	1,455,050	50,370	28.9
South Central Coast	878,484	28,677	30.6
Central Highlands	690,174	22,514	30.7
Northeast South	1,339,325	43,655	30.7
Mekong River Delta	2,030,761	70,370	28.9

Source: MOET (2002a).

Table 2. Enrolment, number of teachers, PTR by region (1981–1999).

	1981–1982	1990–1991	1994–1995	1997–1998	1998–1999
Enrolment	8,092,071	8,862,292	10,431,337	10,431,337	10,247,576
No. of teachers	204,104	252,413	288,173	324,431	336,294
PTR	39.6	35.1	36.2	32.2	30.5

Sources: Socialist Republic of Vietnam (1995), National Committee for EFA Assessment (1999).

impossible to use local finance for this purpose. Consequently, the number of teachers paid through local finance may well be greater in regions with high economic standards. However, there is no distinct correlation between economic standards and the ratio of teachers based on local finance. This is because regions with high economic standards, which are financially well off by definition, are able to secure teachers without using local finances. In the meantime, there are programmes

Table 3. Ratios of female, ethnic minority, and government-funded teachers (2001).

	Number of teachers	Ratios of female teachers	Ratios of ethnic minority teachers	Ratios of government-funded teachers
Whole country	347,833	78.3	10.3	94.1
Red River Delta	63,926	89.7	0.2	94.1
North East	52,272	84.8	30.1	92.5
North West	16,049	73.9	43.5	96.2
North Central Coast	50,370	84.9	9.5	97.8
South Central Coast	28,677	76.2	2.5	95.6
Central Highlands	22,514	81.2	16.9	88.1
Northeast South	43,655	81.5	1.8	95.1
Mekong River Delta	70,370	57.4	4.1	92.6

Source: MOET (2002a).

Table 4. PTR, ratios of female teachers, and ethnic minority teachers in Bac Giang (2004).

Districts	Number of teachers	PTR	Ratios of female teachers	Ratios of ethnic minority teachers
1. Son Dong	632	15.5	78.3%	27.7%
2. Luc Ngan	1100	24.0	80.8%	13.3%
3. Luc Nam	1209	18.3	75.4%	4.1%
4. Yen The	518	18.4	87.6%	12.0%
5. Lang Giang	988	18.9	90.9%	1.4%
6. Yen Dung	837	19.4	77.1%	0.2%
7. Viet Yen	725	20.6	88.0%	0.4%
8. Hiep Hoa	980	21.1	84.6%	0.2%
9. Tan Yen	850	18.0	86.1%	1.4%
10. Bac Giang Town	269	30.6	98.1%	0.4%
Total	8108	20.0	83.3%	5.7%

Source: Questionnaire survey in DOET, Bac Giang.

to allocate public subsidies preferentially to poverty-struck regions, which help them to employ teachers. As such, poor regions or those with higher ratios of ethnic minorities also have relatively higher ratios of government-funded teachers. Consequently, regions with high economic standards and poor regions alike have a higher ratio of government-funded teachers, destroying any correlation that might have been found between economic standards and the ratio of government-funded teachers. And yet, in regions that, despite their low economic standards, are unable to receive adequate subsidies for some reason, or where the size of the subsidy itself is insufficient, the ratio of government-funded teachers is low.

Table 4 provides more detailed district-wise data on the PTR, ratio of females, ethnic minority teachers, etc. The data obtained for the paper from DOET of Bac Giang Province are believed to be of value because it is difficult to obtain district-wise data in Vietnam. As the table shows, the ratio of ethnic minority teachers varies considerably even within Bac Giang Province, which consists of 10 districts. Further, the PTR and ratio of female teachers vary widely. For instance, Son Dong District has a relatively high ratio of ethnic minority teachers (27.7%), whereas its ratio of female teachers is low (78.3%). In such areas, the schools tend to be smaller, with a greater number of satellite schools, resulting in a low pupil-to-teacher ratio (15.5). In contrast, in Bac Giang Town, an urban area within the province, the ratio of ethnic minority teachers is extremely low (0.4%), while the ratio of female teachers is very high (98.1%). This shows that female teachers prefer to work in urban areas with relatively good living conditions, and that in urban areas, school size tends to be bigger, leading to a higher pupil-to-teacher ratio.

One of the biggest problems in Vietnam is that teachers are reluctant to take posts in rural areas. Attempts are being made to recruit teachers locally in order to eliminate the understaffing in mountainous and/or remote areas. And yet, it is difficult to secure competent teachers in remote places. Despite the higher salaries teachers receive in remote areas thanks to special allowances (said to be 30–50% of the salary), teachers are still very reluctant to move to such places. This is because the cost of living in remote areas is high due to extra travel costs required for purchasing daily necessities as well as to the lack of opportunities for side work, signifying that life is poorer and more difficult. Another major reason for the understaffing in remote and/or mountainous areas is the different linguistic and cultural environments, as ethnic minorities prevail in such areas. Personnel affairs are handled very rigidly, and there are virtually no transfers of teachers. Teachers can submit a request for transfer to another workplace for family-related or other reasons, but such relocations seldom take place in reality. This is important for understanding the quantitative and qualitative problems with teachers in rural areas.

The Education Law of Vietnam 1988 stipulates, 'The State adopts policies of rotating teachers working in areas with exceptionally difficult socio-economic conditions, encourages teachers and give preferences to teachers in areas with advantageous conditions to go and work in areas with exceptionally difficult socio-economic conditions, creating conditions for teachers in these areas to feel reassured in their work' (Article 72). In reality, however, the 'preferences' described in this article has not been sufficient to make the number of teachers in remote areas adequate.

Introduction of the new curriculum and learning of new teaching methods

Vietnam has basically achieved the quantitative expansion of its primary education, and its policy focus is now shifting to qualitative improvements. The centrepiece of the qualitative improvement of the education in Vietnam is the effective implementation of the new curriculum that was introduced in 2002. In Vietnam, as part of the educational reform, a new curriculum is being introduced that mandates 35 weeks a year, amounting to 165 weeks in the five years of primary education (MOET 2001). The new curriculum was introduced starting in September 2002 and has been implemented in phases, for grade 1 in 2002 and for grade 2 in 2003. By 2006, the new curriculum will cover all the grades. Prior to its introduction, there were three types of curriculum (165 weeks, 120 weeks, and 100 weeks over five years), based on the circumstances of each region. However, the new curriculum mandates a uniform 165 weeks of schooling throughout the country, and schools that in the past adopted 120 or 100 weeks of classes are required to move to the 165 weeks curriculum.

Under the new curriculum, six subjects are obligatory for grades 1–3, and nine subjects for grades 4 and 5. In addition to Vietnamese, arithmetic, and science, the new curriculum makes compulsory the subjects of health and physical education and art (drawing and manual arts), which in the past were not often taught. In addition to these mandatory subjects, foreign languages, information, and extracurricular activities can be incorporated as optional subjects in higher grades (MOET 2002b).

Another significant characteristic of the new curriculum is the promotion of 'child-centred learning'. Unlike the conventional teaching method adopted in Vietnamese primary schools, where teachers unilaterally impart knowledge to children, the new curriculum places children, the learners, in the centre of the learning process. The new curriculum aspires for a teaching method that encourages children to engage in thinking, class participation, and problem-solving. Textbooks have also been subjected to major revisions to reflect these perspectives. For example, many illustrations and pictures have been adopted to make the textbooks more appealing. Further, contents that were redundantly addressed by multiple subjects have been reorganised with a clearer focus on the knowledge that should be imparted. In the meantime, the amount of time devoted to having children think about how to utilise their knowledge in the real world and everyday life was dramatically increased.

It is evident from various policy documents (Socialist Republic of Vietnam 2001, 2002, 2003) that the introduction of this new curriculum is the centrepiece of the qualitative improvement of education in Vietnam. Teacher education is the key to achieving this task. More specifically, in order to introduce effectively the new curriculum, first, it is important for teachers to learn new teaching content and methods. In addition, 'teacher education' needs to be improved to allow them to learn new teaching methods. Second, educational conditions should be developed and improved with a view toward the implementation of the new curriculum. Specifically, a 'transition from a two-shift system to full-day schooling' has to be realised in order to secure the required number of classes. The implementation of the new curriculum will be impossible if the required number of classes is not secured. In order to secure the required number of classes, either the work system of teachers, who in the past commonly worked half days, must change or additional teachers need to be hired. Even today, two-shift schooling is conducted in many schools, and in fact is hampering the effective implementation of the new curriculum.

The introduction of the new curriculum poses two challenges to teacher education. The first is the need for teachers to learn the new content and the second is to learn the new education/teaching methods. On the first task, subjects such as music, physical education, and drawing and handicrafts (art), which were not taught in the past, have been added in the new curriculum. In addition, the teaching content of major subjects has been significantly increased for every grade. Gaining knowledge about these new contents and studying educational tools for this end will be a great challenge.

The second, learning the educational methods, is an even more important and difficult challenge. Teacher training in Vietnam was traditionally influenced by the French intellectualism-oriented education, with the teaching of a series of systematised pieces of knowledge in print being considered the basis of education. Particularly in Vietnam, teachers traditionally provided pupils with textbook contents unilaterally in classes, and this in turn engendered an emphasis on rote memorisation and a passive learning attitude. Teacher training also placed a focus on knowledge about the subjects and on the Ho Chi Minhism (Pham Minh Hac 1998), while little attention was paid to 'teaching methods'. The concept of the new curriculum, which is currently being introduced, seems to have been developed against this backdrop. It is presumably due to these considerations that MOET (Ministry of Education and Training) is also placing an emphasis on child-centred learning. New textbooks are laid out like workbooks so that children can write in them. Furthermore, a set of teaching materials (toolbox) has been made available so that classes can be handled in an ingenious manner. Judging from these tools, it seems that the new teaching methods are certainly well on their way to introduction. Voluntary workshops by teachers are already taking place. Additional training will be needed to make the new teaching methods and the usage of the teaching materials more effective.

Upgrading teachers' skills

Upgrading teachers' skills is important for allowing them to learn the new teaching methods in line with the new curriculum. The current teacher training policy in Vietnam focuses on upgrading the skills of primary school teachers (Tran Kieu 2002).

In this context, I will make a few comments on the teacher training system in Vietnam. Teacher Training Institutes (TTIs) train teachers for pre-school, primary, and secondary school levels. A TTI is established in every province, and the enrolment limit for each TTI is determined at the provincial level, and authorised by MOET. The Education Law of Vietnam stipulates 12 years of general education plus two years of teacher training education (12+2) as the minimum academic requirement for teachers. In this regard, however, it is only a minimum requirement and there are higher qualifications.

For example, for primary school teachers, attending a two-year course at a TTI after completing 12 years of general education (12+2) is the minimum standard in the Vietnamese qualification system. In addition, a three-year course (12+3) and four-year course (12+4) are also available. There is also a teacher's qualification for those with bachelor degrees. In Vietnam today, 12+2 is deemed the state norm. However, it is said that 12+2 teachers, while meeting the norm, will lack qualifications and abilities when the present educational reform gets underway, and MOET is making efforts to raise the levels to 12+3 or 12+4, or even to the university bachelor level. TTIs are gradually shifting toward the university level.

For example, in Bac Giang Province, the data for 2001/2002 include no '5+3' teachers, 104 '9+3' teachers, 6311 '12+2' teachers, 1205 '12+3 or 12+4' teachers, and 70 classified as 'other'. At that time, 12+2 teachers accounted for 80% or more of total, but at the time of our field investigation in 2003, in-service teacher training was being conducted at the TTI to upgrade their qualifications to 12+3. In some provinces, there are still 9+3 or 5+3 teachers, and in provinces with many such teachers, the quality of education has been a big problem. MOET needs urgently to upgrade the qualifications of teachers at the 9+3 or lower levels. Some provinces have recommended that such teachers retire.

In order to gain a more detailed understanding of teachers' academic records, I conducted a questionnaire survey of all the provinces in 2005. Table 5 shows the findings from the 35 provinces from which valid answers were received (the provinces are listed in ascending order in terms of the ratio of teachers at the 9+3 or lower level). Let us first look at the 9+3 or lower levels. There are major differences among the provinces, ranging from Da Nang and Hai Duong with no 9+3 teachers at all, to Ca Mau where 86.2% of the teachers are of 9+3 level or lower. Looking at 12+3 or higher, the difference is also considerable, ranging from 77.2% in Ha Noi to 5.1% in Ca Mau. This big regional gap seems to derive from the social and economic backgrounds of the provinces, their education policy and the extent the policy trickles down to the rank and file, and the degree of intensity of guidance from the central government (MOET).

Challenges facing in-service training (INSET) in Vietnam
Current status of INSET

As was pointed out in the preceding section, the present policy is to hold down the training and recruitment of new teachers and instead focus on upgrading the

Table 5. Academic background of teachers by province (2005) (%).

	12+4 or more	12+3	12+2	9+3	Under 9+3	9+3 or less	12+3 or more
Da Nang	17.3	32.8	49.9	0.0	0.0	0.0	50.1
Hai Duong	11.0	32.4	56.6	0.0	0.0	0.0	43.4
Nghe An	13.5	19.1	67.2	0.2	0.0	0.2	32.6
Thai Binh	9.6	45.7	43.8	0.9	0.0	0.9	55.3
Thai Nguyen	15.2	14.8	68.7	1.2	0.0	1.2	30.0
Ha Noi	18.2	59.0	21.5	1.2	0.0	1.3	77.2
Ha Nam	3.3	49.4	45.1	2.2	0.0	2.2	52.7
Ha Tay	18.7	52.3	26.7	2.3	0.0	2.3	71.0
Quang Nam	4.0	43.9	49.1	1.8	1.1	2.9	47.9
Quang Binh	6.8	19.5	70.5	3.2	0.0	3.2	26.3
Vinh Phuc	16.5	13.1	65.4	4.2	0.9	5.0	29.6
Thanh Hoa	10.4	13.1	70.0	6.5	0.0	6.5	23.5
Hoa Binh	5.6	13.5	73.4	7.1	0.4	7.5	19.1
Bac Kan	4.0	11.2	77.3	6.6	1.0	7.5	15.2
Yen Bai	2.9	31.3	51.6	0.0	14.1	14.1	34.3
Phu Yen	6.7	23.3	55.1	13.7	1.2	14.9	30.0
Binh Duong	20.8	19.6	42.8	16.8	0.0	16.8	40.5
Bac Giang	2.4	15.2	64.7	2.6	15.2	17.7	17.6
B. Ria-V. Tau	2.6	5.3	71.8	20.3	0.0	20.3	7.9
Dak Lak	8.0	4.0	66.7	7.6	13.6	21.3	12.1
Dong Thap	2.3	31.9	44.2	18.6	3.0	21.6	34.2
Dong Nai	3.0	3.6	66.9	25.3	1.1	26.5	6.6
Cao Bang	3.2	4.1	63.1	22.4	7.2	29.6	7.3
Long An	7.5	18.9	42.9	25.1	5.7	30.8	26.4
An Giang	5.3	22.7	33.6	36.7	1.8	38.4	27.9
Bac Lieu	11.3	11.6	37.4	39.3	0.4	39.7	22.9
Ninh Thuan	2.0	20.5	36.1	36.8	4.5	41.4	22.5
Binh Thuan	1.9	5.0	51.1	35.2	6.6	41.9	7.0
Lai Chau	2.3	10.6	38.7	44.3	4.1	48.4	12.9
Gia Lai	7.5	10.8	33.2	42.9	5.6	48.5	18.3
Lao Cai	0.8	5.5	42.3	47.1	4.3	51.4	6.3
Kon Tum	18.4	2.3	20.3	47.5	11.5	59.0	20.7
Tay Ninh	2.4	17.0	20.5	60.1	0.1	60.2	19.3
Kien Giang	12.0	0.0	20.3	59.3	8.4	67.7	12.0
Ca Mau	4.5	0.7	8.7	84.9	1.2	86.2	5.1

qualifications and abilities of existing teachers through INSET. INSET in Vietnam includes summer training, qualification improvement training, demo lesson training, and in-school training.

Summer training

The training, which is conducted making use of the summer vacation, has been implemented in conjunction with the introduction of the new curriculum. Teachers in charge of grades 1 and 2 were trained in 2002 and in 2003, respectively, and in each year, the target grade of the training will rise. The training takes place over approximately 20 days from July to August covering all the subjects included in the new curriculum. There are two kinds of summer training. One is conducted at the central level, with the participation of provincial and BOET representatives. The other is at the district level, with the participation of every teacher (of the target grade) within the district.

Qualification improvement training: intensive training conducted at TTIs

For primary education, the objective is to upgrade the qualification from 12+2 to 12+3. The expenses are borne by the trainees themselves. The training is conducted on weekends. The training period is one to two years and in the case of Bac Giang Province, it is said to continue for 18 months.

'Demo lessons' given by supervisors

The supervisor of each district visits primary schools to conduct demonstration lessons. After the lesson, a meeting is organised to exchange views about the lesson. Taking Bac Giang Province as an example, there are 55 supervisors within the province (five from each of the 10 districts of the province and five from DOET [the provincial Department of Education and Training]) and each supervisor conducts a demo lesson in the district under his or her charge. Several teachers from neighbourhood schools attend, observing the lesson and participating in the discussion.

In-school training

Teachers voluntarily conduct a demo lesson, exchange views on the lesson, etc., in their schools. In some schools, the training is conducted regularly, and in others on an irregular basis.

The challenges for INSET

As described above, INSET has been implemented in Vietnam to a certain degree. However, in view of the need for the acquisition of the new teaching methods under the new curriculum, or more broadly in view of competency upgrading, the following challenges have to be considered.

Establishing a regular training system

Upgrading teachers' competency requires a scheme that enables every teacher to participate regularly and continuously in training. At present, demo lessons are given by supervisors on weekends, but not every teacher can attend the demo lessons. Furthermore, schools differ in the implementation of in-school training. Some engage enthusiastically in in-school training, while others have no interest whatsoever. In other words, as things stand now, a training system in which 'every teacher can take part' 'on a regular basis' is still unavailable in Vietnam and consideration must be given to how such a system can be established.

Practical training

Currently, teacher training in Vietnam is primarily carried out in lecture style. This is true not only with INSET but also with pre-service training, and this poses another challenge to teacher education. Although teaching practice training such as the demo lessons given by supervisors as described earlier is implemented, summer training and qualification upgrading are largely done in lecture style and with an orientation on theory. This is because the faculty of the TTIs and teacher training colleges are strongly theory-oriented, and this is reflected in the training content. However, what is required of Vietnamese teachers of today is not theory, such as 'what exactly is child-centred learning?' but 'how to implement it in actual lessons'. The future challenge therefore is to increase practical teacher education with the help of international aid.

Implementation of school administrative staff training

Training for principals, assistant principals, and other school administrative staff is also included in the 'Education for All Action Plan', a programme component for the qualitative improvement of education. Effective school studies have demonstrated that better school management and administration enhance educational effects. School administrative staff members have a great role to play in planning INSETs, transition to full-day schooling, etc., as well as in developing and improving the educational environment, including the development of annual school plans, management of teachers' work, and control of educational quality. In addition, communicating with parents and local communities (organising Parents' Associations, publication of school papers) is also an important task of school administrative staff. Furthermore, in rural areas where many schools have satellite schools, administrative staff members play a critical role as they have to manage the satellite schools and teacher staffing there. At present, there is virtually no training for school administrative staff on these matters, and this is a matter for future consideration.

International aid for teacher training

Given the Vietnamese teachers and teacher education situation, what kind of international aid is being provided? In the 2000s, there was an increase in international aid to Vietnam to achieve the EFA (Education for All). In primary education, international aid has been provided in various fields including the construction of schools, curriculum development, education plans, and teacher education (MOET and JICA 2002; World Bank 2001). In the following section, I will discuss major aid with regard to teacher education projects.

The World Bank

As Vietnam has nearly accomplished universal primary education and is shifting its focus to qualitative improvement, the World Bank is providing support to teachers.

The World Bank's Primary Teacher Development Project (PTDP) supports teachers directly. It is being implemented in 10 target provinces starting in 2002 and is scheduled to continue until 2007. Specific activities include, first, the development of teacher professional standards. These standards, called a 'teacher profile', deal with what professional competence teachers need to acquire and what should be the criteria for evaluating teachers, and are to be used as evaluation criteria in teacher training. The second is the development of teacher training materials and the implementation of the training programmes that utilise these tools. Assessing the needs and specifying the content of training packages, institutional strengthening of teacher training colleges, provinces, districts, programme coordination, capacity strengthening, monitoring, etc., are included (World Bank 2000). The programmes incorporate Active Teaching Learning (ATL), a teaching method that emphasises independent thinking on the part of children. With regard to the training method, key trainers are first selected at the provincial level, and trained. They then return to their districts or schools, where they distribute what they have learned. This is the so-called cascading system, and the Belgian project described later adopted this method.

Belgian Technical Corporation

The Belgian Technical Corporation (BTC) implemented teacher training projects for primary and secondary education for seven provinces in the northern mountainous area (LaiChau, LaoCai, Son La, Ha Giang, Cao Bang, Tuyen Quang, Lang Son) from 1999 to 2003. The target group comprised 13 teacher trainers, one training institute director, and one training school director per province, totalling 105 target trainees in seven provinces. These trainees received training, and upon their return to their respective provinces, trained other teachers by distributing the content of what they had learned.

Following this, BTC launched a primary and lower secondary teacher education project (both pre-service training and in-service training) planned for 2005–2009 in 14 provinces in the northern mountainous area including the seven target provinces of the prior project. It is entitled 'Project for Improving Pre- and In-service Training of Primary and Lower Secondary Teachers in the Northern Highlands of Vietnam'. The project consists of teacher education with a focus on learning Active Teaching Learning (ATL), a method that fits with the new curriculum.

Japan International Cooperation Agency (JICA)

Japan is implementing an 'In-service Teacher Improvement Programme'. This INSET-oriented programme began in 2004 and was scheduled to continue until 2007. Its objective is to develop an effective trial model of the new curriculum in targeted pilot provinces. It is designed to develop a system of cluster training and school-based training, to develop a cluster training system for enhancing school administration and to improve the planning and management ability of provincial educational administrators.

The project's aim is to develop training materials, implement training, and strengthen the abilities of administrators with a view to introducing new teaching methods in line with the new curriculum. In the first year of the project, training was given to school administrators and key trainers and the latter, after receiving the training, conducted school-based training. In this training, a number of schools in the same neighbourhood were grouped into a cluster, indicating that importance was attached to cooperation among schools in the same neighbourhood. In the second year, support was provided for school management. Each of the target schools submitted a management plan, which was reviewed by the project and persons in charge from each district, and small-scale financial support of around US$200–400 was given to plans that were deemed appropriate.

The teaching method emphasised in the training is 'child-centred learning'. As for the teaching method required by the new curriculum, the World Bank and BTC use the terminology of ATL, while JICA emphasises a 'child-centred' approach. The child-centred teaching promoted under the JICA project is not just a simple 'teaching method', but involves a change in the mindset of teachers, and looks deeply into how the teachers' mindset underpins the teaching method.

Analysis

International aid for teacher training is still being conducted by these three donors, and it is too early to evaluate the outcome. However, it is interesting to note some differences in the approaches of those projects despite their shared objective of providing 'support to teacher training in response to the introduction of the new curriculum'.

Both the World Bank and BTC emphasise the 'teaching methods (educational methods as a skill)'. Moreover, the number of target provinces is almost identical: 10 for the World Bank and 14 for BTC (seven provinces from 1999 to 2003). They share a training style, which is based on TTI and keeps an eye on both pre- and in-service training, as well as the adoption of the cascading system as means of communication. As such, the World Bank and BTC have much in common. The only difference between them, perhaps, is that the World Bank deals with the 'rigid' part of the new curriculum, namely the part for which the teaching method is fixed, while BTC addresses the 'flexible' part that can be operated with flexibility in response to regional conditions.

JICA's approach is slightly different from that of the World Bank and the Belgian projects. First, its project does not include pre-service as a direct target and is designed only for INSET. Further, its target area is Bac Giang province alone, which is designated as a pilot province. The ultimate objective of the project is to establish an effective new curriculum implementation model to be used widely throughout the country. Based on the goal to establish in-service training as a 'system', the target of the training is not limited to teachers but includes school managers and administrators, who are trained for capacity development, and this is a characteristic of JICA's project. The teaching method advocated by the project is different from that under the World Bank and BTC, in that it attempts to change the mindset of teachers.

While the World Bank and BTC are implementing their training in a cascading system based on TTI, JICA's project, in addition to the cascading system, organises several schools in a neighbourhood into 'clusters', providing support to a system under which all the teachers belonging to the cluster gather in a designated school to organise and participate in the training, as well as a system to implement in-school trainings based on their own schools. This makes JICA's assistance unique.

Conclusion

The paper, after reviewing the general situation of the Vietnamese teachers, has pointed out that the attention of primary education reform in Vietnam is shifting from quantitative expansion to qualitative improvement, and that the centrepiece of the qualitative improvement of education is the introduction of a new curriculum and teacher training to this end. It has also clarified that while upgrading the qualification of teachers is essential for adopting new teaching methods, the current status of teachers' qualifications varies a great deal among regions and there has only been slow progress in the establishment of in-service training. And lastly, I compared and discussed international aid for teacher training as exemplified by the World Bank, Belgian, and Japanese projects.

In order to realise effective teaching in the classroom, teachers must possess three important elements. First, teachers must have adequate knowledge about the contents of education. Second, they must be equipped with appropriate educational methods, and third, they must be highly motivated. As it stands now, the educational policy of the Vietnamese government as well as the international aid are concentrated into the first and second points, and measures to enhance the motivation of teachers have been inadequate. In Vietnam, a teacher's salary is 1.7 times the per capita GDP, less than half of the EFA/FTI Indicative Framework target of 3.5. Furthermore, this figure is significantly below the Asian average (2.4). The Education Law of Vietnam 1988 stipulates, 'The salary scale and grades of teachers is one of the highest in the system of salary scales and grades of the administrative and non business sector of the State' (Article 71), and yet, the salaries of primary school teachers are too low to even allow them to support themselves. Teachers have no choice but to do second jobs. Rural areas are experiencing serious shortfalls of teachers in terms of both quantity and quality. It is essential to develop a scheme to enable teachers to take jobs in rural areas.

Further, teacher education in Vietnam needs to be seen in the larger context of decentralisation (World Bank 1999a, 1999b) and 'socialisation of education'. In Vietnam, the 'socialisation of education' is being promoted amidst the trend toward decentralisation. This signifies that the society as a whole supports education, and thus implies that education funds should be provided by a variety of actors outside the central government.

The 'socialisation of education' is generally interpreted as the expansion of the cost burden to parents and communities and some believe that it leads to greater regional gaps. However, a closer look at the reality of socialisation reveals that things are not so simple. Socialisation is not a system for expanding the burden on parents, but involves community participation in various forms (Nguyen 2004). In many parts of Vietnam, there are 'Study Encouragement Associations', a form of community organisation to collect education funds from the community. They function as a scheme for gathering educational funds from community residents, parents, local corporations, and other entities. In other words, this represents an attempt to seek financial resources from a broad range of sources, not limited to parents. As such, it is not simply a 'self-payment burden'. The Study Encouragement Associations are engaged in a variety of educational promotion activities (encouraging enrolment, improving educational facilities, support for establishing community education centres, etc.) at the commune, district, and provincial levels, capitalising on the funds collected. On the issue of teacher training, the funds of the Study Encouragement Associations are apparently used to finance in-school training and to honour highly competent teachers. The 'socialisation of education' is an activity based on originality and ingenuity at the community level, involving many forms of activities to support basic education. When the central government lacks ample resources, such activities at the community level seem also to play a valuable role in teacher training. Various stakeholders are involved. International aid for teacher training needs to be implemented with full consideration of policy trends in Vietnam such as decentralisation and the socialisation of education.

References

IIEP (International Institute for Educational Planning). 2001. *Educational financing and budgeting in Viet Nam*. Paris: UNESCO.
MOET (Ministry of Education and Training). 2001. *Primary curriculum*. Hanoi: MOET.
MOET (Ministry of Education and Training). 2002a. *Vietnam education statistics in brief 2000–2001*. Hanoi: MOET.
MOET (Ministry of Education and Training). 2002b. *National primary development programme*. Hanoi: MOET.
MOET and JICA. 2002. *Vietnam support programme for primary education development phase – final report main text*. Tokyo: Padeco.
National Committee for EFA Assessment. 1999. *The assessment of Education for All: Vietnam 1990–2000*. Hanoi: MOET.
Nguyen Cong Giap. 2004. Results from the survey of implementation on our nation's education socialization in recent years. In *Symposium: Social mobilization of education and training*. Hanoi: Education Publishing House.
Nguyen, N.N. 2002. *Trends in the education sector from 1993–1998*. Washington, DC: World Bank.
Pham Minh Hac. 1998. *Vietnam's education: The current position and future prospects*. Hanoi: Gioi Publishers.
Poverty Task Force. 2002. *Providing quality basic education for all*.
Rose, P. 2002. *Financing of education in East Asia: EFA and beyond*. Preliminary Report prepared for Oxfam GB.
Socialist Republic of Vietnam. 1995. *Sectoral aid coordination meeting on education*. Hanoi: Socialist Republic of Vietnam.
Socialist Republic of Vietnam. 2001. *Education development strategic plan 2000–2010*. Hanoi: Education Publishing House.
Socialist Republic of Vietnam. 2002. *The comprehensive poverty reduction and growth strategy (CPRGS)*. Hanoi: Education Publishing House.
Socialist Republic of Vietnam. 2003. *National Education for All (EFA) action plan 2003–2015*. Hanoi: Education Publishing House.
Tran Kieu. 2002. *Education in Vietnam: Current state and issues*. Hanoi: Gioi Publishers.
World Bank. 1996a. *Vietnam: Fiscal decentralization and the delivery of rural services*. Washington, DC: World Bank.
World Bank. 1996b. *Vietnam: Education financing*. Washington, DC: World Bank.
World Bank. 2000. *Vietnam – Primary Teacher Training Project (APL), volume 1*. Washington, DC: World Bank.
World Bank. 2001. *Project appraisal report – Primary Teacher Training Project*. Washington, DC: World Bank.
World Bank. 2004. *Vietnam: Poverty Reduction Strategy Paper (PRSP) annual progress report*. Washington, DC: World Bank.
World Bank. 2005. *Vietnam: Managing public expenditure for poverty reduction and growth (volume: Sectoral issues)*. Washington, DC: World Bank.

Afterword

Shin'ichi Suzuki

Saitama-ken, Japan

In the preceding chapters, the authors have identified several important issues for teacher education and training. Themes identified cover such items as (1) system innovation of teacher education, (2) standards and qualifications of teaching professions, (3) curriculum designs for the teachers' certificates, (4) policy trends of on-the-job teacher training, (5) English teaching and new roles of school teachers, and (6) e-learning and teacher education. In addition, (7) teachers' cultures were analysed, and (8) the urgency of building sound theories for teacher education was argued. Methodologically, some are comparative and ethnomethodological and others descriptive-explanatory. Almost all of the practical innovations are related to the national policies of economic, social and cultural development of societies in the respective country.

What is common to all the topics examining teacher education innovation and what is latent in analyses of the trends is *nationalism*. In 2006 Japan repealed the Fundamental Law of Education, first enacted in 1946, which was closely connected with the conservative revival of *Hinomaru*, the national flag and *Kimigayo*, the national anthem, both of which were institutionalised as the Law, for the first time in its history, enacted by the Lower and Upper Parliaments. As a result, the National Council for Educational Reform submitted reports, all of which asserted the necessity of habituating and ritualising patriotic attitudes in school life and introducing re-nationalised history and the traditional cultures of Japan into the school curriculum.

In Korea, responding to the social needs of re-establishing social justice and solidarity against the negative effects of cultural relativism caused by post-modernism, the state took as a policy priority the need to educate school teachers as moral actors who would realise social justice among citizens through education. Teacher education was laid on the table of discussions for social and national stability (Kaneko 2007; Cho 2008).

The Chinese government, in its 11th five year plan issued in 2006, stated that the national progress by way of science and education should be the ground principle of all strategies for central and local governments. Quality education was given the first priority among all others. Finding a solution for the disparity between urban areas and non-urban zones, particularly the agricultural regions, was taken as most urgent. Innovation and investment in school education was the first need and hence teacher education had to be radically improved (Higurashi 2007). These policy choices are induced cross-nationally with accelerated globalism in trades and economy, and enhanced 'information age'. Thus, 'knowledge-society' has been interpreted into national idioms and ideologies, resulting in either common policy choices or individual prerequisites. This is a common feature of teacher education innovation in the industrialised countries in Asia.

In the countries in the midst of developing various stages of modernisation, nationalism takes unique expressions in education and teacher training. It has been argued that Education for All (EFA) should be implemented in every context of national education world-wide. Asian nation-states have accepted the task of EFA. Especially, in the Southeast Asian regions, the nation-states are too young to implement all the ideals and ideas expressed in and by the international reports on or recommendations for EFA. In such a case, the urgent tasks for the central government of a given country are to educate its national people in line with rationalised and politicised aims of national unities and identities, regardless of different religious creeds and ethnicities.

A series of confrontations results for these young nation-states as they face the internationalised model(s) of educational innovations and teacher education. It is clear that there are significant gaps between the western models and the de facto situations younger states' schools and teachers face. For example, the UNESCO Bangkok Office launched successive workshops on teacher education from 2001, inviting experts from the regions and countries concerned. The argumentations reflected rather a limited range of national policy interest in teacher education, teacher training and teaching personnel managements.

For the Mongolian local governors, for example, it was urgent to introduce a more teacher-supporting administrative service such as a national pension and service subsidies for teachers working in the rural regions in Mongolia (Nyam Jadamba 2004).

A delegate from Indonesia mentioned that 'teachers play an important role in national development, particularly the human resource development' (Ali 2003), while a Chinese expert recognised that in the twenty-first century basic education in China must be regarded as the new condition for national industrialisation, knowledge economy and information society. 'Therefore, strategic transformation must be accomplished in teacher education that serves basic education' (Ren 2003).

EFA was taken by the Cambodian Prime Minister as a basic step for Cambodia to launch its modernisation and economic growth so that lead nation could resolve the problems of poverty and realise prosperity. Teacher education is part of the national policy of EFA (Samnang 2003).

In Myanmar development of school provisions and educational reforms are ongoing and teacher education is given the key role of supporting the national development of EFA. The core issue of the Myanmar educational reform was the improvement of educational quality (Than 2001). To the Vietnamese human resource education is critical and the first priority is given to school education and teachers (Nguyen 2004).

Regarding the background paradigm of these policy orientations observed in the developing countries in East and South East Asia, there lie some models of/for teaching, learning, and teacher education. A typical model of learning is Dolor's 'Four Pillars of Learning'. Rosas (2003) explained the Philippines' experience. In Thailand the state government introduced national educational acts in 1999 (Worainthara 2003) in response to UNESCO's framework of EFA. In many cases, the USA, EU and Australian models of teacher education are more influential upon these countries, partly because of their earlier relations with suzerains and partly because of overwhelming power of models exported from the highly advanced knowledge states.

The conflict between regional nationalism and a globalised uniformity of model building indicates various contradictions among nation-states in the regions covering Southeast and Northeast Asia. Contradictions become apparent when the basic images of teachers, or those who teach, are set in juxtaposition: educational labourers, persons committed to a sacred calling, morally sound examples of matured citizens, local leaders, literati, researching practitioners, professionals for teaching, learning facilitators, and so forth. In the Japanese context state school teachers are educational public servants while they are more presumed 'matured clerisy' in the private sector. Deep contradictions exist, historically rooted between secular teaching and religious instruction, between modern enlightenment and traditional wisdom, between exogenous civilisation and endogenous culture. Any image of a teacher has an intrinsic concern with the proto-image of governance of the country. The Japanese case can be compared with others in the region.

Whatever the interpretations of a knowledge-society can be, knowledge itself is an intellectual activity of human beings. Each culture has its own ways and idioms of intellectual communication, discourse, representation and problem-solving. Literacy matters in this context. Literacy is not the simple three Rs but has a much wider connotation. Literacy relates to 'literate', namely, to 'widely read'. It means a higher capability of reading in the present day situation.

First, within the multi-lingual circumstances teachers should be capable of managing several tongues. In this case, teachers are expected to know and to manipulate the 'trilogical' system of a given language: ontological, epistemological and methodological dimensions of the grammar and the semantics of the language in question. In the Asian circumstances it is not an easy task for all teachers of all countries to be acquainted with many languages in the regions.

Second, in the highly developed internet communication networks, advanced and developed by the hyper-technology of information, more people young and old, join a widespread communication system mostly controlled by English. In addition, 'e-literacy' or 'digital literacy' affects ordinary literacy. Nowadays it is more and more common for schools, universities and other educational institutions to adopt ICT in teaching and learning. In addition, more educational/learning opportunities are provided by various bodies in the internet spheres. The e-university is now widely spread not only locally but over the world. Educational institutions in the conventional sense, and other bodies including commercial organisations or agencies, now provide people with course opportunities leading to teaching certificates. In addition, more independent bodies offer chances to intending teachers, teachers and teacher educators who are required to be assessed by the bodies as such regarding their professional proficiency. The trends are more common in the hyper-knowledge societies.

In developing countries, the agencies, bodies or relevant organisations in the advanced countries offer these services by way of inter-collegiate, inter-university, inter-governmental, or other possible collaborations among institutions concerned with international accreditations and assessment. All has been worked out within the virtual sphere of e-literacy. It follows that e- (or digital) literacy is now a universal literacy crossing over the differences of indigenous literacy in respective cultures. Major media in the universal literacy is normally English. There are, however, many 'Englishes' over the world.

In 2002, AOL Time Warner Foundation and Bertelsmann Foundation together issued a White Paper entitled *21st Century Literacy Summit*. The White Paper, assuring the positive aspects of digital technologies and their productive effects on industry, defined twenty-first century literacy. The ability to use information and knowledge effectively rests on a set of abilities that extend beyond the traditional base of reading, writing, math and science. Teachers must now incorporate the following components to enhance our knowledge and critical thinking:

(a) technology literacy (the ability to use new media),
(b) information literacy (the ability to gather, organise, filter and evaluate information, and to form valid opinions based on the results),
(c) media creativity (the growing capacity of individuals to produce and to distribute content to audiences of all size),
(d) social competence and responsibility (the competence to consider the social consequences of an on line publication and the responsibility *vis-à-vis* children).

This form of literacy can be seen as a possible challenge to a society, to education, to workplace skills, and to civic engagement (21st Century Literacy Summit 2005). Such strands as above seem to be widely accepted by the political, industrial, social, cultural and educational publics in the Asian states.

Before the publication of the White Paper, the Prometeus Community issued in 2001 its Position Paper on Technology Supported Learning. The paper pointed out sets of research topics for the Prometeus Community, touching pedagogical and organisational issues, technologies and infrastructures, and new approaches for ubiquitous learning. As an alternative approach the Alliance for Childhood issued a new literacy of technology (Alliance for Childhood 2004). They asserted seven key reforms for a new literacy of technology: (1) make human relationship and a commitment to strong communities a top priority at home and at school, (2) colour childhood green to emphasise children's relationship with the rest of the living world, (3) foster creativity every day, with time for art and play, (4) put community-based research and action at the heart of the science and technology curriculum, (5) declare one day a week an electronic entertainment-free zone, (6) end marketing aimed at children, and (7) shift spending from unproven high-tech products in the classroom to children's unmet basic needs (Alliance for Childhood 2004).

This suggests a need for a more elaborate analysis of e-learning processes and in particular there is a high need for a conceptual framework for lifelong learning, and for the development of models derived from non-formal settings and self-organising communities of learners. 'The concept of the learning community is an especially important area. It is likely that supporting constructivist approaches will prove especially fertile' (Prometeus 2001).

Within Europe, there are some problems in developing the literacy required for the new ubiquitous spheres of e-learning and the new abilities to be acquired by children and adults in expanding digital society. Western culture had a common background for the modern nation-states to develop national language policies respectively, that is, Latin and Greek. Literacy (=being literate) and literati (=people widely read), as social, cultural and political products, have together influenced European historical processes since medieval times.

Historically, in the Asian context, *Hanzi* (Chinese square letters) had played to some extent the part of Latin in Europe. However, after contact with European civilisations, the background of national literacy of each country in Asia changed. Japan in the 1870s, for example, introduced English to secondary schools and European languages like French and German were taught at higher schools for boys (aged 17–19), with Spanish, Italian, and Russian introduced to the courses for advanced learning at various universities. Advanced literacy for the selected few, both boys and girls, became complex; these included modern and classic Japanese, Chinese classics, and modern European languages (Suzuki 2008b). Such complex literacy became prevalent among the Asian cultures. Nowadays more Japanese young people acquire Asian tongues such as Korean, Chinese, Indonesian, Filipino, Malaysian, Mongolian and others. In the age of digital knowledge and technology, what kinds of measures should/could be developed to enhance e-learning against the complex of multiple literacy? Is English good enough?

Teacher educators should commit themselves to the discovery of a common base of 'literacy' for all teachers from, and to, Asia, by which they may cultivate their own frame-of-reference. This would be not only acculturate the learners' digital literacy but also enrich their higher competencies in synthesising complex literacy upward to higher-order literacy for teaching. New literacy for new teachers is an urgent need.

One way to tackle the task as such is the development of an international network of learning communities, and to build a global Institute of Education within the network, wherever it is possible for those responsible with teacher education. At such an Institute of Education teacher educators from colleges and universities and the teachers from schools of all levels could meet. They could talk more about the required knowledge-base for the teaching profession, professional standards, teachers' status, recruitment to profession, and professional independence and autonomy. There they could establish any type of partnership among those concerned with teacher education, inviting advisors and those from the communities around the Institute, who are highly interested in education and lifelong learning. It is important for there to be more opportunities for the informal learning groups to join and discuss much about ubiquitous learning including teaching certificate qualifications.

As for a new knowledge-base for teaching I believe that the knowledge-base once established in the universities or elsewhere should be reviewed and re-examined through a complex of advanced learning, to include brain-, life-, cognitive sciences, cybernetics, information and computer science, cultural studies, new social sciences and advanced interdisciplinary research. It is desirable for teacher educators to envisage the possibility of establishing a classificatory inventory of endogenous and exogenous knowledge which are both the base of interpretation of foreign knowledge and the base of interpretation of endogenous knowledge into international learning.

In this way, any universal literacy, either of digital or e-learning, can be at once nationalised on the one side and reciprocally re-internationalised on the other backed by a local knowledge (Suzuki 2006). Lee suggests there is a high potential of IT integration in teacher education in Hong Kong (Lee 2008). However, the issues of digital literacy are so tense that e-learning, together with the rapid growth and spread of new communication tools and sites, may change the institutional forms of higher learning and hence teacher education and training conventionally maintained by the universities and colleges (Gilroy 2003; Williams 2005).

In each country there should be a general teaching council built on the network of local institutes of education. An Asia-wide International Teaching Council (ITC) could be built on the networks of the national, the regional General Teaching Councils and International Institute of Education. The latter would be composed of the Asia-wide ITC. Any strong theory of teacher education, an idea developed by Bates, for example, could be developed, attested and become more generative and heuristic through such a new international and inter-regional collaboration (Suzuki 2004; Suzuki 2008a).

In the early 1970s Harvard dropped its formerly highly regarded teacher education programmes (the Master of Arts in Education) and reduced its principal and superintendent preparation effort (the Administrative Career Programme). In doing so, Harvard turned its attention to issues of research, social policy, planning, and learning environments (often those not connected with schools or colleges). Most other schools of education in leading research universities in the US did the same thing, either eliminating their schools of education entirely (Duke, Yale and Johns Hopkins), or shifting their focus from schooling (Chicago, Stanford, Teachers College). Some came within a whisker of closing (Chicago), and both Harvard and Stanford had discussions on their campuses about closing or eliminating their status as Schools and making them departments (as happened at Chicago before the department was eliminated) (Garaham 2003). Against such trends, there arose a serious reflection on the role of universities as teacher education institutions (Graham 2003). In this sense it is important, as papers in this issue of the journal indicate, for researchers and teachers to reflect upon what are ontological realities for teaching, what perspectives can or should be developed as epistemological frames-of-reference of teaching and what methodology has to be cultivated internationally and interculturally.

References

21st Century Literacy Summit. 2005. *A global imperative, the report of the 21st Century Literacy Summit*. Stanford: New Media Consortium.

Ali, M. 2003. Teacher professional standard. Paper presented at Sub-regional Seminar on Social Dialogue for Teacher and Quality in EFA, 15 December.

Alliance for Childhood. 2004. *Tech tonic towards a new literacy of technology*. College Park, MD.

Cho, Y-D. 2008. Innovation in teacher education: The development of Korean education through a new system for challenge of education. In *Proceedings of the First East-Asia International Forum*, 41–49, Seoul, 20–23 March.

Gilroy, P. 2005. Commercialization of education: Teacher education in the market-place. *Journal of Education for Teaching* 31, no. 4: 275–77.

Graham, P.A. 2003. Forward. In *American education twenty years after nation at risk*, ed. T. Gordon and P.A. Graham. Cambridge, MA: Harvard Education Press.

Higurashi, T. 2007. Chugoku (China), In *Recent trends in education overseas 2006*. Tokyo: The Monbusho (Ministry of Education, Science, Sports and Culture).

Kaneko, M. 2007. Kankoku (Korea), In *Recent trends in education overseas 2006*. Tokyo: The Monbusho (Ministry of Education, Science, Sports and Culture).

Lee, K.T. 2008. IT integration in teacher education: Supporting the paradigm shift in Hong Kong. Paper presented at the 1st East Asia International Symposium for Teacher Education, 20–23 March, Hosei University, Tokyo.

Nguyen, T.S. 2004. Country discussion paper. In *File of Background and Working Document, UNESCO experts meeting on teacher education reform and teacher professional standards*, 51–54. Bangkok: UNESCO.

Nyam, J. 2004. Academic rank of teachers. In *File of the background and working documents, UNESCO experts meeting on teacher education reform and teacher professional standards*. Bangkok, UNESCO.

Prometeus. 2001. *Report: Open consultation process*, Prometeus Position Paper. Prometeus Community.

Ren, Y. 2003. About decision on teacher education. Paper presented at Sub-Regional Seminar on Social Dialogue for Teacher and Quality in EFA, 15 December.

Rosas, N.L. 2003. The Philippine experience. Paper presented at Sub-Regional Seminar on Social Dialogue for Teachers and Quality in EFA, 15 January.

Samnag, S. 2003. Opening address. Presented at Sub-regional Seminar on Social Dialogue for Teacher and Quality in EFA, 15 December.

Suzuki, S. 2004. Who are the learning-facilitators? Where should they be educated? Geopolitic and geo-cultural impacts on knowledge-base for learning facilitators. Paper presented at 2004 CESE meeting, Danish University of Education, 28 June–1 July.

Suzuki, S. 2006. Toward holistic knowledge-base for learning facilitators: Conflict between the global and the local? In *Identity, education and citizenship – multiple interrelations*, ed. T. Winther-Jensen and J. Sprogoen. (Komparatische Bibliothek, Band 13), 239–59. Frankfurt am Main: Peter Lang.

Suzuki, S. 2008a. Toward renewed knowledge-base for teaching profession: School university complex experimented at the Advanced Institute of Teacher Education, Waseda University. Paper submitted to the Workshop for Teacher Educators – School University Partnership, 1st East Asia International Symposium for Teacher Education, 20–23 March, Hosei University, Tokyo.

Suzuki, S. 2008b. Toward learning beyond nation-state: Where and how? Conflicting paradigms of nationalism; East Asia and Europe. In *Changing knowledge and education – communities, mobilities and new politics in global societies*, ed. M. Pereyra, 85–103. Frankfurt am Main: Peter Lang.

Than, U.T. 2001. Teacher education in Myanmar. Paper presented at the South-east and East Asia Sub-regional Workshop on the reform of Teacher Education and Training, 5–7 January 2001, Manila.

Williams, P. 2005. Lessons from the future: ICT scenarios and the education of teachers. *Journal of Education for Teaching* 31, no. 4: 319–39.

Worainthara, S. 2004. Teacher professional standard development in Thailand. In *File of Background and Working Documents*, 47–50. Bangkok: UNESCO.

Index

Abbs, P. 15
Active Teaching Learning: Vietnam 166
all trained and all graduate policy 33-4
Alliance for Childhood 173
alternative pathways 29, 34-6
America: colleges for teacher education 3; online universities 59-68
appointment examination 138
art: curriculum integration 13-14; integrated subject 19
Asia: educational space 48; music education polices 11-15; national and individual identity 9
assessing ability 17
assessment: objective 13-14; problem of validity 52-3; teacher education 103
authentic assessment: concept 12-13

Bates, R.: and Townsend, T. 42
Belgian Technical Corporation 166-7
Bologna Declaration 46
Brennan, M.: and Nofke, S. 53
British Columbia 102-3; College of Teachers 100; education 101; higher education 101-2; teacher education 102-3
Broadfoot, P. 44
burnout 93

Cambodia: education for all 171
Canada: enrolments 102; public education 105
Canada and Japan: comparative study 96-108
Century Literacy Summit: white paper 173
certification 27
Cheng, Y.: Chow, K. and Mok, M. 42
child-centred learning 167; Vietnam 160-1
children's total development 12
China 124-5; early childhood 122-30; education quality 170; educational spending 113; environment and institutions 110-12; government policies 110; improving quality 114; information technology 115-16; kindergarten curriculum reform 126; kindergarten-based training 128; kindergartens 123; merged institutions 111; model of *four plus X* 117-18; model of teachers' cultivation 116-17; model of *three plus one* 117; model of *two plus one plus one* 117; model of *two plus two* 117; modes of adjustment 111-12; music curriculum 14-15; priorities and developments 113-18; professional development 113-15; professional development rural teachers 128-9; qualifications 114-15; reform 109-21, 118-20; resources and programming 125; response at institutional level 110-11; staffing issues 113-14; teacher education programmes 124-5; The Teachers' Law 113
Chow, K.: Mok, M. and Cheng, Y. 42
classical music: music education 16
classroom management: lessons focused 105
Clay, J.: and George, R. 47
college English classes 71-4
commoditised learning 62
compulsory education: Japan 71
corporate ethos: domination 67
corporate influence: higher education 59-68; increased 66-7
cost-effectiveness 45
Couturier, L.: Scurry, J. and Newman, F. 67
creativity: flexibility and lifelong learning 44-5
cultural role 11-25
culture and tradition: teacher education 46-9
curriculum: art 13-14; Chinese kindergarten 126; development in China 129; problem of focus 51

Decision on the reform of the education system (Ministry of Education) 110
defensible theory 41-57, 50-4
demo lessons by supervisors: Vietnam 164
DETYA: report 54
digital literacy or e-literacy 8-9, 172
Dore, R. 15

early childhood teacher education in China 122-30; problem 123-7, 127-9; recommendations 127; trends 125-7

economic gap: urban/rural 18
education: British Columbia 101; children's total development 12; incoherent government policies 37; industry and online learning 59; Japan 96-100; North American 96-7; partnership 6; practices 95; socialisation 168-9; teaching idioms 2-3
Education for All 6; Cambodia 171
Education Bureau: Hong Kong 30
education industry: emerging market 59
Education Law: Vietnam 160
education policies 23; Korea and Japan 143
education quality: China 170
education systems: ICT integration 8
educational idioms 2-3
educational reform: Vietnam 157-69
educational space: Asian 48
educational structures: Korea and Japan 151-2
effective teaching 168
elementary school: English course 79; teacher certification 137; teacher programme 103
Elliott, J. 52
English: communication tool 142; compulsory subject Korea 145; global literacy 7-8; important role South Korea 140-1; international language 131; Japanese primary schools 7-8; Korean context 136; Korean society 146; learning hour 151; second language 59; social differences affecting 150-1
English education: East Asian countries 154; as foreign language 135; Korea 144-6; reform plans Korea 146; South Korea 131-41, 135
English Experience Facilities 149-50
English Programme in Korea (EPIK) 149
English Teacher Assistants 143; recruitment 152; system 149
English teachers: South Korea 131-41, 141
English Village: creation 152; Korea 150
enrolments: Canada 102
Erziehungsformen (Jaspers) 2
Europe: literacy development 173
evaluation system: South Korea 139-40

feedback cycle programmes 70
female teachers: Vietnam 157
flexibility: creativity and lifelong learning 44-5
foreign language: opportunity 145
Four Pillars of Learning (Dolor) 171
French intellectualism-oriented education 161
Fundamental Law of Education: Japan 170
Furlong, J. 38

gender awareness 89-91
gender bias: coping strategies 87; practices 85-9; reluctant to resist 87; women teachers 81-94
gender inequality: ethnographic case study 82-3; Japan 81-94; policy implications 91-2; post-secondary participation 102; research questions and methodologies 82
General Teaching Council: establishment 33; Hong Kong 38; need for 175; United Kingdom 3
George, R.: and Clay, J. 47
gifted education: South Korea 135
Gipps, C. 12
Giroux, H. 66-7; and Myrsiades, K. 61, 66, 67
global competition: implications 45
global context: teacher education 41-57
global learning 1-2
global literacy: English 7-8
global market 45
globalisation 11, 126; teacher education reform 49-50
government policies: China 110
government-funded teachers: Vietnam 157
Graduate Teacher Programme 28

Hardt, M.: and Negri, A. 4
Harvard: teacher education programmes 175
high school education: South Korea 133
higher education: at risk 66-7; British Columbia 101-2; corporate influence 59-68; government intervention 67; Japan 97-9; Japan's private sector 98; Korea 144; South Korea 133-4
Ho Chi Minhism 161
holistic assessments 72
Hong Kong 30; changing policy context 31-2; General Teaching Council 38; in-service teacher training 30; teacher education 30; teacher preparation system 30-1; teacher qualifications 30; untrained teachers 27
human resource development 171

in-school training: Vietnam 164
In-service Courses of Training for Teachers (ICTT) 30
in-service training: challenges 164-5; Japan 166-7; pre-service education 105-6; preference 35; programmes 77-9; refresh

seminars 70; South Korea 138-9; Vietnam 162-5
industry: online learning 59
information technology: application China 115-16; influence China 115-16; integration 8; skill acquisition 11
initial and in-service training: Korea 146-9
initial teacher training: alternate routes growth 27-8; government control 28; school or site-based models 29-30; United Kingdom 28
Instructional Management Systems 59
integrated study 16-17
international aid: Vietnam 165-7
international language: English 131
international network 174
internet communication networks 172
interns 34-5

Jansen, J. 42-3
Japan 99-100; compulsory education 71; education 96-100; educational reforms 106; English ability cultivation 74; exchange and teaching programme 152; Fundamental Law of Education 170; high school teachers 81-94; higher education 97-9; in-service teacher training 166-7; International Cooperation Agency 166-7; primary schools 7-8; private sector higher education 98; teacher education 99-100; University Council 98
Japan and Canada 103; comparative study 96-108
Japan and Korea: educational policies languages 143; educational structures 151-2; learning opportunity equality 152-3; social backgrounds 153
Jaspers, K. 2

Ke-Ju: paradigm 7
Keiwa College: curriculum accreditation 80; English language programme 70; local networking English education 69-80; pre-service training 70-4
kindergarten: China 123
kindergarten teacher: China 123, 128; South Korea 137
knowledge economy era 126
knowledge instrumentalization 61
Knowledge Network 101
knowledge-base for teaching 174
knowledge-society: interpretation 170, 172

Koh, A. 48-9
Korea: English as compulsory subject 145; English education 143, 144-6; *English Village* 150; equalisation policy 144-5; higher education 144; initial and in-service English training 146-9; National Common Basic Curriculum 144; primary teacher training 146-9; relationship English-speaking countries 151; school teachers as moral actors 170; teacher policies 136-7; teacher training and primary English education 142-5
Korea and Japan: educational policies 143; educational structures 151-2; learning opportunity equality 152-3; social backgrounds 153

Lai, K. 36
language proficiency 32
Language Proficiency Requirements (LPR) 32
Law for Certification of Educational Personnel 99
Law, F. 33
Lawn, M. 47
learning: commoditised 62; communities 174; opportunity equality 152-3; practice 36
Lee, K. 174
Li, W.: Zhao, X. and Xie, J. 18
licences temporary 33-4
licensing system 4
lifelong learning 5; flexibility and creativity 44-5; South Korea 134
Lincicome, M. 48
Lipman, P. 58
literacy: development Europe 173; digital 8-9; regional and international policies 6-7
local networking: English education 69-80; programmes 74-7
local traditional music 20-2
localisation 53

MacDonald, B. 53
male-dominant occupational culture 86
management courses 66-7
managerial positions: training 90
mentorship: Canadian public education 105
middle and high school certification 137-8
middle school: education South Korea 133; teacher programme 103
Ministry of Education: objectives 74
minority teachers: Vietnam 157
Mok, M.: Cheng, Y. and Chow, K. 42

Monbukagakusho 98, 105; authorised university or college 100
Mongolia: administration service 171
multiculturalism: global trend 16
Murata, Y.: and Takakura, S. 100
music: curriculum China 14-15; instruments 21; learning to play 22; perception 17
music education: classical music 16; national identity 14-15; policies in Asia 11-15
Myanmar 171; teacher education 171
Myrsiades, K.: and Giroux, H. 61, 66, 67

national identity: and individual Asia 9; music education 14-15
national literacy: Asian Countries 174
National Meeting on Secondary and Primary School Teachers 110
national policies 4-6
Native Speaker English Teachers (NSET) 135-6
Negri, A.: and Hardt, M. 4
Newman, F.: Couturier, L. and Scurry, J. 67
Nofke, S.: and Brennan, M. 53
non-traditional pathways 27
North American: education 96-7

objective assessment 13-14
occupational culture 83-5; male-dominant 86
online: course provision 60; environment knowledge and learning 61-3; instructors 65-6; learning 59, 60-1; students 64, 66; universities 63
online teaching: communication pattern 63; income supplement 65; nature of 59; workload 64
Open Learning Agency 101
Organisation for Economic Cooperation and Development (OECD) 44

pedagogy: problem of motivation 51-2
performance-based assessment 17
Perkins, D. 106
personal touch 63-4
Peters, O. 62
Piaget: reappraisals 1
policy setting: centralisation 44
policy trends: implication 15-16
power relations 90-1; among teachers 90-1; and gender 91
practicum: teacher research 53-4
pre-school education: South Korea 132
pre-service: training 70-4, 105-6

primary education: South Korea 132-3; Vietnam 157
primary English education: Korea 142-5
primary and secondary education 5
Primary Teacher Development Project: World Bank 165-6
primary teacher training: Korea 146-9
primary teaching 31
private providers: global education market 45
professional counselling: South Korea 138
professional development: model 106; rural teachers 128-9
Prometeus Community 173
public funding 66
pupil-teacher ratio: Vietnam 157

qualification improvement training: Vietnam 164
qualifications: Hong Kong 30
Qualified Teacher Status (QTS) 27-8

recruitment programmes 27
Refresh Seminars: in-service teacher training 70
regional identities: promotion 47
research practicum 53-4
Robins, K.: and Webster, F. 60-2, 67
Rohlen, T. 95-6
Rosas, N. 171
rote learning 15
routes and models of preparation 35
rural v urban areas: development 124

Sakai, A.: and Shimahara, N. 100
Sato, N.: and Shimahara, N. 84
Sayer, J. 46, 47-8
school: administration staff training Vietnam 165; articulations South Korea 131-4; counsellors 92; education global context 1; management assessment 140; system 6-3 3-4 South Korea 132; teachers Korea 170
school partnership 36
school-based models: initial training 29-30
School-Centred Initial Teacher Training (SCITT) 28
Scurry, J.: Newman, F. and Couturier, L. 67
second career 36
secondary school: English teachers 77-9; teacher programme 103
Seiro Middle School: teaching practice 76-7
Seoul Metropolitan Office of Education (SMOE) 135-6

sexual harassment 86-7
Shanghai New Village: Teachers Professional Development 129
Shimahara, N.: and Sakai, A. 100; and Sato, N. 84
shortages: meeting 27-8
skill training 154
social backgrounds: Korea and Japan 153
social differences: affecting English 150-1
socialisation: of education 168-9
South Korea: elementary school teacher certification 137; English education 135; English important role 140-1; English teachers in school education 141; gifted education 135; high school education 133; higher education 133-4; in-service training programmes 138-9; kindergarten teacher certification 137; lifelong education 134; middle and high school certification 137-8; middle school education 133; pre-school education 132; primary education 132-3; professional counselling teacher certification 138; school articulations 131-4; school system (6-3-3-4 system of institutions) 132; special education 134; teacher appointment examination 138; teacher evaluation system 139-40; training principals 139; voluntary professional teacher training 139
Southeast and Northeast Asia 172
special education: South Korea 134
staffing issues: China 113-14
Student Information Systems 59
student retention 65
students online 64
subjects integration 15-16

Takakura, S.: and Murata, Y. 100
talented individuals 37
talented people: deterring 34
Tatto, M. 42, 43-4
teacher: demand for high quality 140; in-service training 104; induction across the Pacific 96-108; programme elementary 103; programme middle school 103; programme secondary school 103; quality problem 18; requirement 32-3; supply flexibility 34; two-tiered system 100; types 87-9
teacher education: accountabilities 44-5; comparison and positioning 44-5; culture and tradition 46-9; global context 41-57; globalisation and reform 49-50; initial 27-40; providers 28; recent reforms 100; shifts 3; and training 6, 170; Vietnam 157-69, 161
Teacher Training Agency (TTA) 28
Teachers' Law 6, 113
Teaching Assistance Programme 70; benefits 73; college English classes 71-4; development 76-7; evaluation 75; improvements 75-6; problems 73; teaching practice 76
Teaching Councils 50
teaching formula theorem 2-3
teaching practice: Japan 71-2; Seiro Middle School 76-7; Teaching Assistance Programme 76
Thaman, K. 43
third year students 72
Touraine, H. 50
Townsend, T.: and Bates, R. 42
tradition and culture 46-9
training: feedback cycle 69-80; gender awareness raising 89-91; international aid 165-7; managerial positions 90; primary English education Korea 142-5; principals South Korea 139; system Vietnam 162, 164-5
transferable skills 61
Tung Chee Hwa 31

United Kingdom: initial teacher training 28
University Council: Japan 98
university entrance: competition levels 134
university-based: training 28-9, 38
untrained teachers 27, 36
urban *v* rural areas: development 124

value gap 23
Vietnam 157; basic education 157; child-centred learning 160-1; decentralisation 168; *demo lessons* by supervisors 164; Education Law 160; female teachers 157; government-funded teachers ratio 157; in-school training 164; introduction of new curriculum 160-1; minority teachers 157; posts in rural areas 159-60; primary education 157; pupil-teacher ratio 157; qualification improvement training 164; school administration staff training 165; summer training 163-4; teacher education importance 161; teacher training system 162; teachers 157; teaching methods 160-1

vocational qualifications 4
voluntary professional teacher training: South Korea 139
Vygoytsky: reappraisals 1

Webster, F.: and Robins, K. 60-2, 67
well-being 93
white paper: Century literacy summit 173
women teachers 81-94

World Bank: Primary Teacher Development Project 165-6
World Trade Organisation 45

Xie, J.: Li, W. and Zhao, X. 18

Yuan, Z. 119

Zhao, X.: Xie, J. and Li, W. 18